EVERYTHING IS Beautiful, AND I'M NOT AFRAID

A BAOPU COLLECTION

YAO XIAO

Andrews McMeel
PUBLISHING®

FOR MOTHER

抱朴

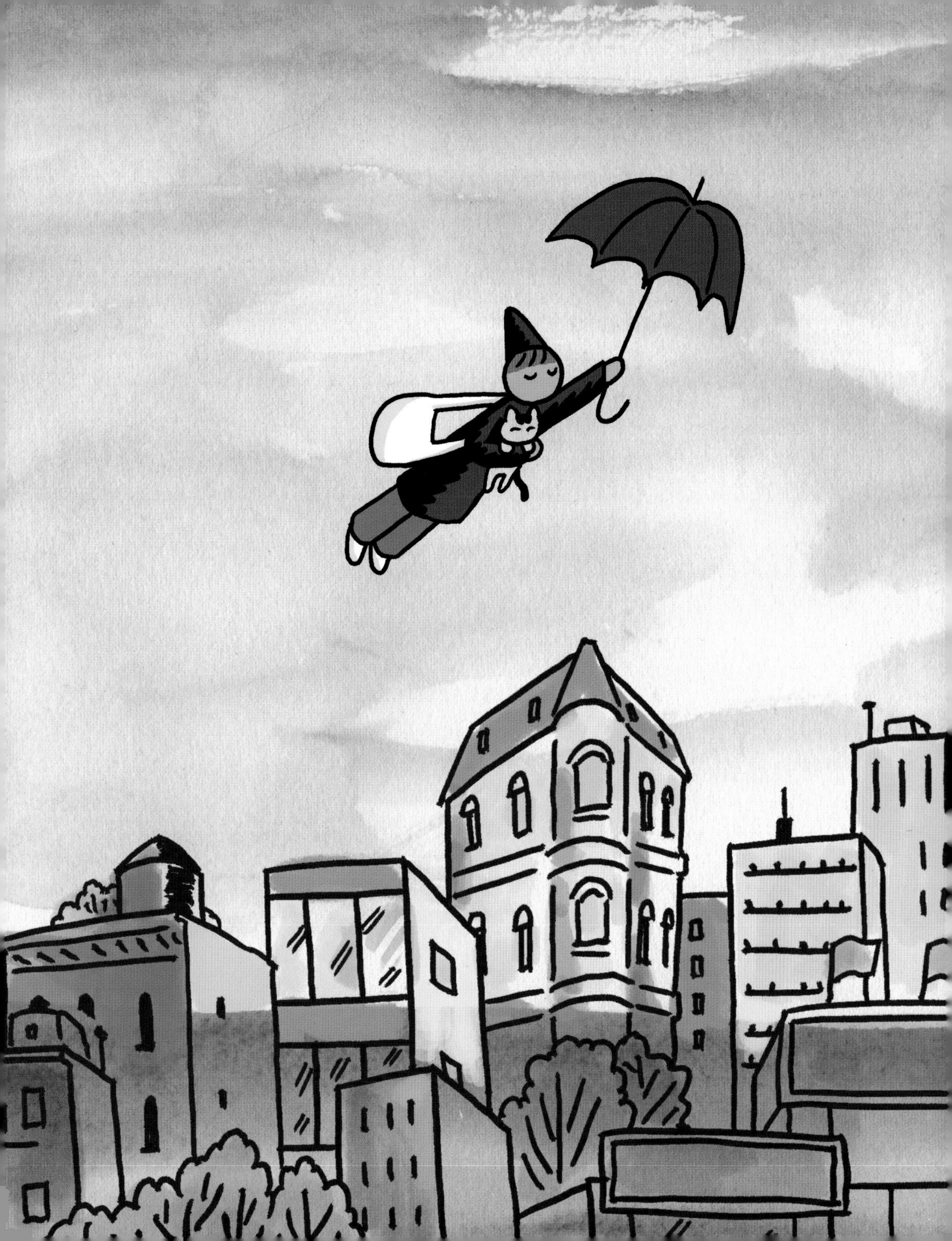

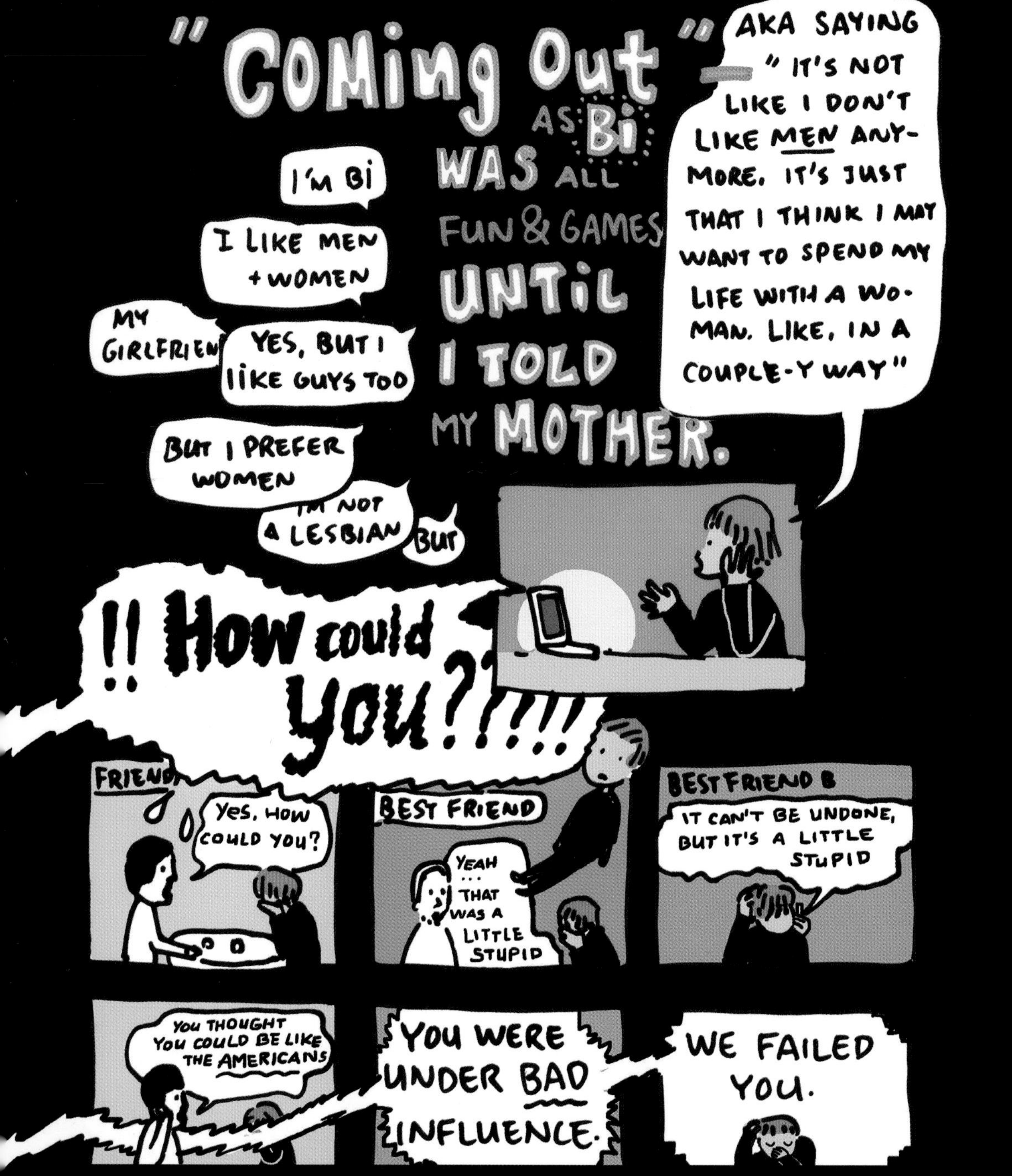

"COMING OUT" AS Bi WAS ALL FUN & GAMES UNTIL I TOLD MY MOTHER.
AKA SAYING "IT'S NOT LIKE I DON'T LIKE MEN ANY-MORE. IT'S JUST THAT I THINK I MAY WANT TO SPEND MY LIFE WITH A WO-MAN. LIKE, IN A COUPLE-Y WAY"
I'M Bi
I LIKE MEN + WOMEN
MY GIRLFRIEN
YES, BUT I LIKE GUYS TOO
BUT I PREFER WOMEN
I'M NOT A LESBIAN
BUT
!! How could you??!!!
FRIEND
Yes, HOW COULD YOU?
BEST FRIEND
YEAH ... THAT WAS A LITTLE STUPID
BEST FRIEND B
IT CAN'T BE UNDONE, BUT IT'S A LITTLE STUPID
You THOUGHT You COULD BE LIKE THE AMERICANS
YOU WERE UNDER BAD INFLUENCE.
WE FAILED YOU.

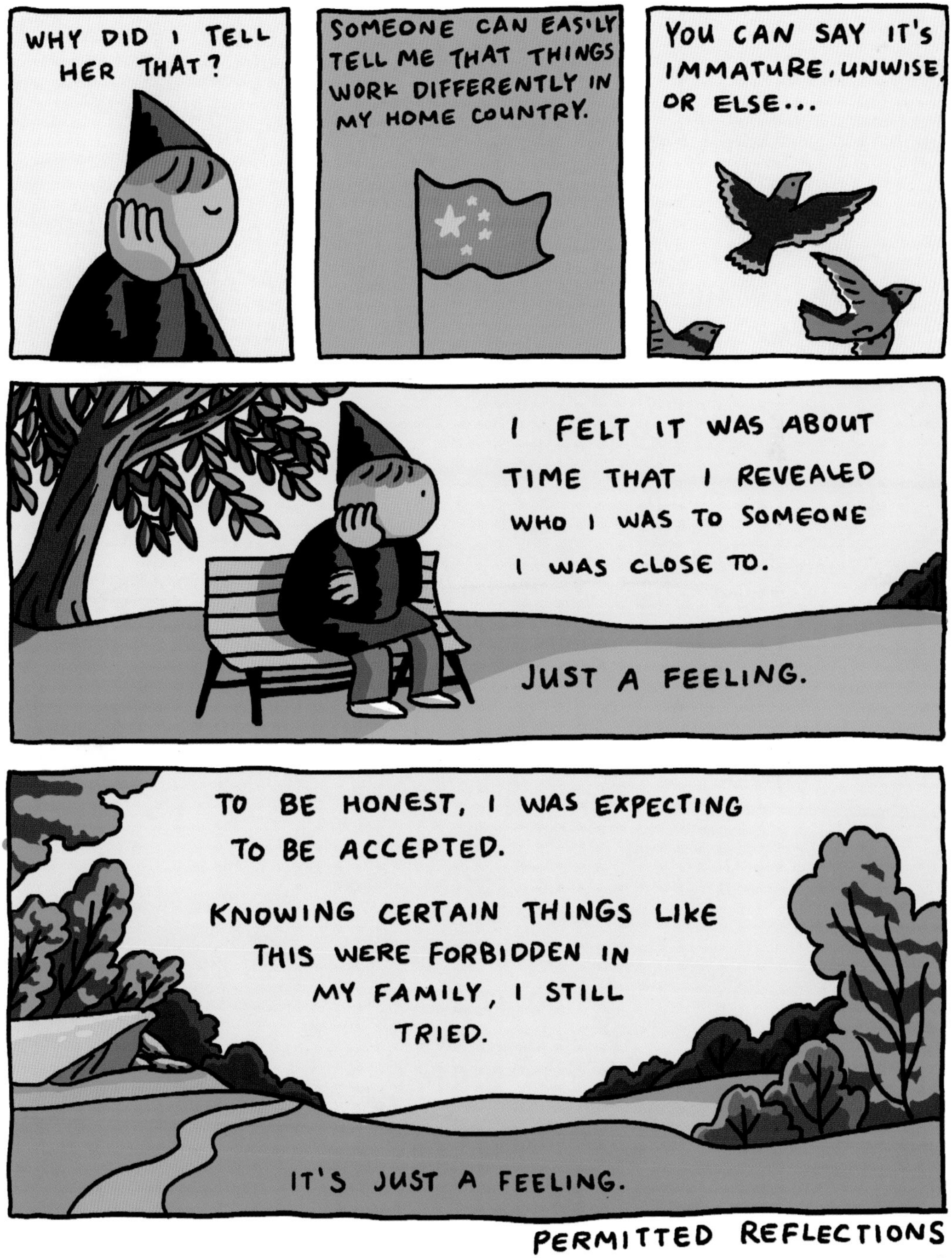
WHY DID I TELL HER THAT?
SOMEONE CAN EASILY TELL ME THAT THINGS WORK DIFFERENTLY IN MY HOME COUNTRY.
YOU CAN SAY IT'S IMMATURE, UNWISE, OR ELSE...
I FELT IT WAS ABOUT TIME THAT I REVEALED WHO I WAS TO SOMEONE I WAS CLOSE TO.
JUST A FEELING.
TO BE HONEST, I WAS EXPECTING TO BE ACCEPTED.
KNOWING CERTAIN THINGS LIKE THIS WERE FORBIDDEN IN MY FAMILY, I STILL TRIED.
IT'S JUST A FEELING.

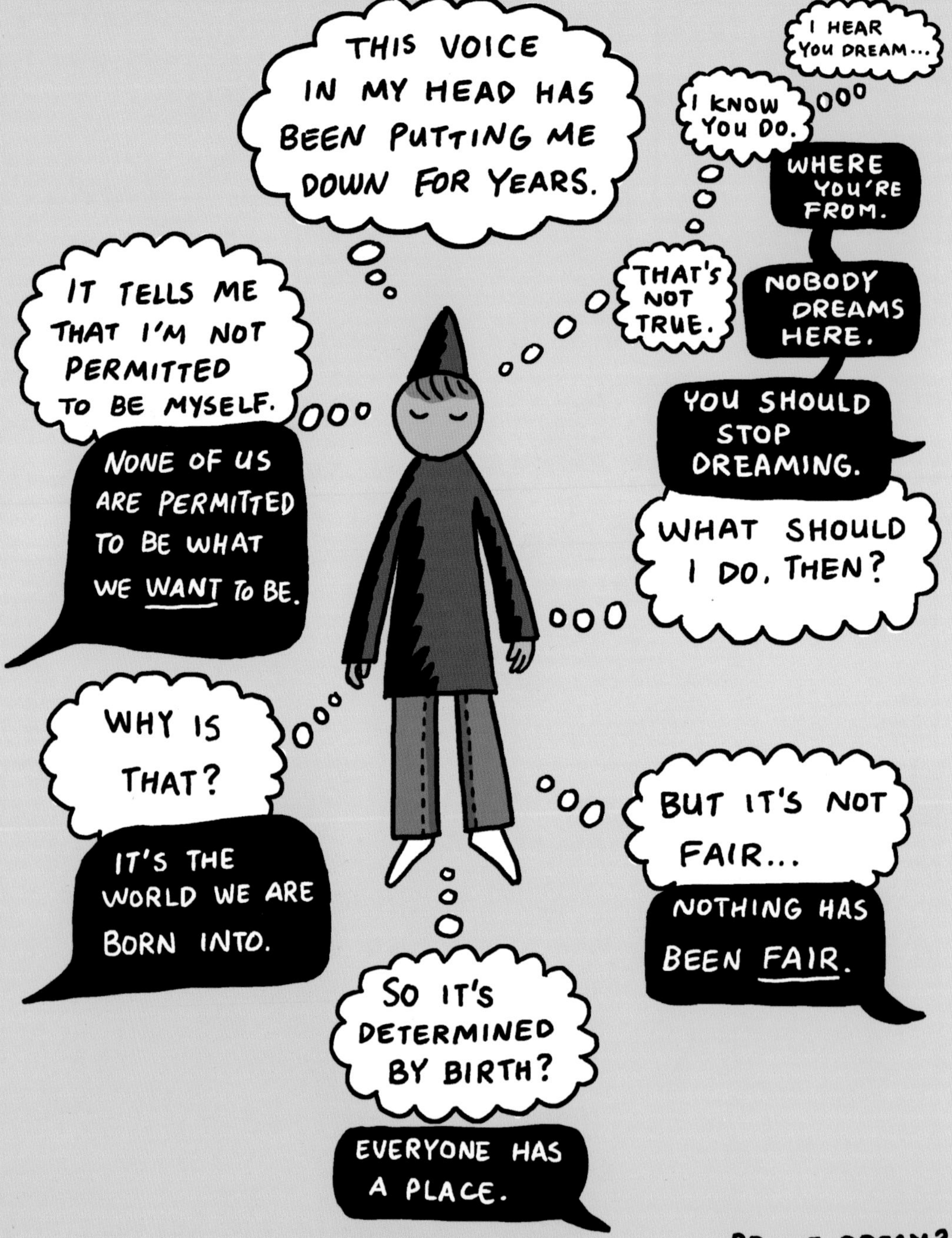
THIS VOICE IN MY HEAD HAS BEEN PUTTING ME DOWN FOR YEARS.
IT TELLS ME THAT I'M NOT PERMITTED TO BE MYSELF.
NONE OF US ARE PERMITTED TO BE WHAT WE WANT TO BE.
THAT'S NOT TRUE.
I KNOW YOU DO.
I HEAR YOU DREAM...
WHERE YOU'RE FROM.
NOBODY DREAMS HERE.
YOU SHOULD STOP DREAMING.
WHAT SHOULD I DO, THEN?
WHY IS THAT?
IT'S THE WORLD WE ARE BORN INTO.
BUT IT'S NOT FAIR...
NOTHING HAS BEEN FAIR.
SO IT'S DETERMINED BY BIRTH?
EVERYONE HAS A PLACE.

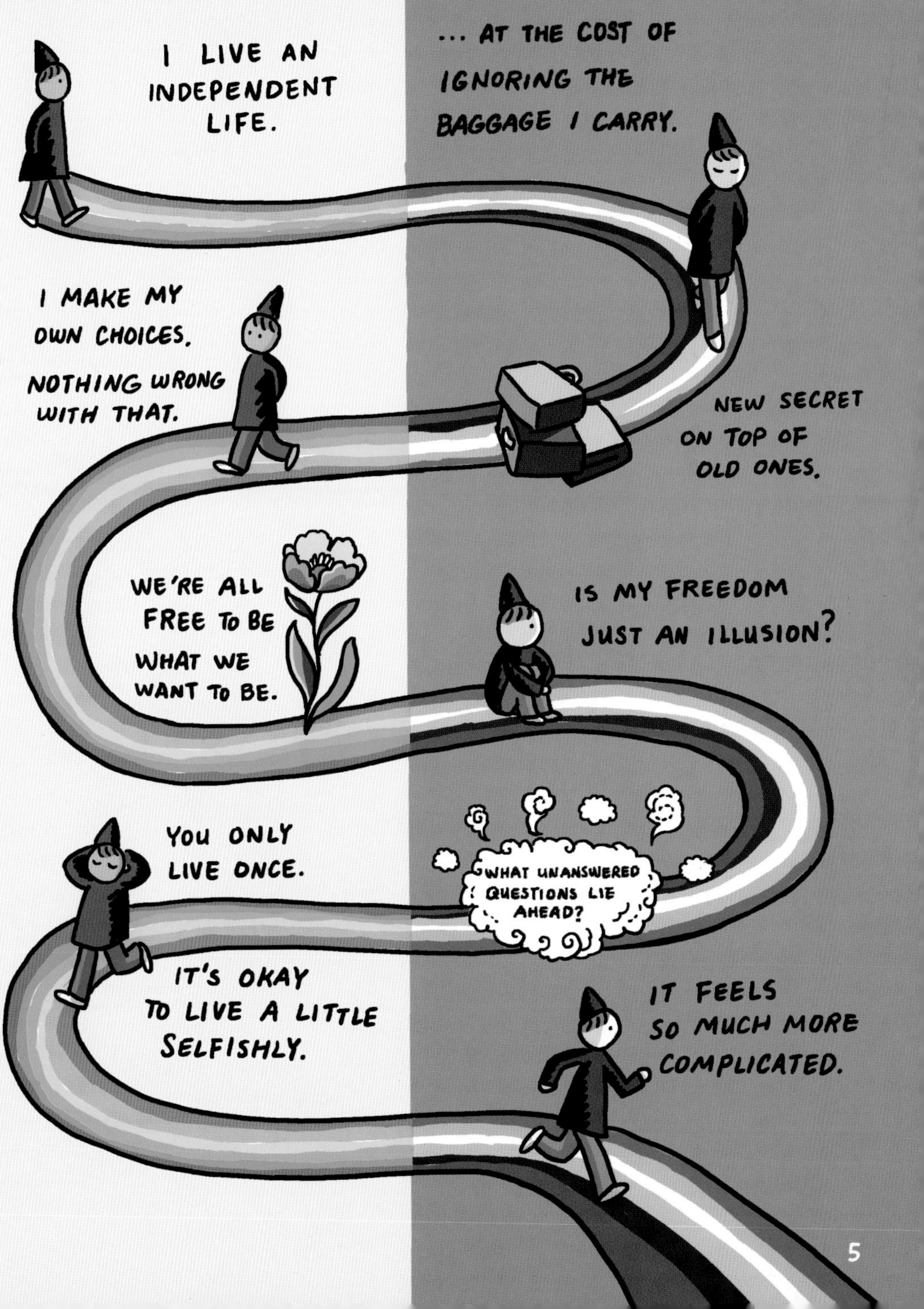

I LIVE AN INDEPENDENT LIFE.
... AT THE COST OF IGNORING THE BAGGAGE I CARRY.
I MAKE MY OWN CHOICES.
NOTHING WRONG WITH THAT.
NEW SECRET ON TOP OF OLD ONES.
WE'RE ALL FREE TO BE WHAT WE WANT TO BE.
IS MY FREEDOM JUST AN ILLUSION?
YOU ONLY LIVE ONCE.
WHAT UNANSWERED QUESTIONS LIE AHEAD?
IT'S OKAY TO LIVE A LITTLE SELFISHLY.
IT FEELS SO MUCH MORE COMPLICATED.

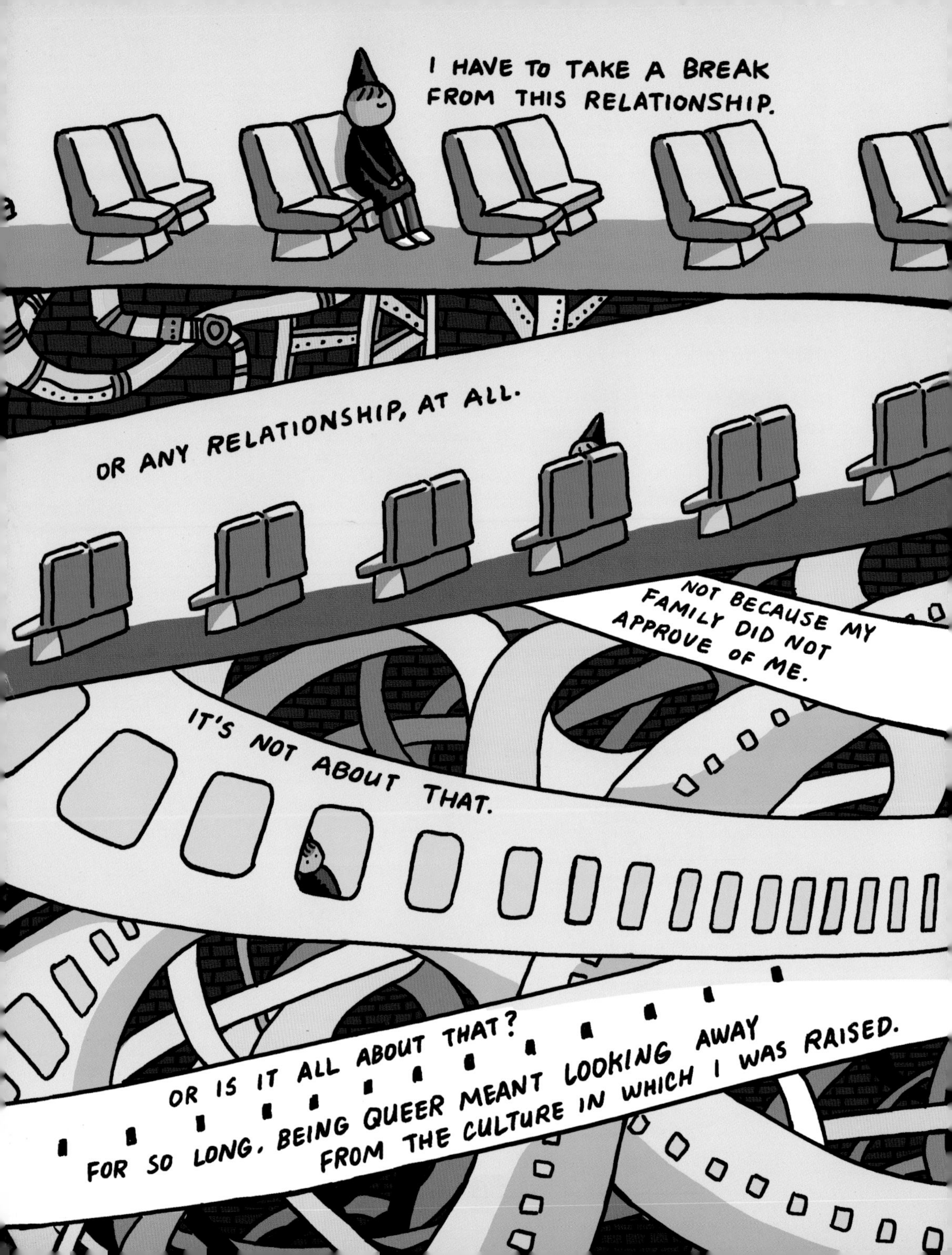
I HAVE TO TAKE A BREAK FROM THIS RELATIONSHIP.
OR ANY RELATIONSHIP, AT ALL.
NOT BECAUSE MY FAMILY DID NOT APPROVE OF ME.
IT'S NOT ABOUT THAT.
OR IS IT ALL ABOUT THAT?
FOR SO LONG, BEING QUEER MEANT LOOKING AWAY FROM THE CULTURE IN WHICH I WAS RAISED.

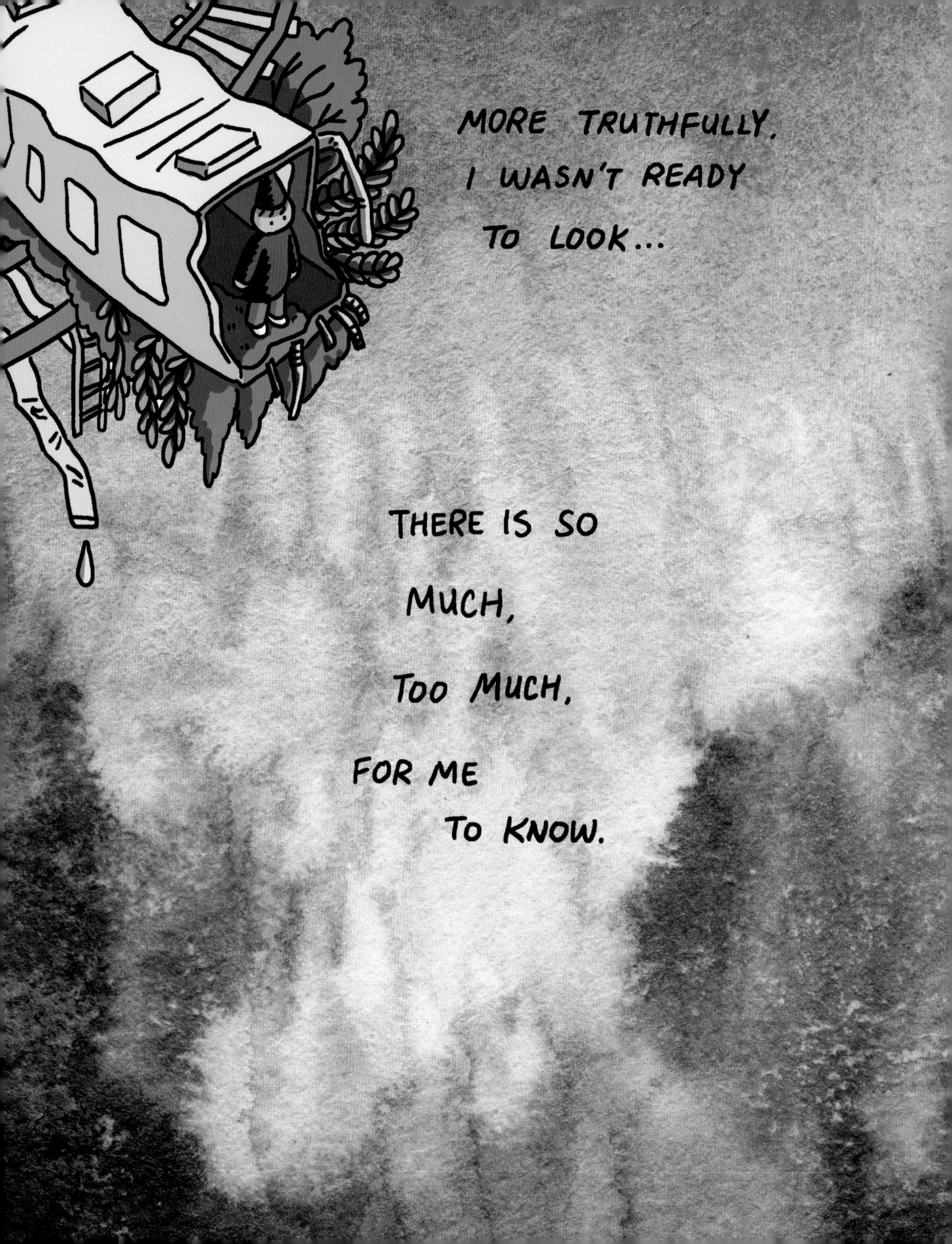
MORE TRUTHFULLY, I WASN'T READY TO LOOK...
THERE IS SO MUCH,
TOO MUCH,
FOR ME TO KNOW.

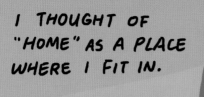

I THOUGHT OF "HOME" AS A PLACE WHERE I FIT IN.

WHERE MY JOURNEY STARTS AND ENDS.

SOMEWHERE TO REBEL AGAINST, PERHAPS.

THESE PLACES ARE DIFFERENT FOR ME NOW.

IF I CAN'T GO BACK,

WHERE CAN I GO?

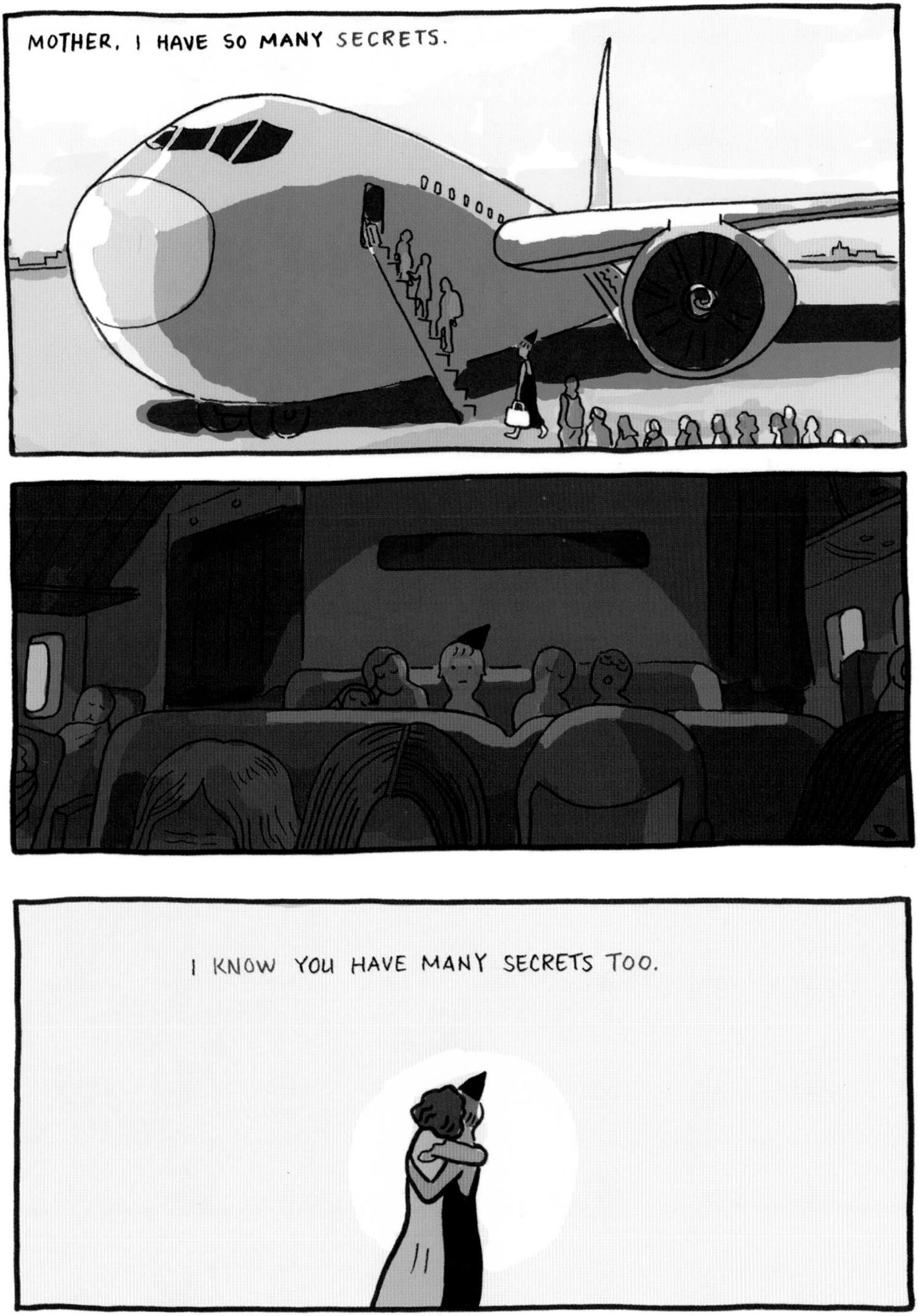
MOTHER, I HAVE SO MANY SECRETS.
I KNOW YOU HAVE MANY SECRETS TOO.

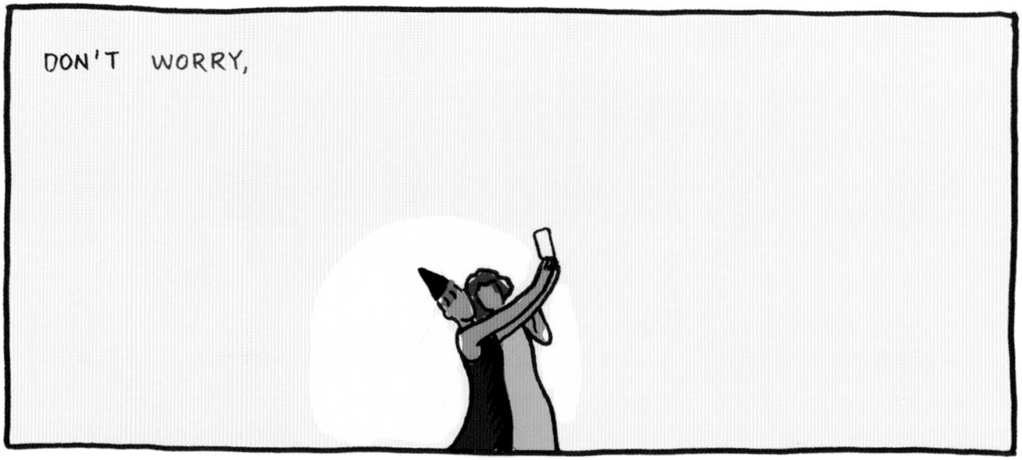
DON'T WORRY,

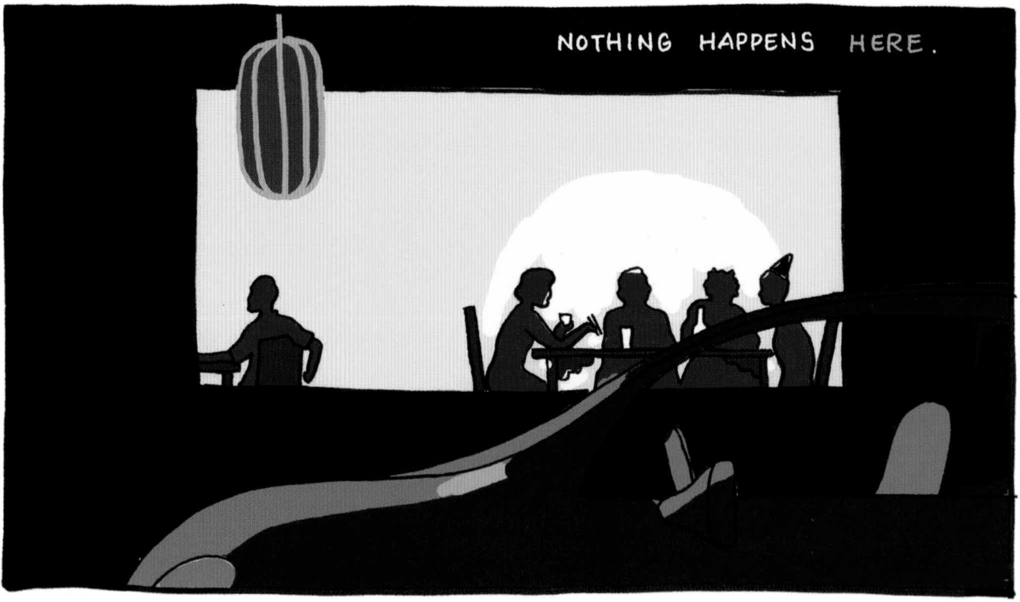
NOTHING HAPPENS HERE.

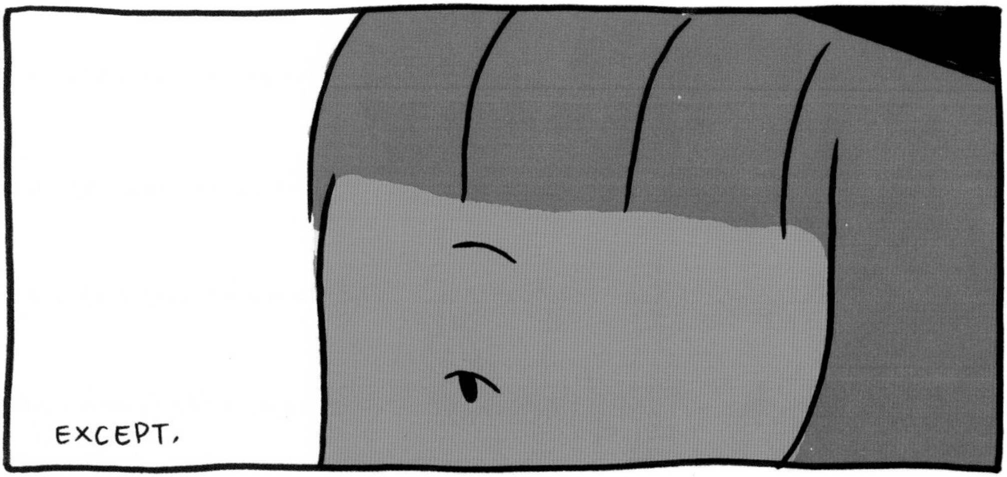
EXCEPT,

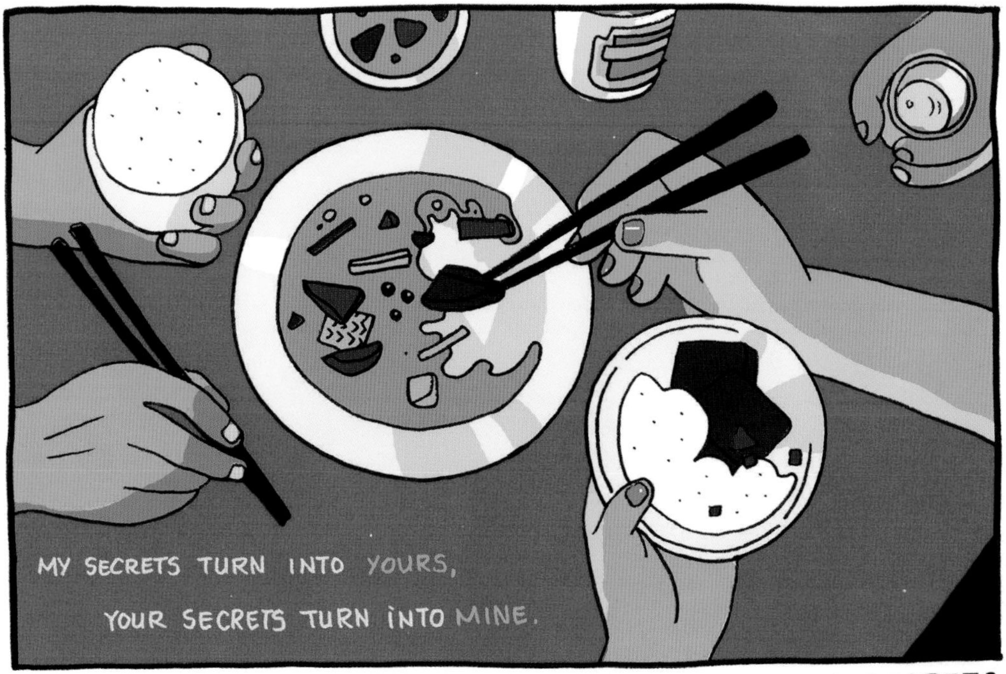
MY SECRETS TURN INTO YOURS,
YOUR SECRETS TURN INTO MINE.

I HAVE SO MANY SECRETS

WHEN YOU WERE A KID

DID THEY TELL YOU STORIES that were full of VOIDS?

in the VOIDS you saw

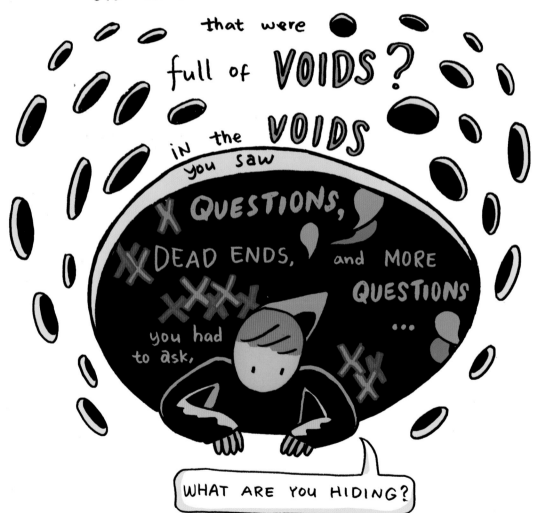

QUESTIONS, DEAD ENDS, and MORE QUESTIONS ... you had to ask,

WHAT ARE YOU HIDING?

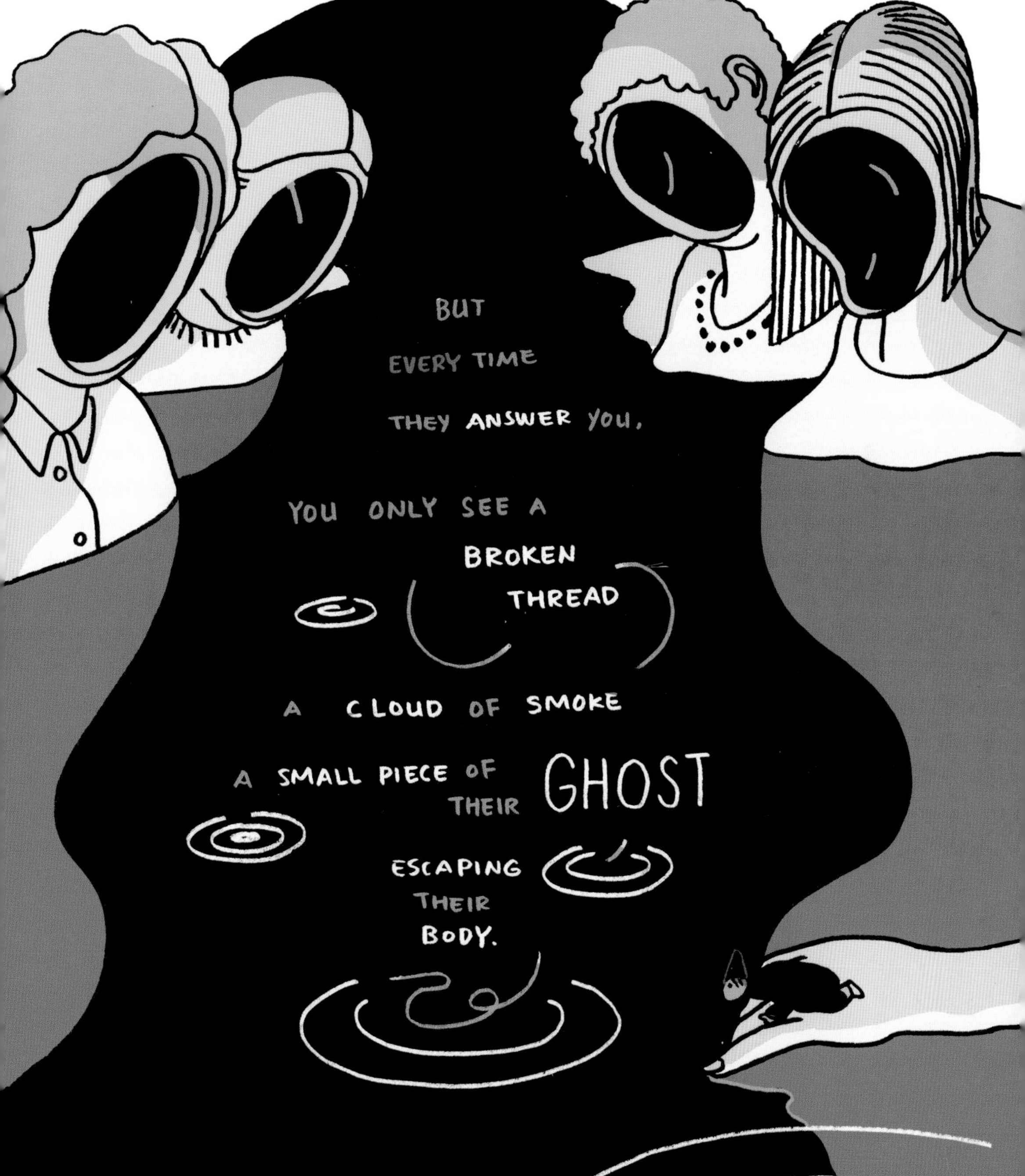
BUT
EVERY TIME
THEY ANSWER YOU,
YOU ONLY SEE A
BROKEN
THREAD
A CLOUD OF SMOKE
A SMALL PIECE OF THEIR GHOST
ESCAPING
THEIR
BODY.

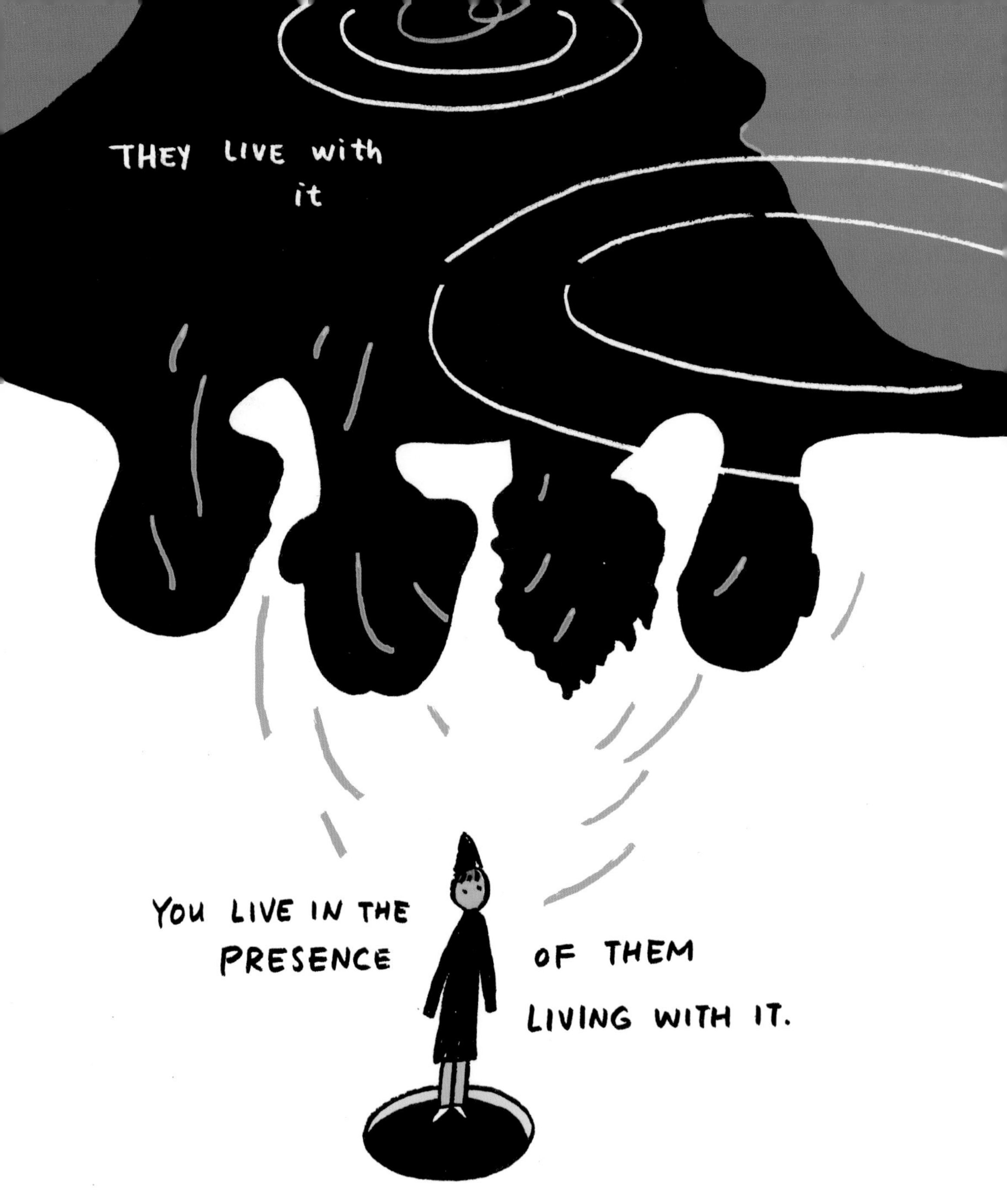
THEY LIVE with it
YOU LIVE IN THE PRESENCE OF THEM LIVING WITH IT.

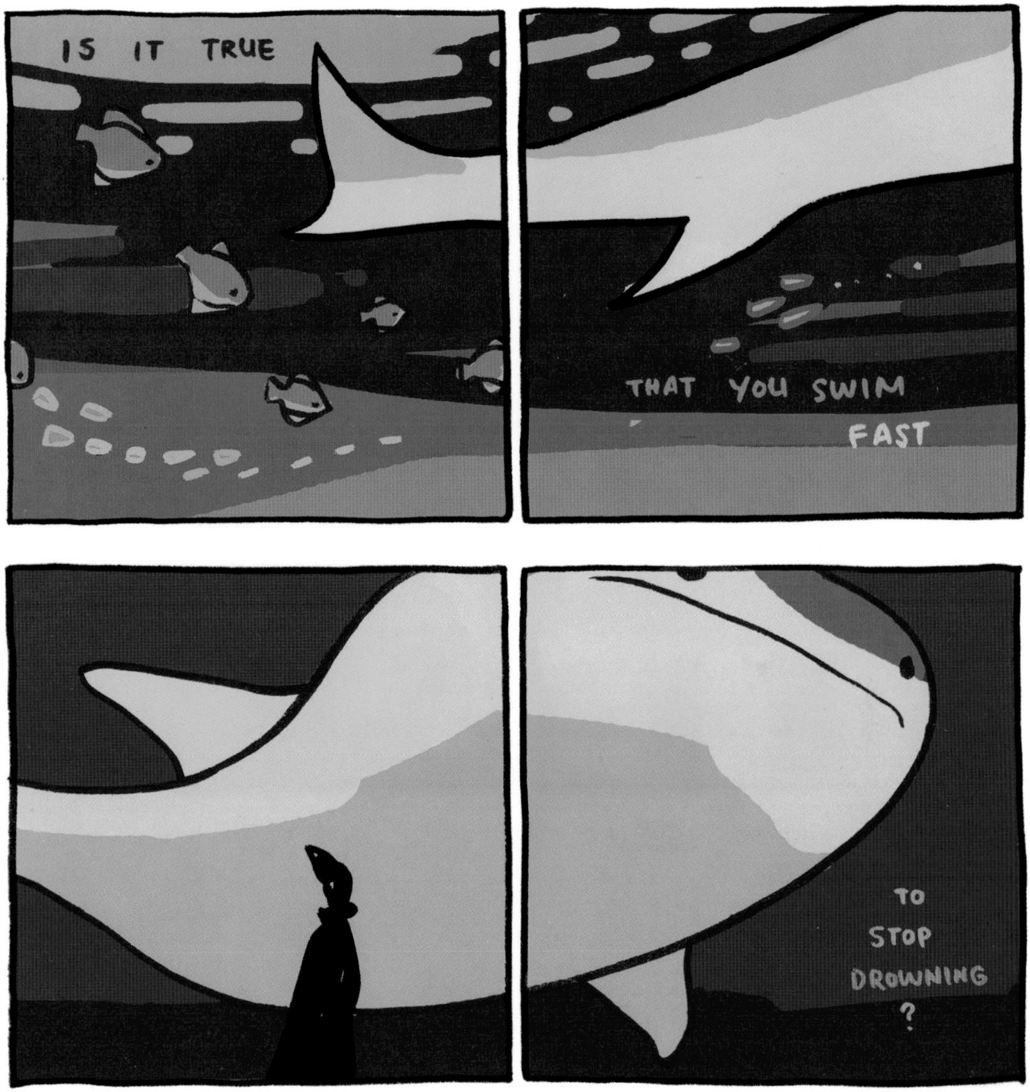
IS IT TRUE
THAT YOU SWIM
FAST
TO
STOP
DROWNING
?

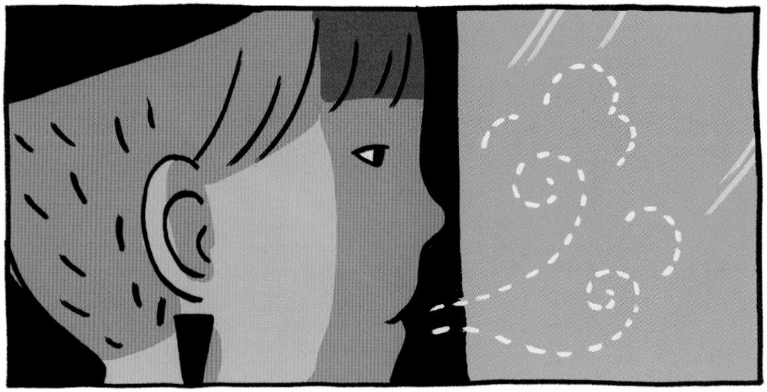

DID YOU HAVE SOMEONE
TO TEACH YOU BREATHING?

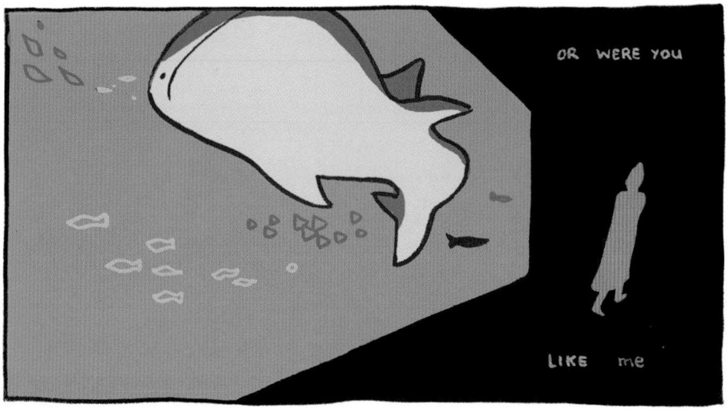
OR WERE YOU
LIKE me

LOOKING FOR FAMILIAR WATER

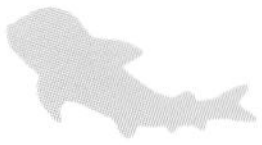

IN A FOREIGN TANK?

QUESTIONS TO ASK A FOREIGN FISH

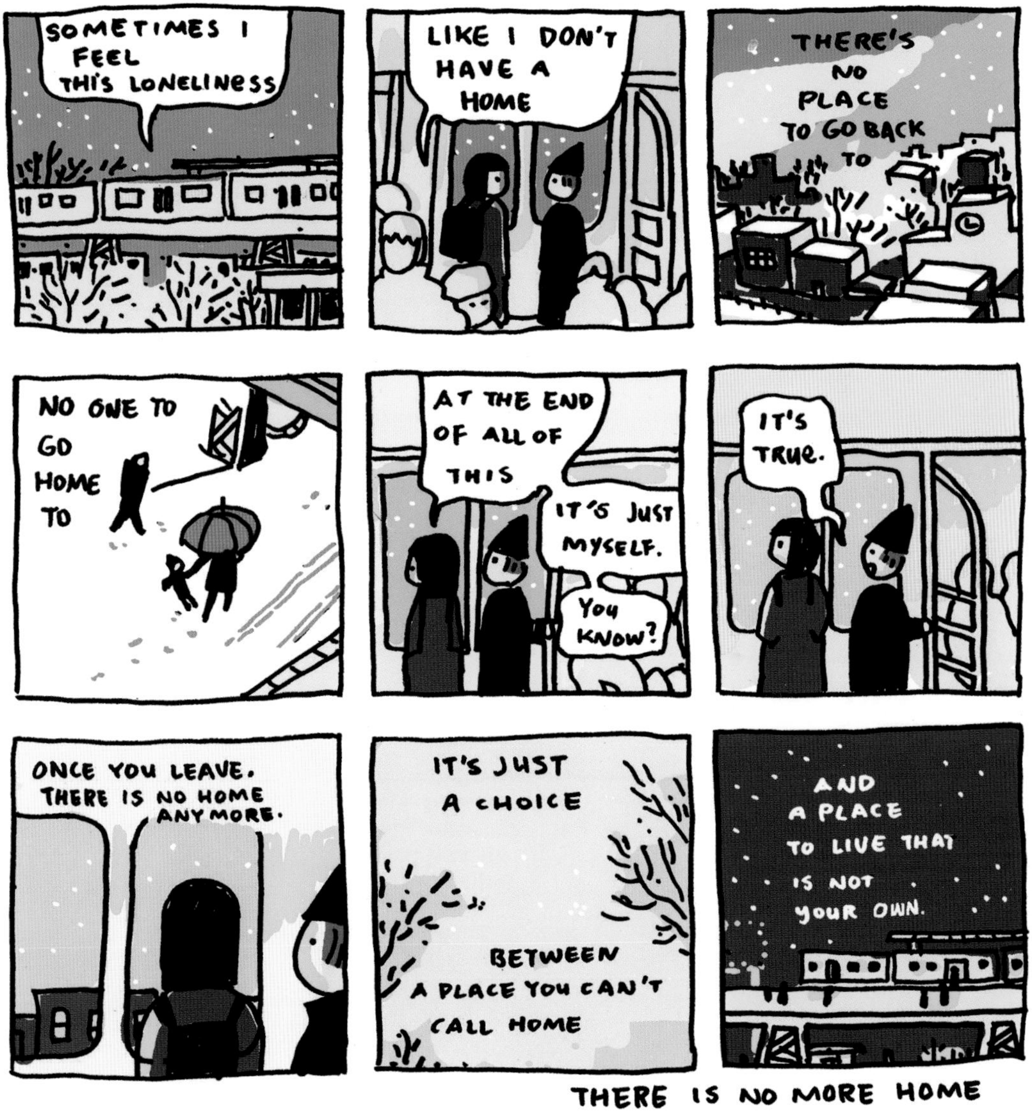
SOMETIMES I FEEL THIS LONELINESS
LIKE I DON'T HAVE A HOME
THERE'S NO PLACE TO GO BACK TO
NO ONE TO GO HOME TO
AT THE END OF ALL OF THIS
IT'S JUST MYSELF.
YOU KNOW?
IT'S TRUE.
ONCE YOU LEAVE. THERE IS NO HOME ANYMORE.
IT'S JUST A CHOICE
BETWEEN A PLACE YOU CAN'T CALL HOME
AND A PLACE TO LIVE THAT IS NOT YOUR OWN.

THERE IS NO MORE HOME

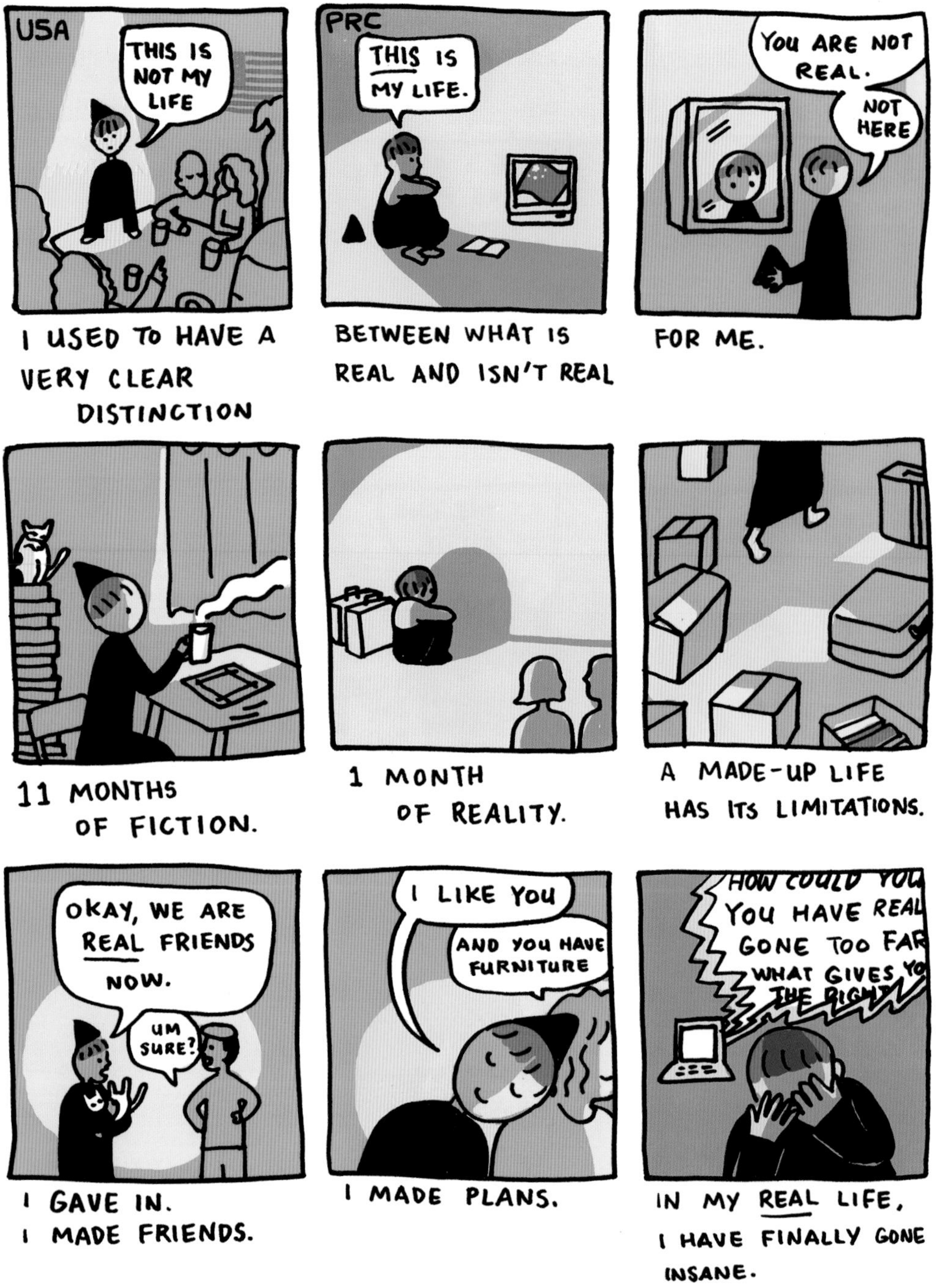
USA
THIS IS NOT MY LIFE
I USED TO HAVE A VERY CLEAR DISTINCTION
PRC
THIS IS MY LIFE.
BETWEEN WHAT IS REAL AND ISN'T REAL
YOU ARE NOT REAL.
NOT HERE
FOR ME.
11 MONTHS OF FICTION.
1 MONTH OF REALITY.
A MADE-UP LIFE HAS ITS LIMITATIONS.
OKAY, WE ARE REAL FRIENDS NOW.
UM SURE?
I GAVE IN.
I MADE FRIENDS.
I LIKE YOU
AND YOU HAVE FURNITURE
I MADE PLANS.
HOW COULD YOU
YOU HAVE REAL
GONE TOO FAR
WHAT GIVES YO
IN MY REAL LIFE, I HAVE FINALLY GONE INSANE.

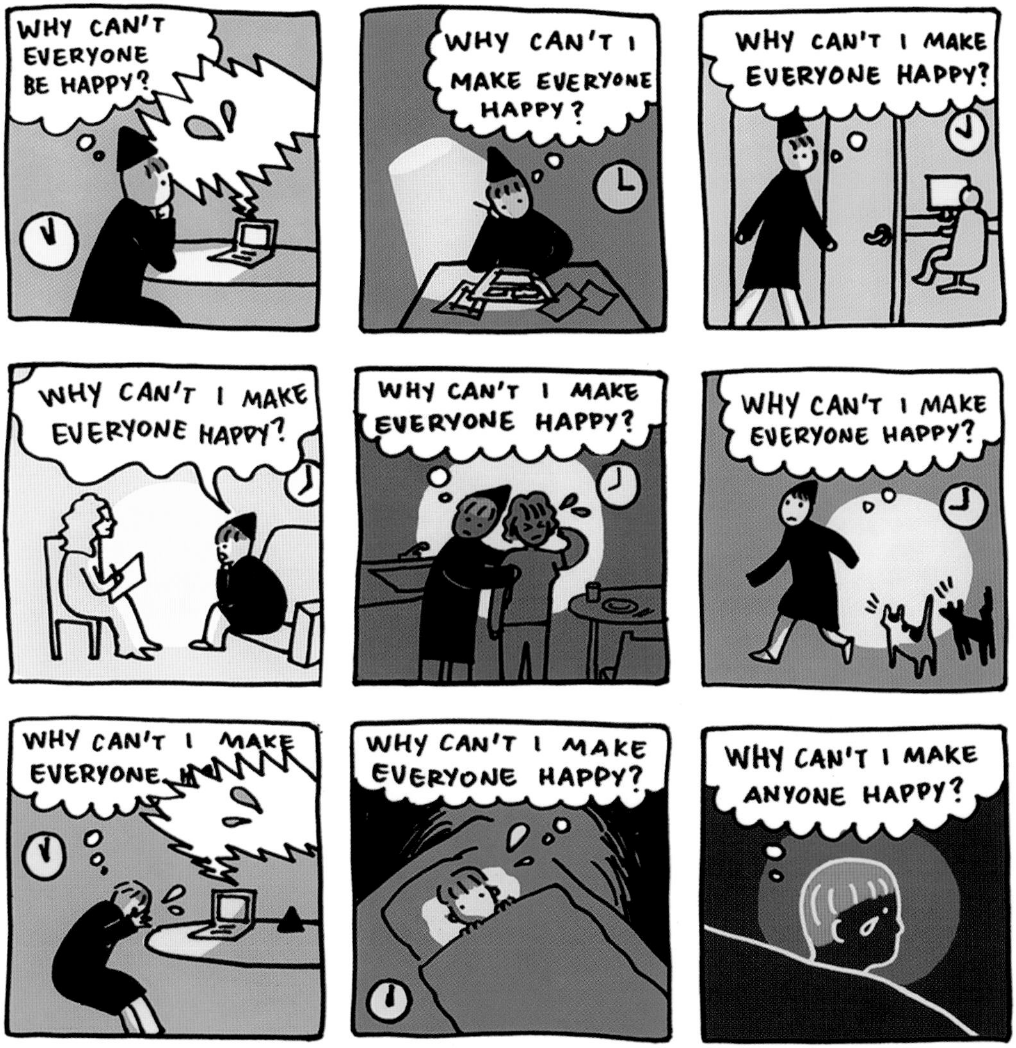
WHY CAN'T EVERYONE BE HAPPY?
WHY CAN'T I MAKE EVERYONE HAPPY?
WHY CAN'T I MAKE EVERYONE HAPPY?
WHY CAN'T I MAKE EVERYONE HAPPY?
WHY CAN'T I MAKE EVERYONE HAPPY?
WHY CAN'T I MAKE EVERYONE HAPPY?
WHY CAN'T I MAKE EVERYONE
WHY CAN'T I MAKE EVERYONE HAPPY?
WHY CAN'T I MAKE ANYONE HAPPY?

WHY CAN'T I MAKE EVERYONE HAPPY?

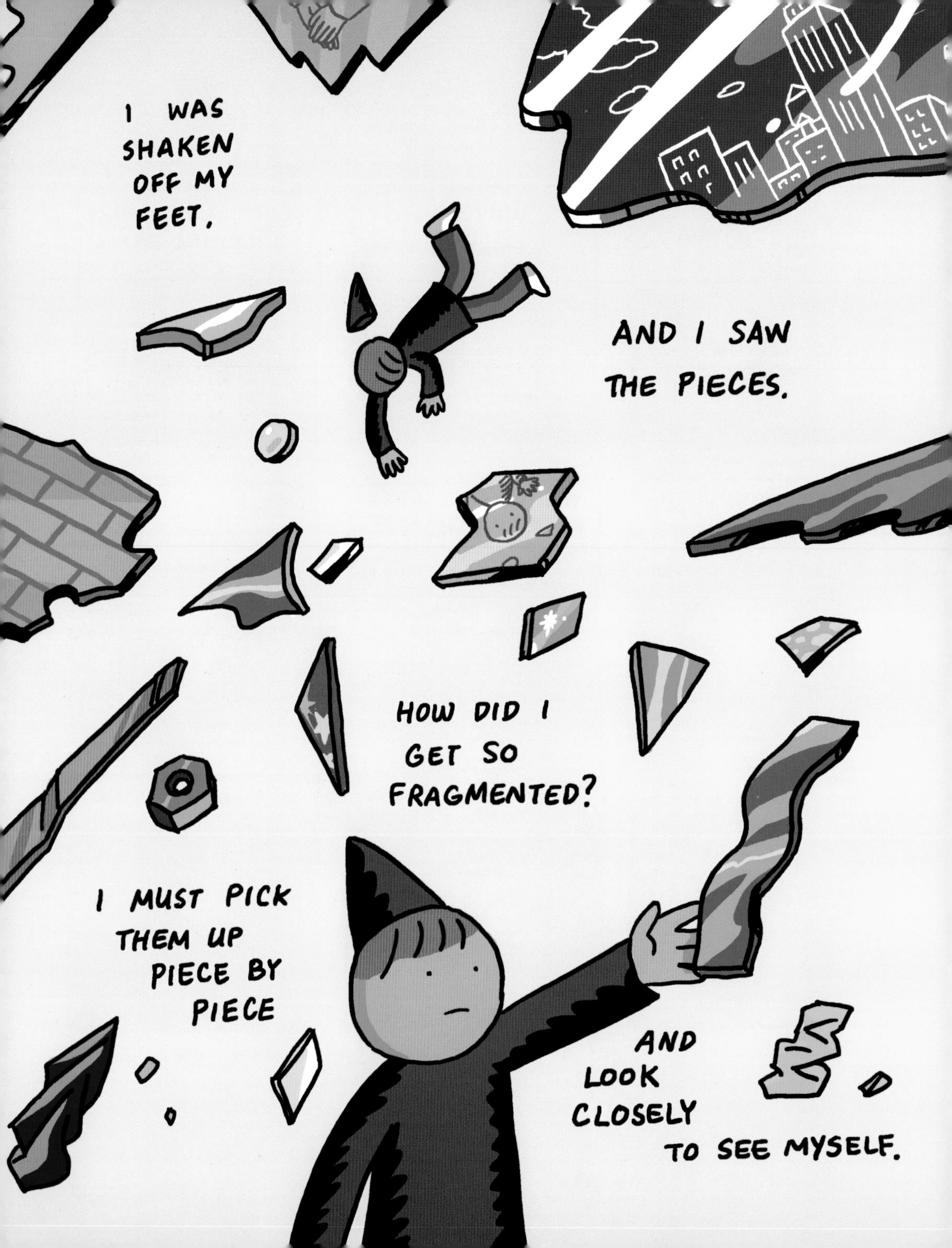
I WAS SHAKEN OFF MY FEET.
AND I SAW THE PIECES.
HOW DID I GET SO FRAGMENTED?
I MUST PICK THEM UP PIECE BY PIECE
AND LOOK CLOSELY TO SEE MYSELF.

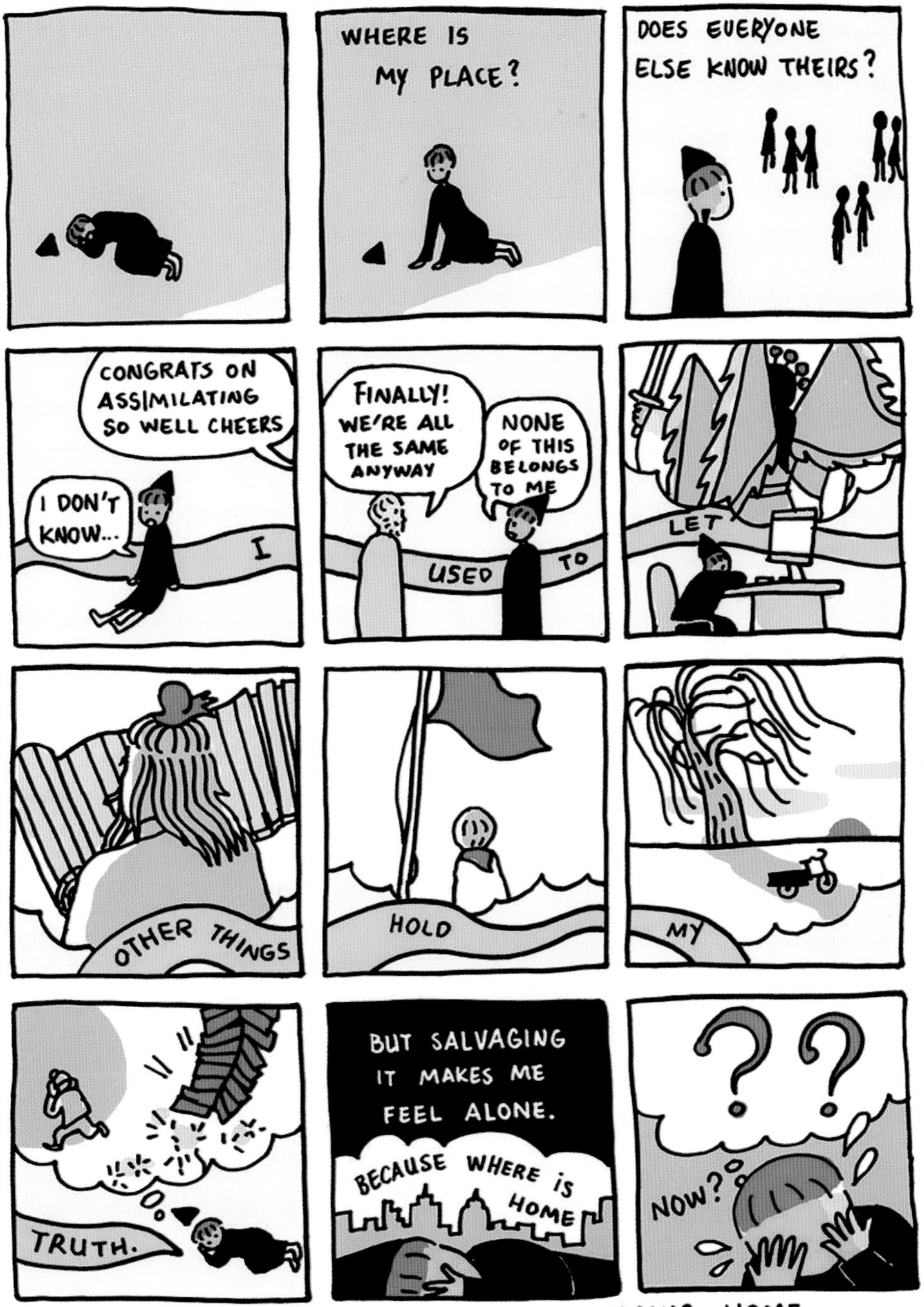

WHERE IS MY PLACE?
DOES EVERYONE ELSE KNOW THEIRS?
CONGRATS ON ASSIMILATING SO WELL CHEERS
I DON'T KNOW...
I
FINALLY! WE'RE ALL THE SAME ANYWAY
NONE OF THIS BELONGS TO ME
USED
TO
LET
OTHER THINGS
HOLD
MY
TRUTH.
BUT SALVAGING IT MAKES ME FEEL ALONE.
BECAUSE WHERE IS HOME
NOW?

SALVAGING HOME

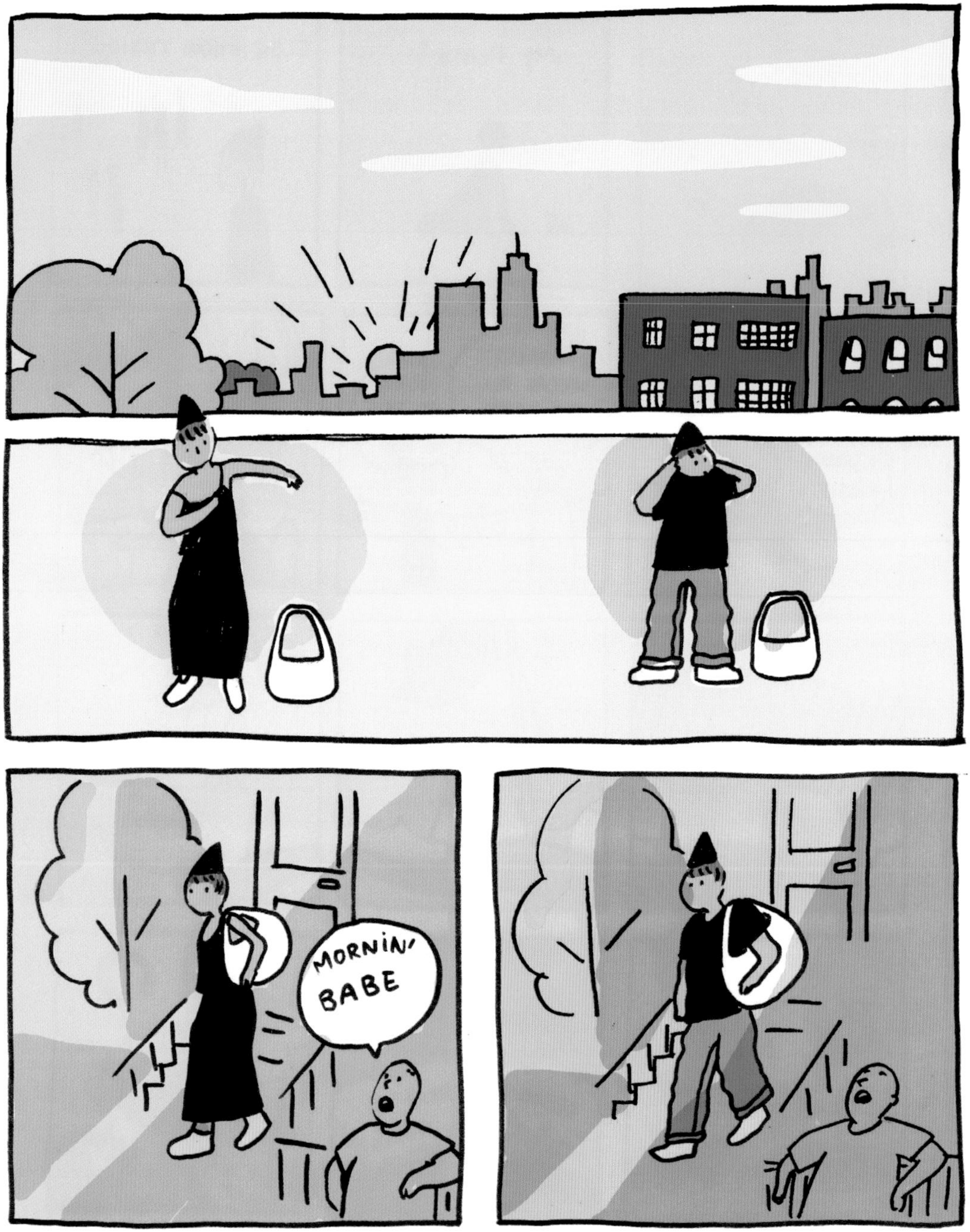
MORNIN' BABE

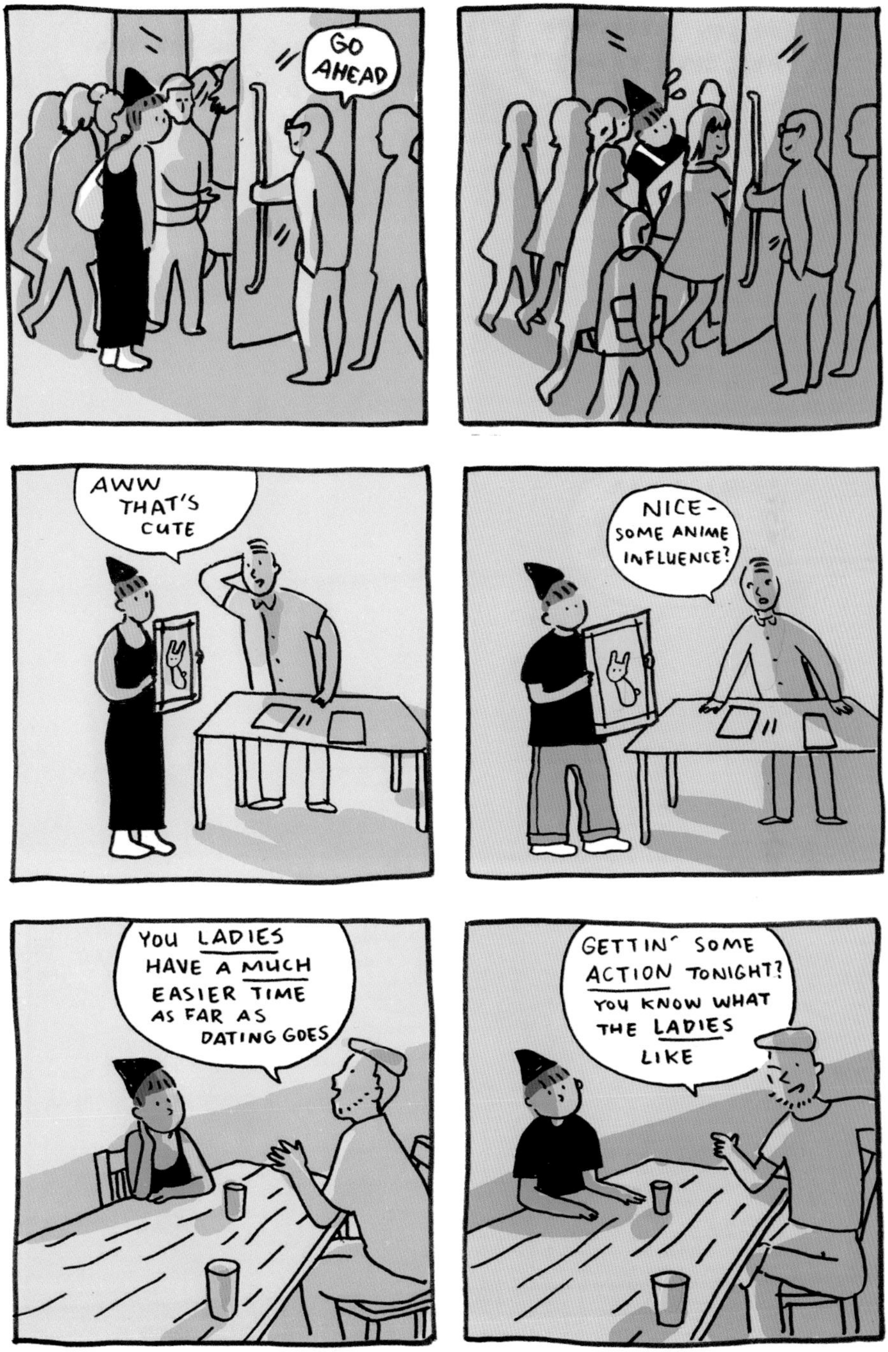
GO AHEAD
AWW THAT'S CUTE
NICE - SOME ANIME INFLUENCE?
YOU LADIES HAVE A MUCH EASIER TIME AS FAR AS DATING GOES
GETTIN' SOME ACTION TONIGHT?
YOU KNOW WHAT THE LADIES LIKE

YOU CAN SLEEP WITH HER, SHE'S FEMME!
WOULD YOU TAP THAT? I'D TAP THAT.
WHOA WHOA, I THOUGHT YOU WERE ONLY INTO GIRLS??
YOU ARE SUCH A TEASE.
?
WHAT'S UP, CHINA DOLL
AWW, MAN.
GO BACK TO WHERE YOU'RE FROM, JACKIE CHAN
AWW, MAN.

DRESSING THE PART

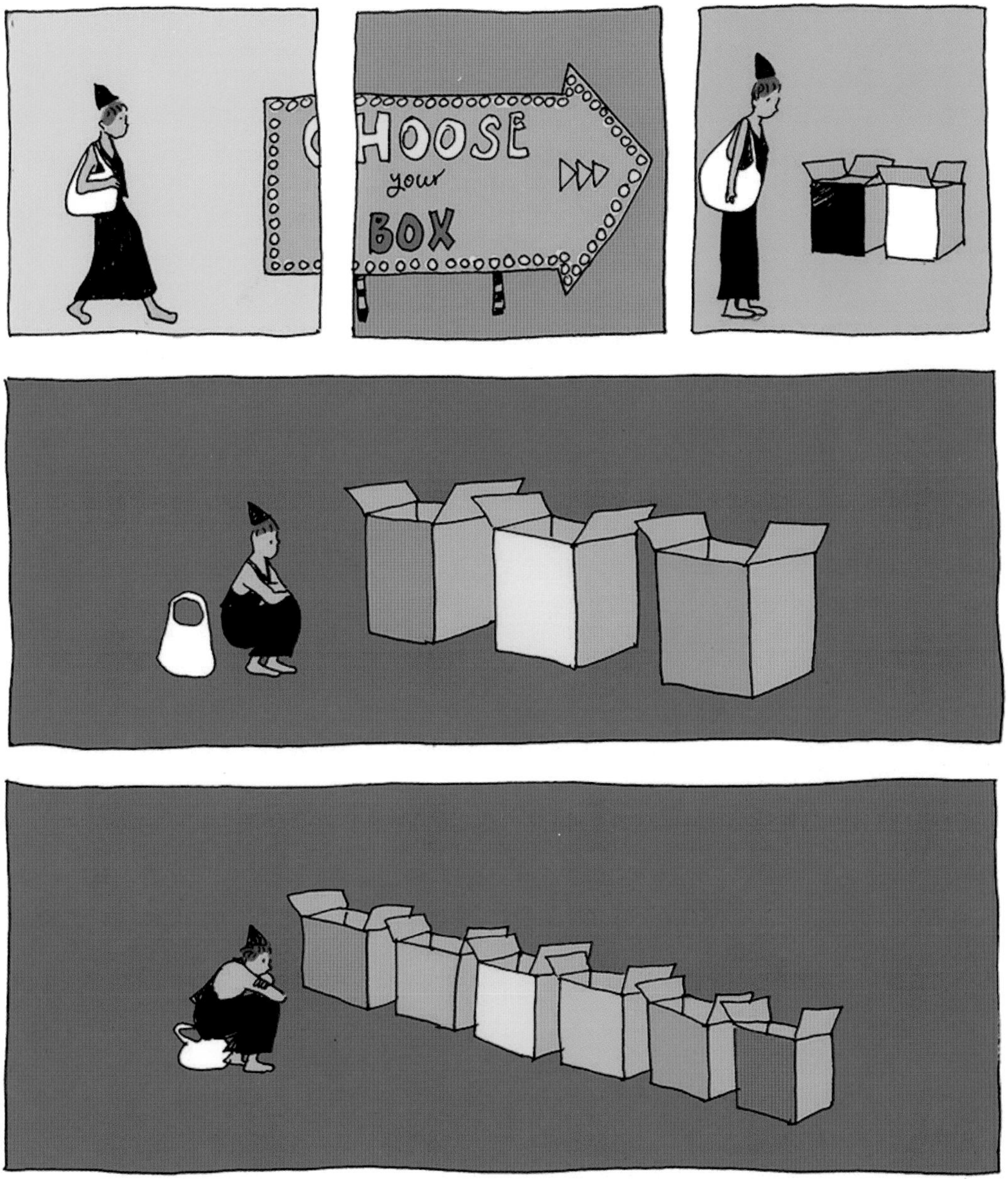
CHOOSE
your
BOX

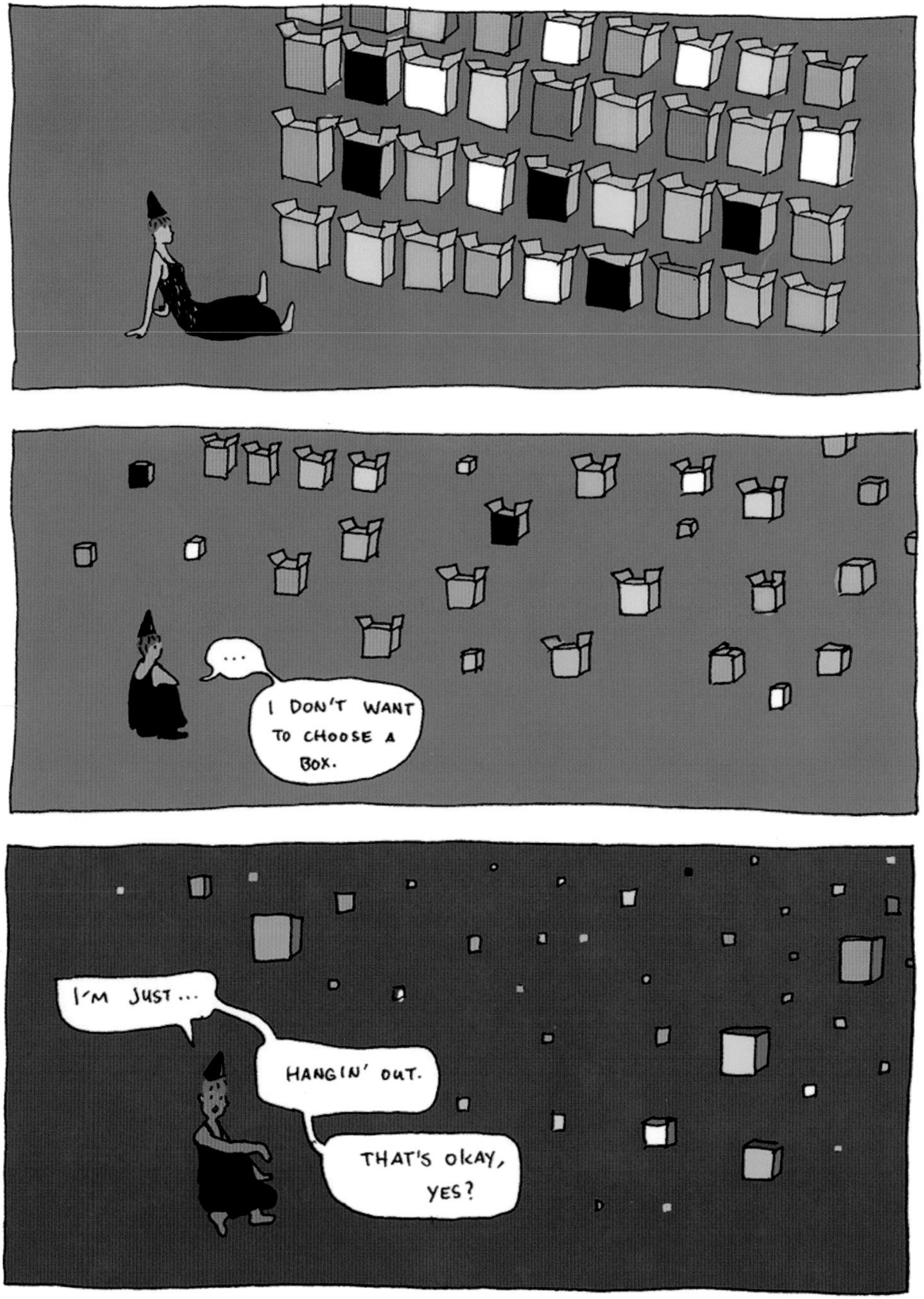
...
I DON'T WANT TO CHOOSE A BOX.
I'M JUST...
HANGIN' OUT.
THAT'S OKAY, YES?

I DON'T HAVE A BOX

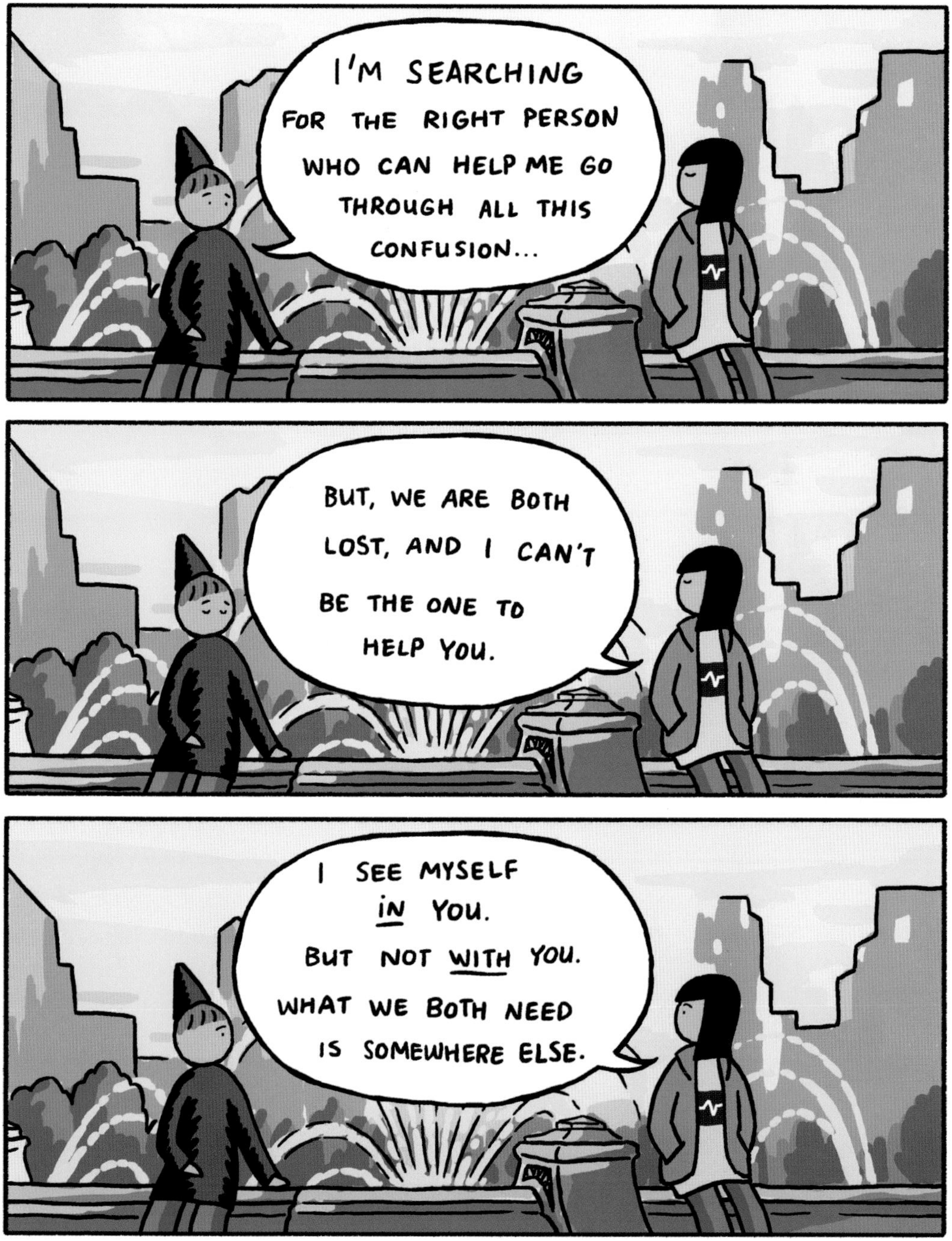
I'M SEARCHING FOR THE RIGHT PERSON WHO CAN HELP ME GO THROUGH ALL THIS CONFUSION...
BUT, WE ARE BOTH LOST, AND I CAN'T BE THE ONE TO HELP YOU.
I SEE MYSELF IN YOU. BUT NOT WITH YOU. WHAT WE BOTH NEED IS SOMEWHERE ELSE.

LOST, WITH DIRECTIONS

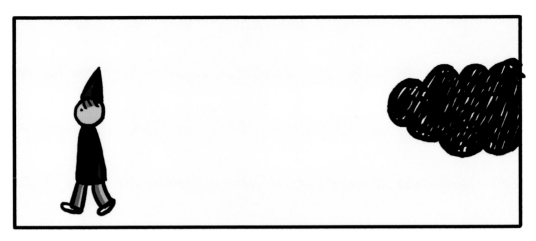

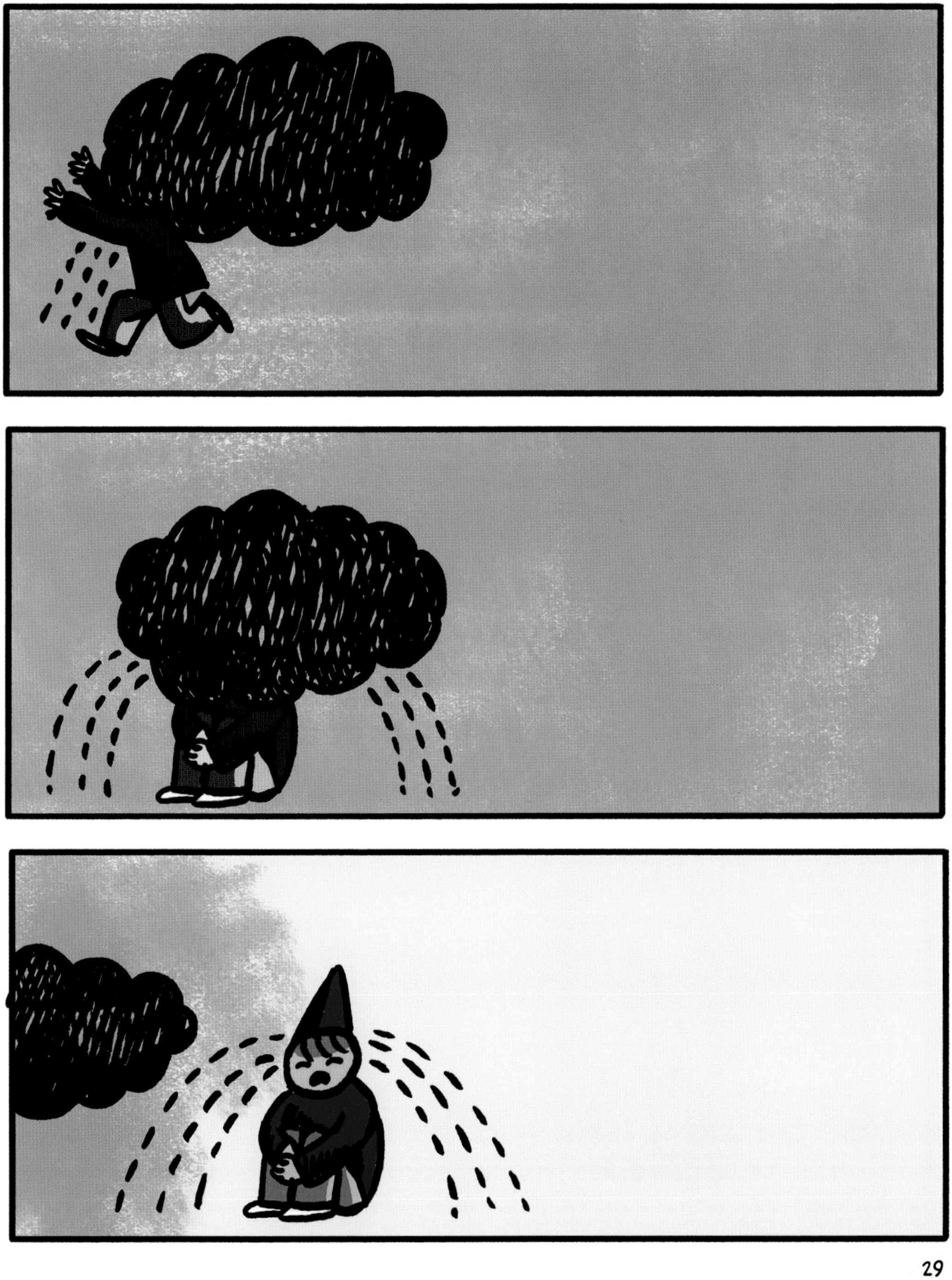

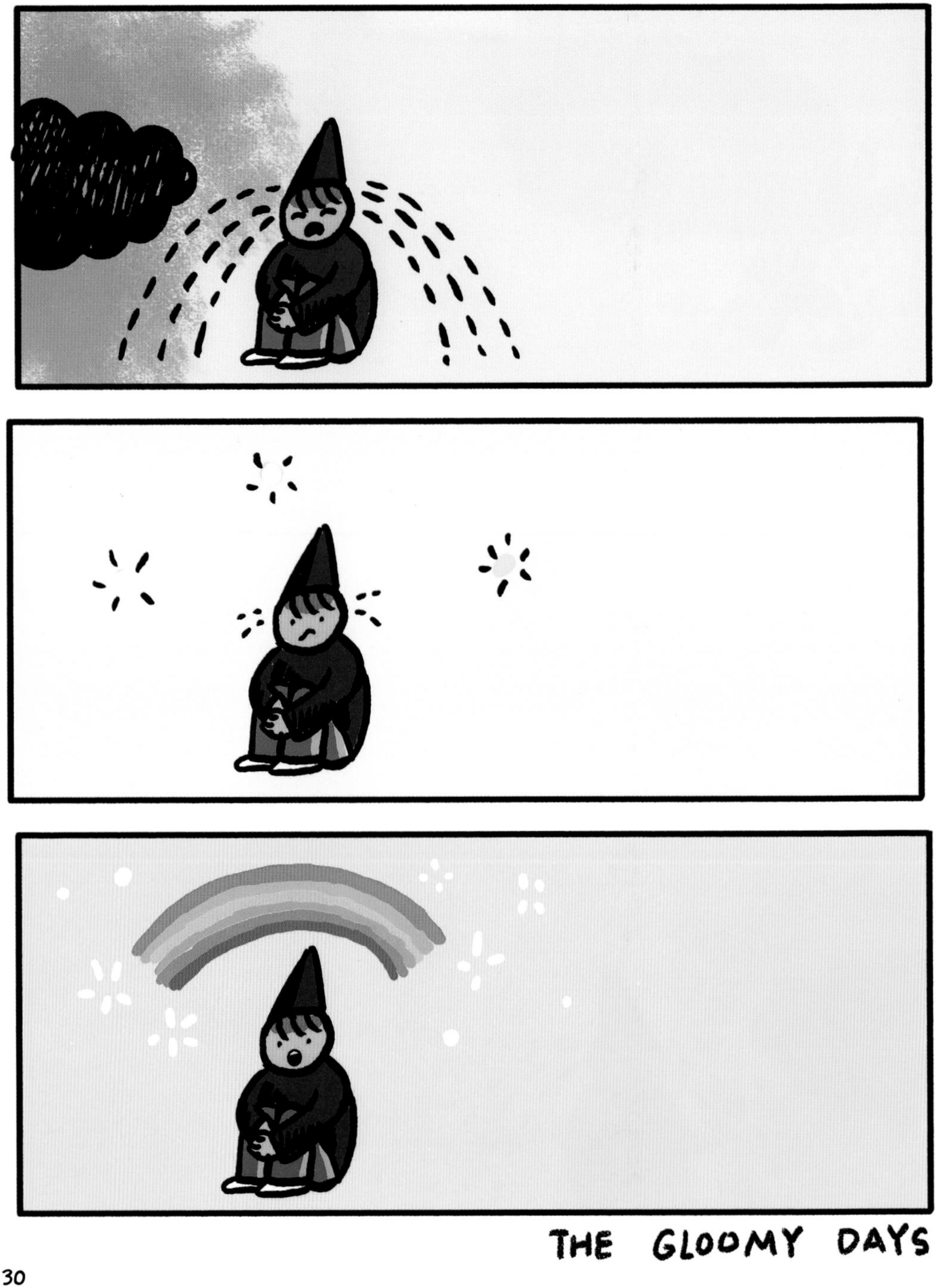

THE GLOOMY DAYS

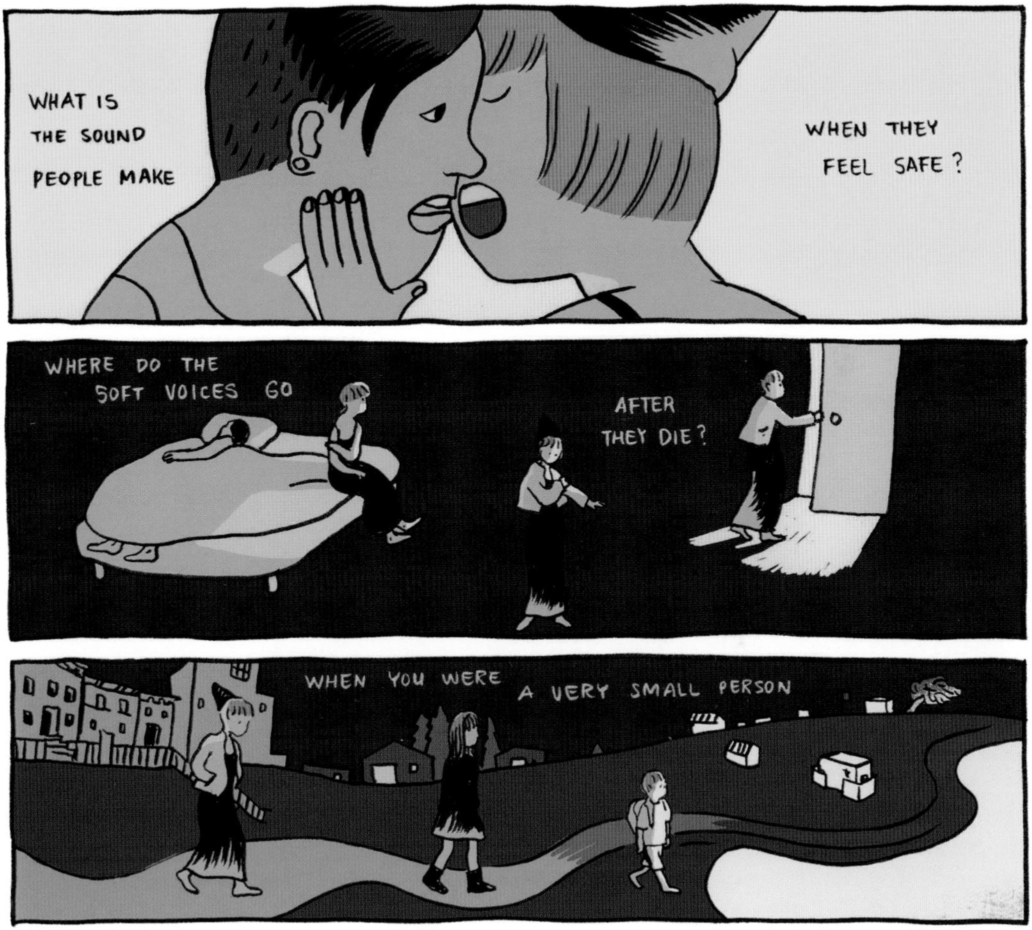
WHAT IS
THE SOUND
PEOPLE MAKE
WHEN THEY
FEEL SAFE?
WHERE DO THE
SOFT VOICES GO
AFTER
THEY DIE?
WHEN YOU WERE
A VERY SMALL PERSON

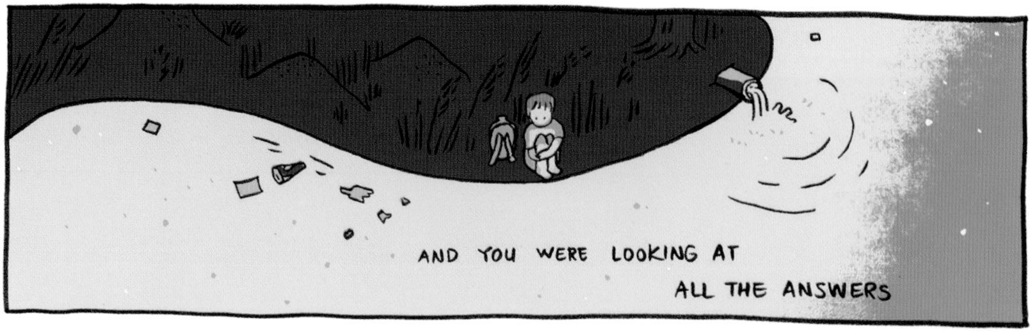
AND YOU WERE LOOKING AT
ALL THE ANSWERS

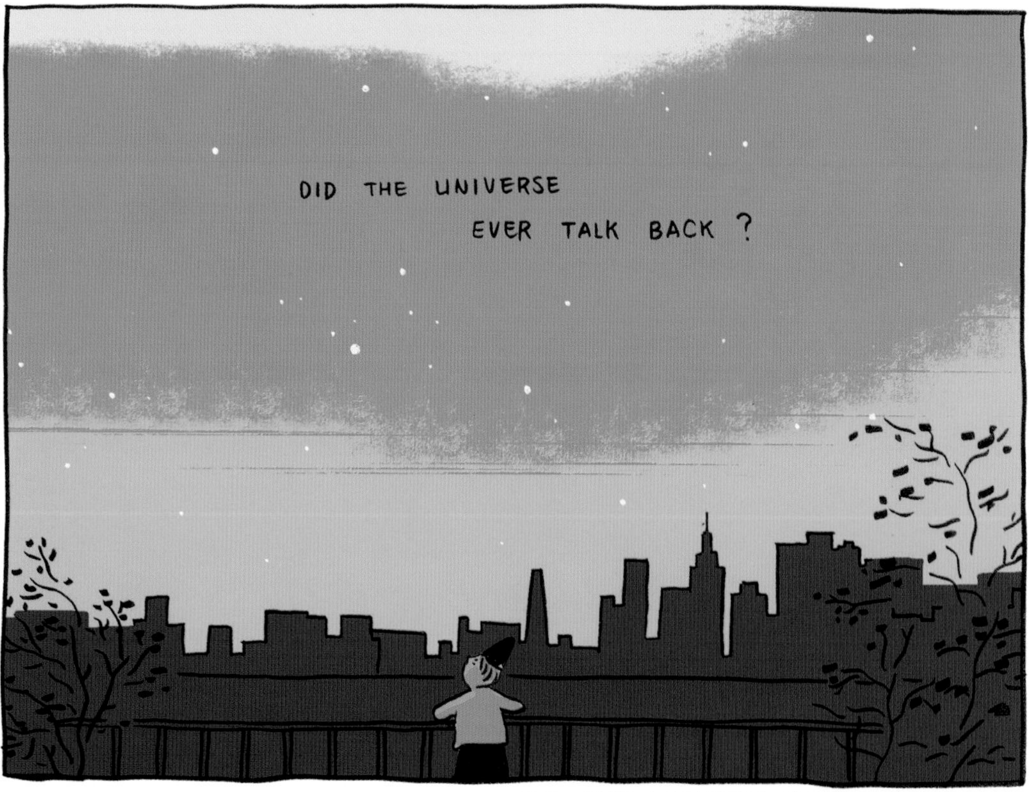
DID THE UNIVERSE
EVER TALK BACK ?

DID THE UNIVERSE EVER TALK BACK

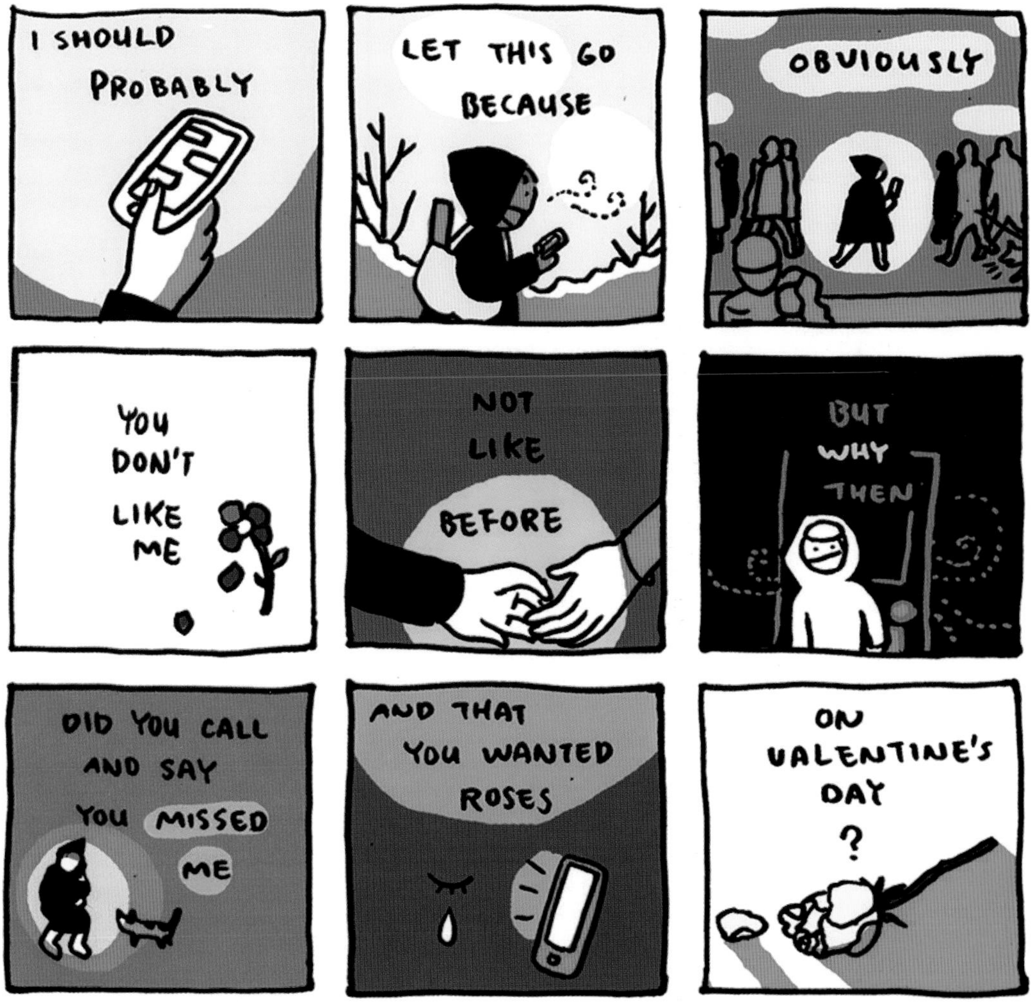
I SHOULD
PROBABLY
LET THIS GO
BECAUSE
OBVIOUSLY
YOU DON'T LIKE ME
NOT LIKE
BEFORE
BUT WHY THEN
DID YOU CALL AND SAY
YOU MISSED ME
AND THAT YOU WANTED ROSES
ON VALENTINE'S DAY
?

WINTER IN THE CITY

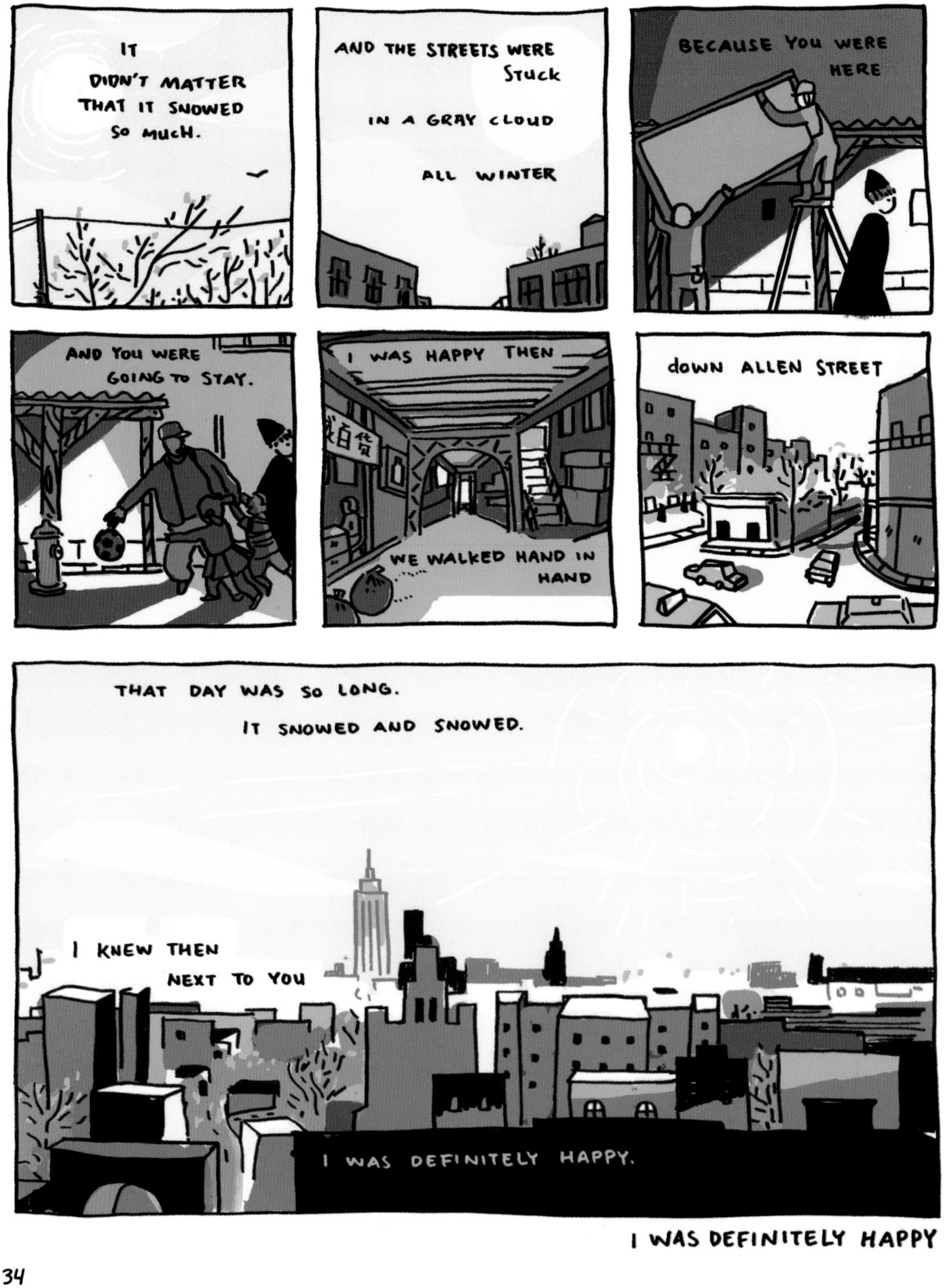
IT DIDN'T MATTER THAT IT SNOWED SO MUCH.
AND THE STREETS WERE STUCK
IN A GRAY CLOUD
ALL WINTER
BECAUSE YOU WERE HERE
AND YOU WERE GOING TO STAY.
I WAS HAPPY THEN
WE WALKED HAND IN HAND
DOWN ALLEN STREET
THAT DAY WAS SO LONG.
IT SNOWED AND SNOWED.
I KNEW THEN
NEXT TO YOU
I WAS DEFINITELY HAPPY.

I WAS DEFINITELY HAPPY

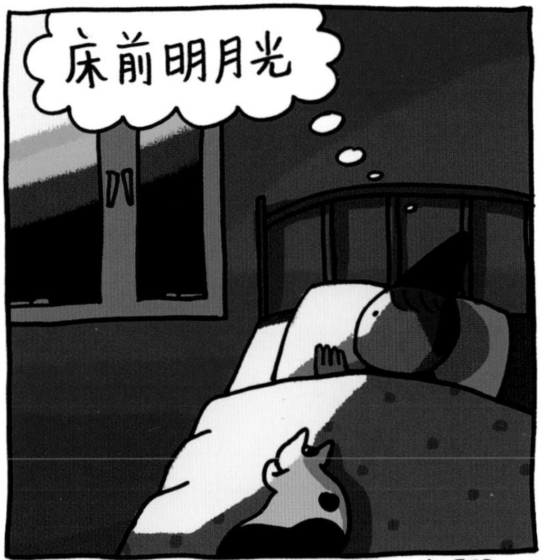
床前明月光

BRIGHT MOONLIGHT FALLS BEFORE MY BED,

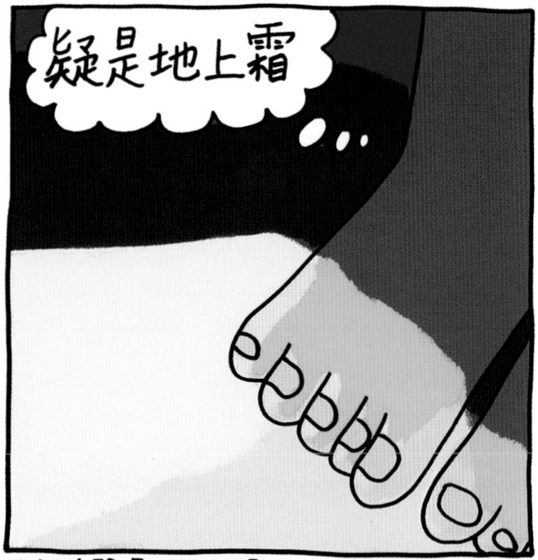
疑是地上霜

IT LOOKED TO ME LIKE A COLD FROST ON THE FLOOR.

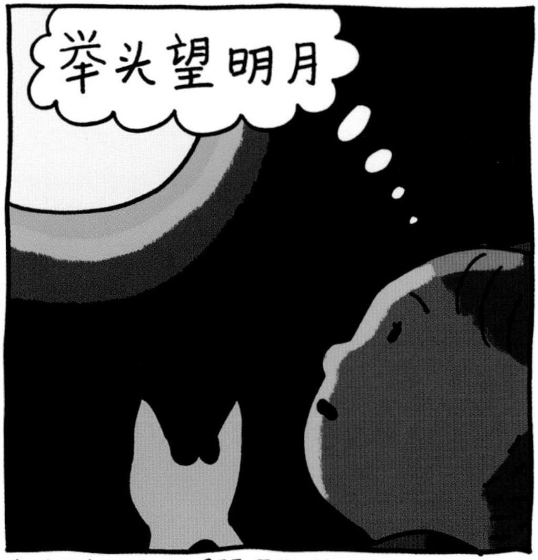
举头望明月

I LOOK UP TO SEE THE MOON...

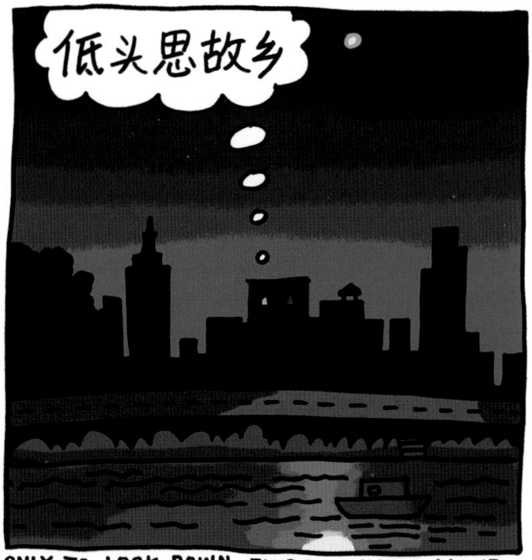
低头思故乡

ONLY TO LOOK DOWN, FINDING MYSELF ALONE, AND MISSING MY HOME.

"QUIET NIGHT THOUGHTS" (ORIGINAL POEM BY LI BAI)

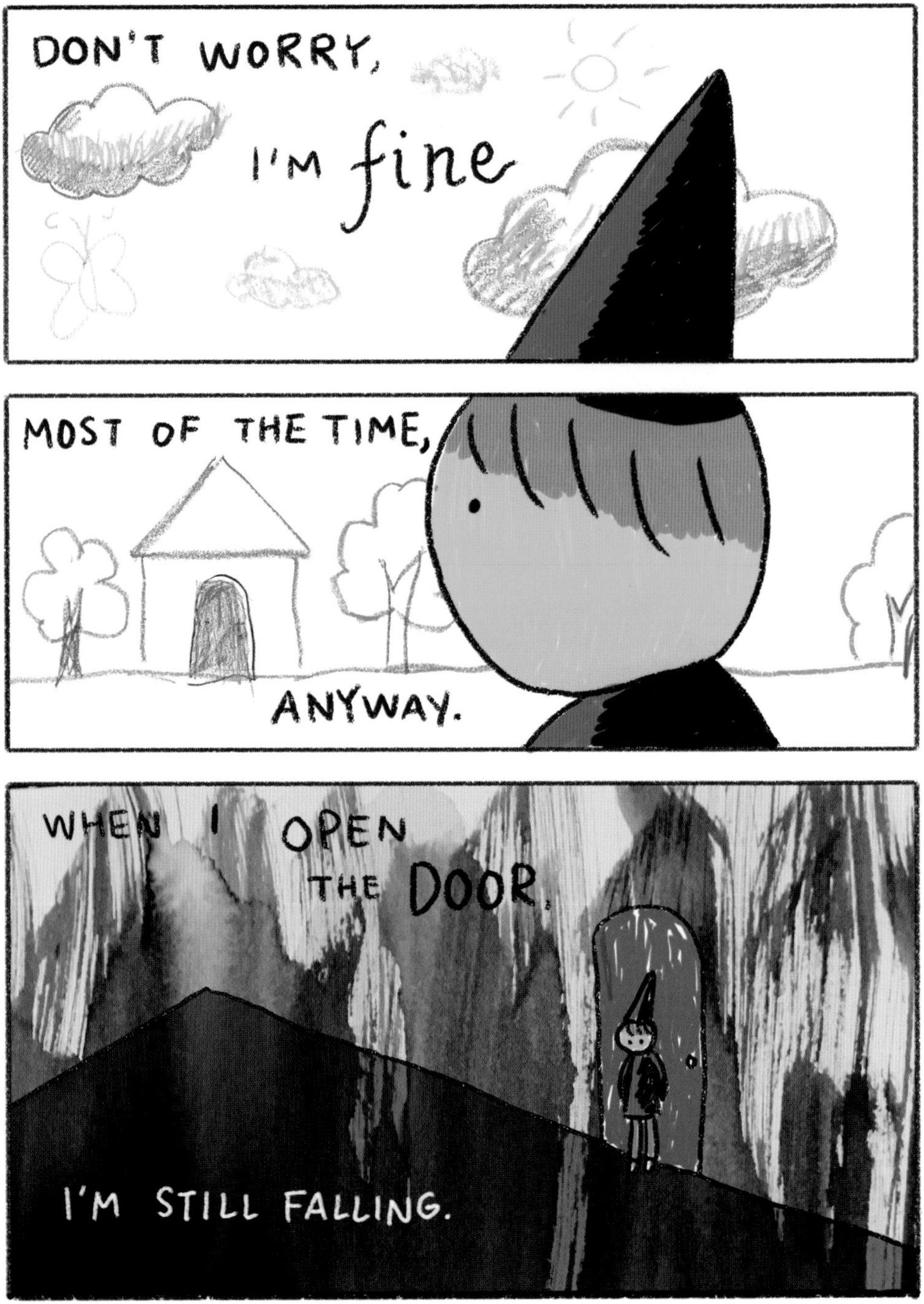
DON'T WORRY,
I'M fine
MOST OF THE TIME,
ANYWAY.
WHEN I OPEN THE DOOR,
I'M STILL FALLING.

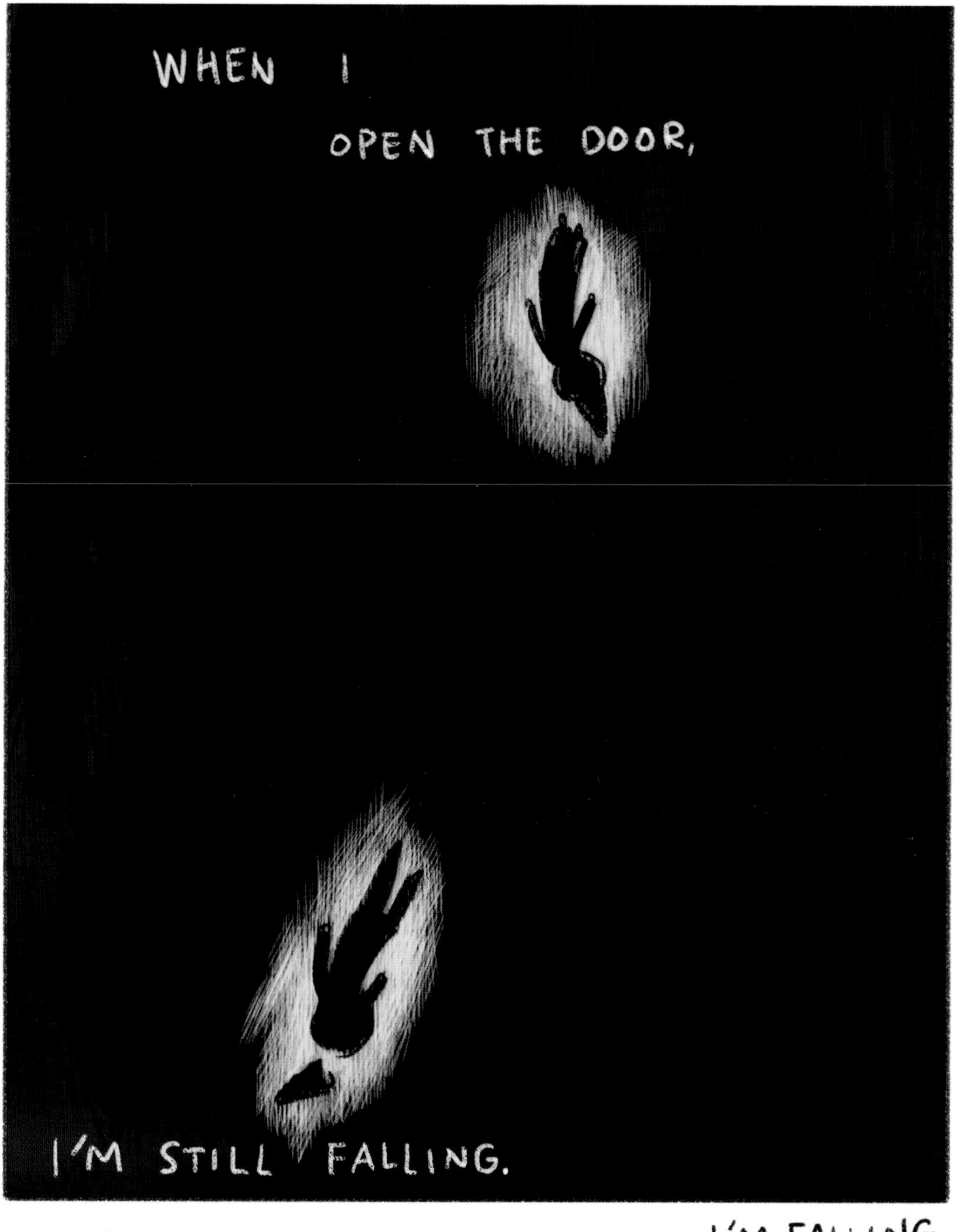
WHEN I
OPEN THE DOOR,
I'M STILL FALLING.

I'M FALLING

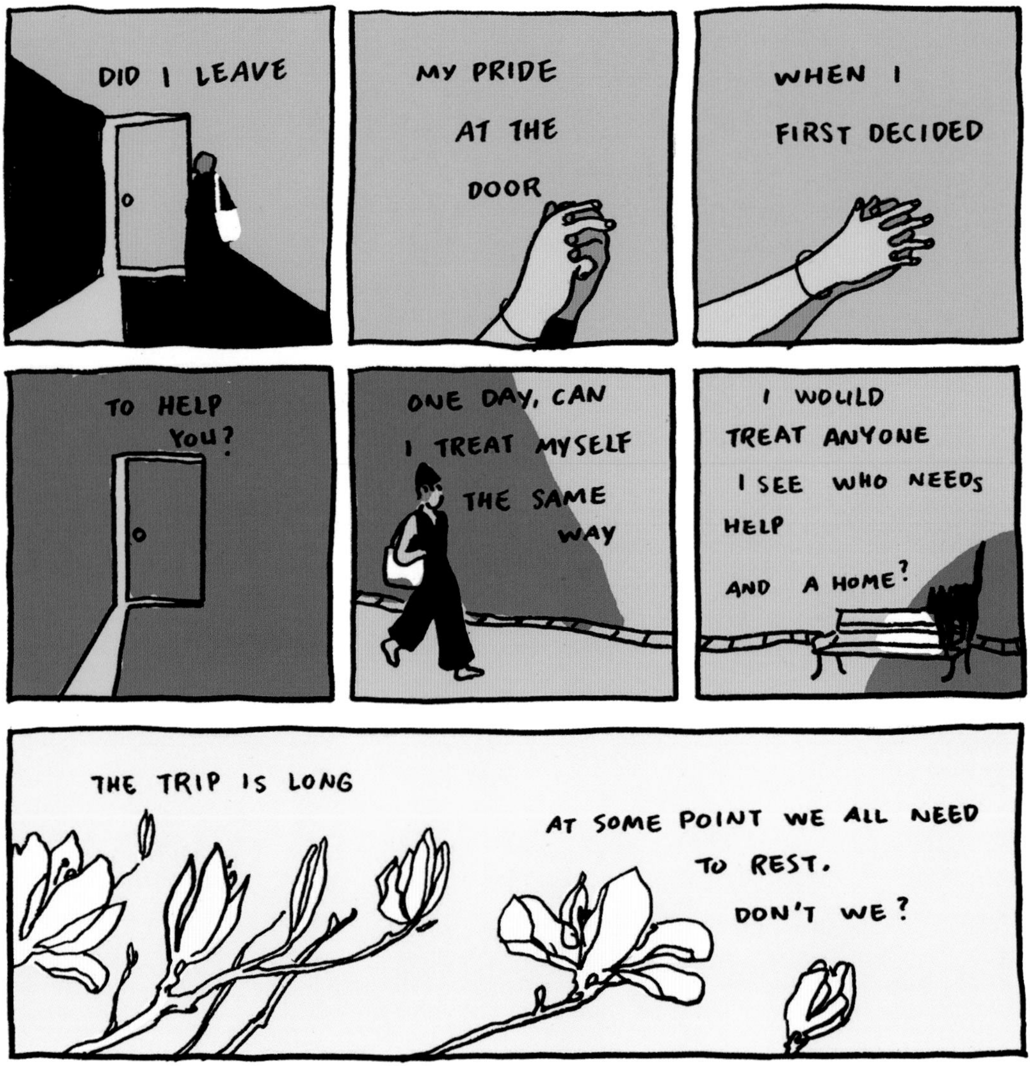

DID I LEAVE
MY PRIDE
AT THE
DOOR
WHEN I
FIRST DECIDED
TO HELP
YOU?
ONE DAY, CAN
I TREAT MYSELF
THE SAME
WAY
I WOULD
TREAT ANYONE
I SEE WHO NEEDS
HELP
AND A HOME?
THE TRIP IS LONG
AT SOME POINT WE ALL NEED
TO REST.
DON'T WE?

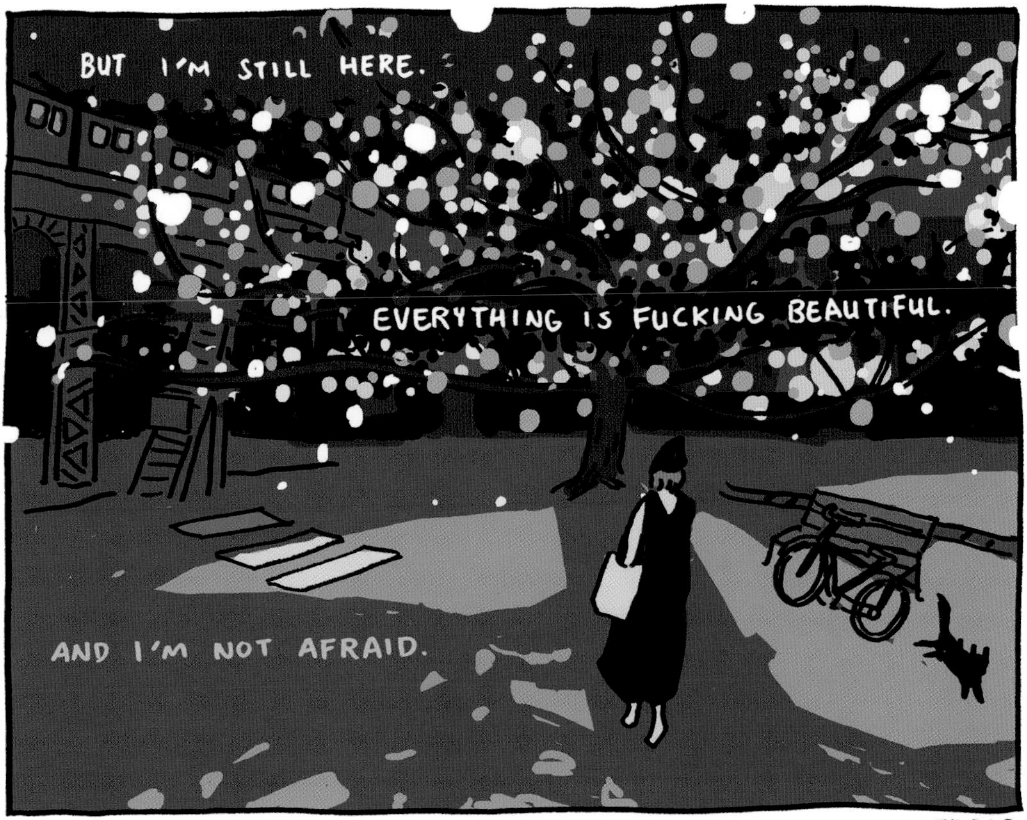
BUT I'M STILL HERE.
EVERYTHING IS FUCKING BEAUTIFUL.
AND I'M NOT AFRAID.

I'M NOT AFRAID

LIKE A CLIMBING VINE,

HOWEVER WEAK,

HOWEVER UNWANTED,

HOWEVER FORGOTTEN,

I'M...

ALWAYS LOOKING FOR A SPACE TO EXIST...

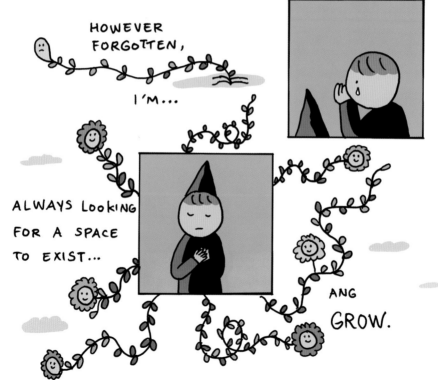

ANG GROW.

LIKE A CLIMBING VINE

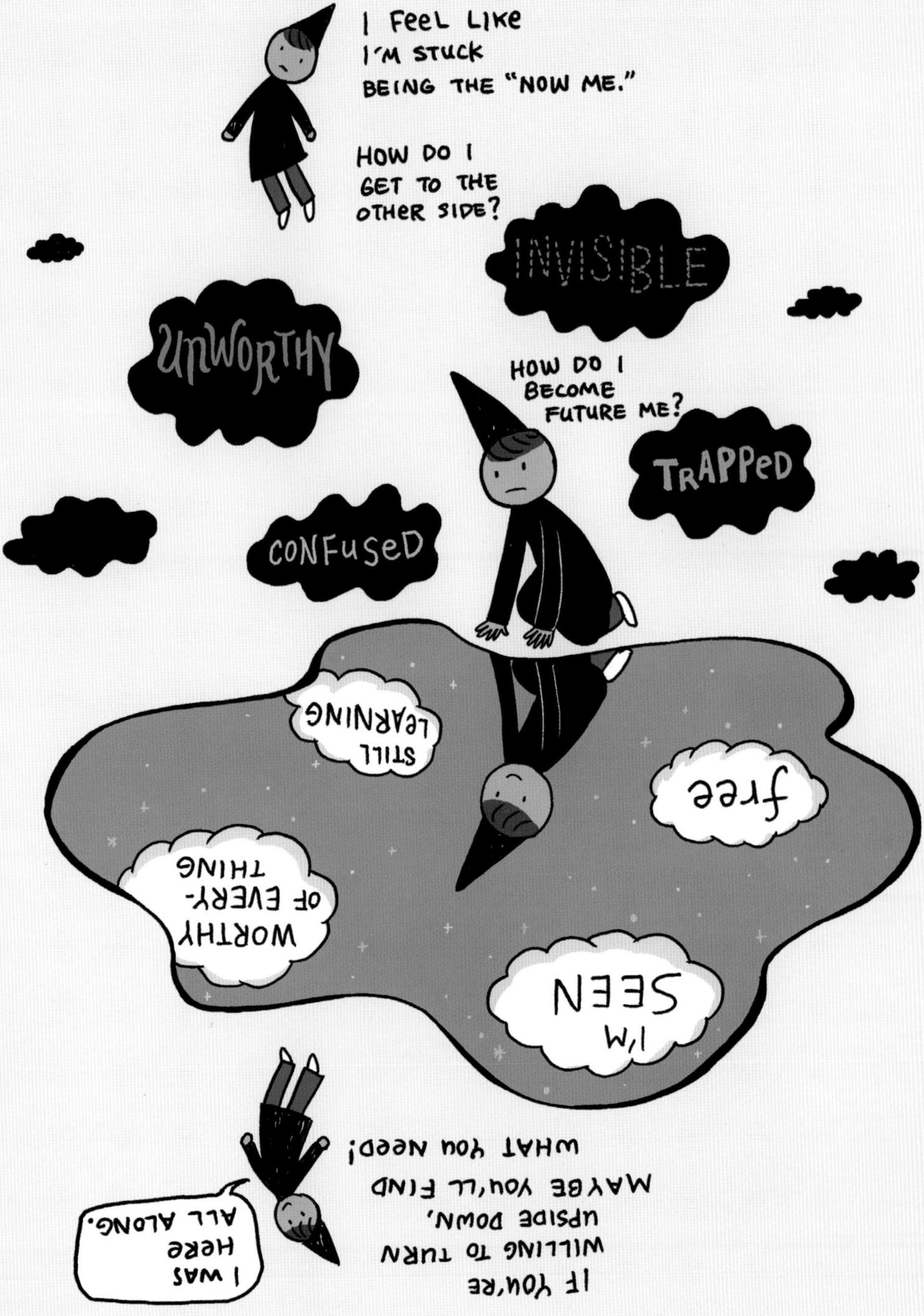
I FEEL LIKE I'M STUCK BEING THE "NOW ME."
HOW DO I GET TO THE OTHER SIDE?
INVISIBLE
UNWORTHY
HOW DO I BECOME FUTURE ME?
TRAPPED
CONFUSED
STILL LEARNING
free
WORTHY OF EVERY-THING
I'M SEEN
IF YOU'RE WILLING TO TURN UPSIDE DOWN, MAYBE YOU'LL FIND WHAT YOU NEED!
I WAS HERE ALL ALONG.

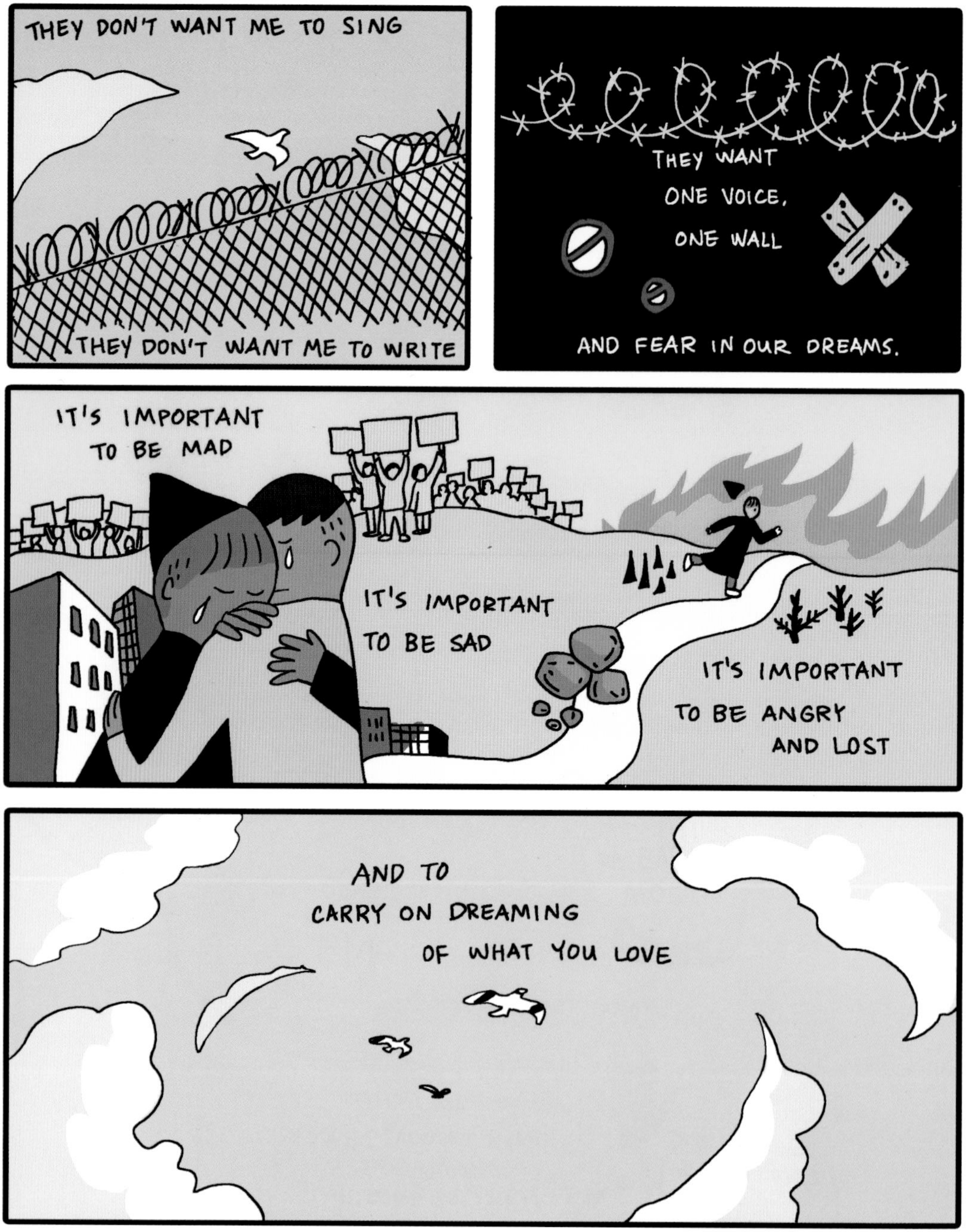
THEY DON'T WANT ME TO SING
THEY DON'T WANT ME TO WRITE
THEY WANT ONE VOICE, ONE WALL
AND FEAR IN OUR DREAMS.
IT'S IMPORTANT TO BE MAD
IT'S IMPORTANT TO BE SAD
IT'S IMPORTANT TO BE ANGRY AND LOST
AND TO CARRY ON DREAMING OF WHAT YOU LOVE

DON'T CENSOR FEELINGS

THE What are you AFRAID of? BINGO
Rejection
Not being liked
Depression
Racist comments when I'm unprepared
Heartbreak
cancer
"You're NOT ____ ENOUGH."
Feeling alone
Failure
Calling my family
Losing control
Unable to Tell the TRUTH
All-nighters
Bedbugs
Throwing up
Getting lost
Being Lied to
Car Accidents
Feeling betrayed
Small talk
Height
Being bullied
Food poisoning
Moving

WE CREATED MONSTERS

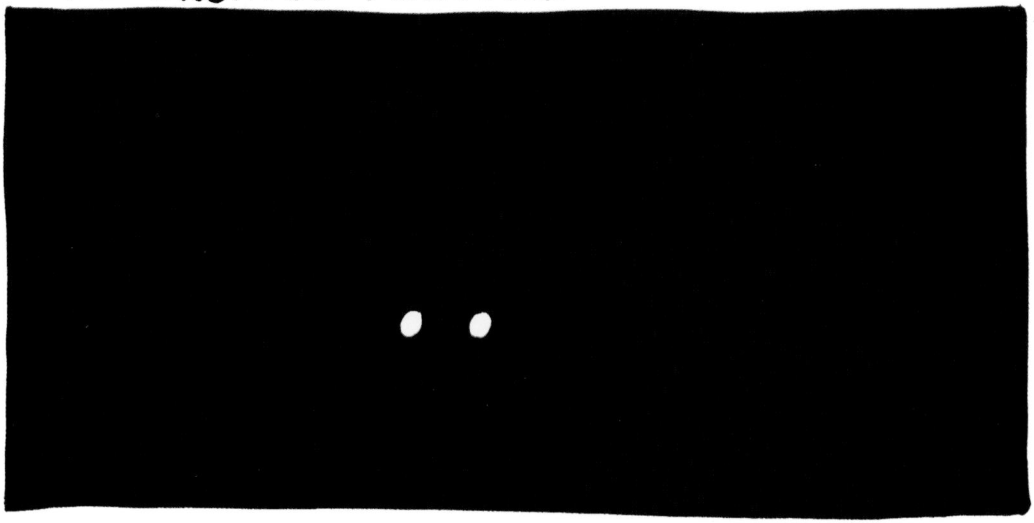

TO PROTECT US FROM THE DARK.

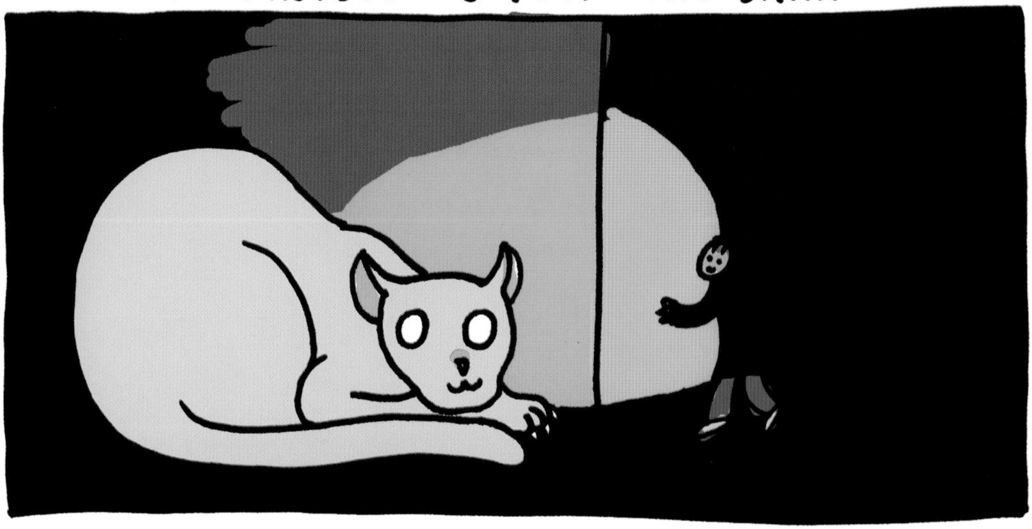

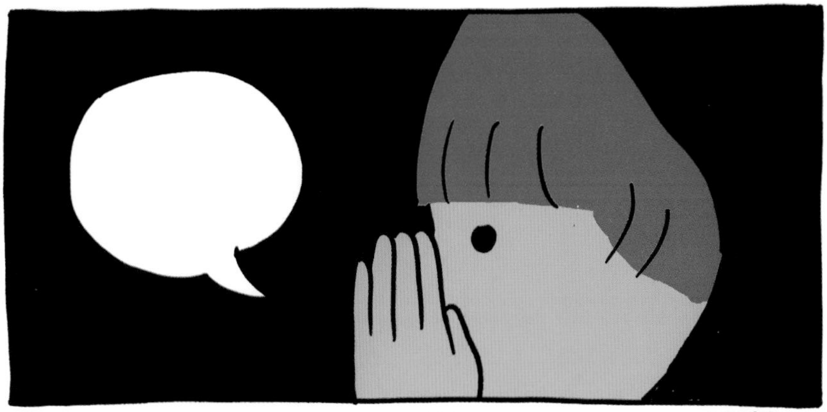

TELL SOMEONE ABOUT YOUR NIGHTMARES.

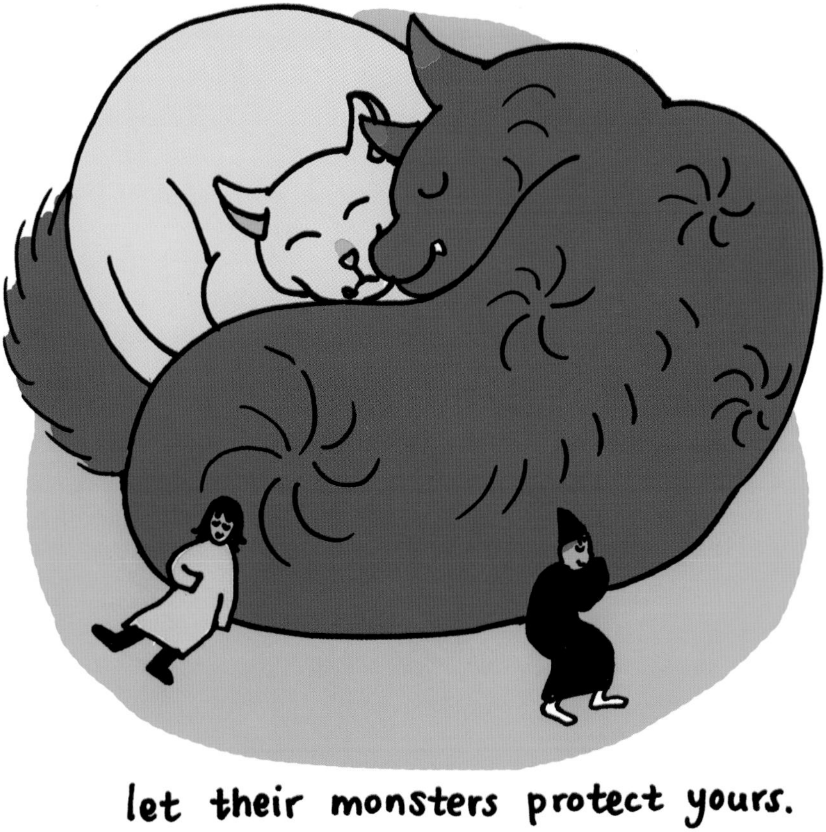

let their monsters protect yours.

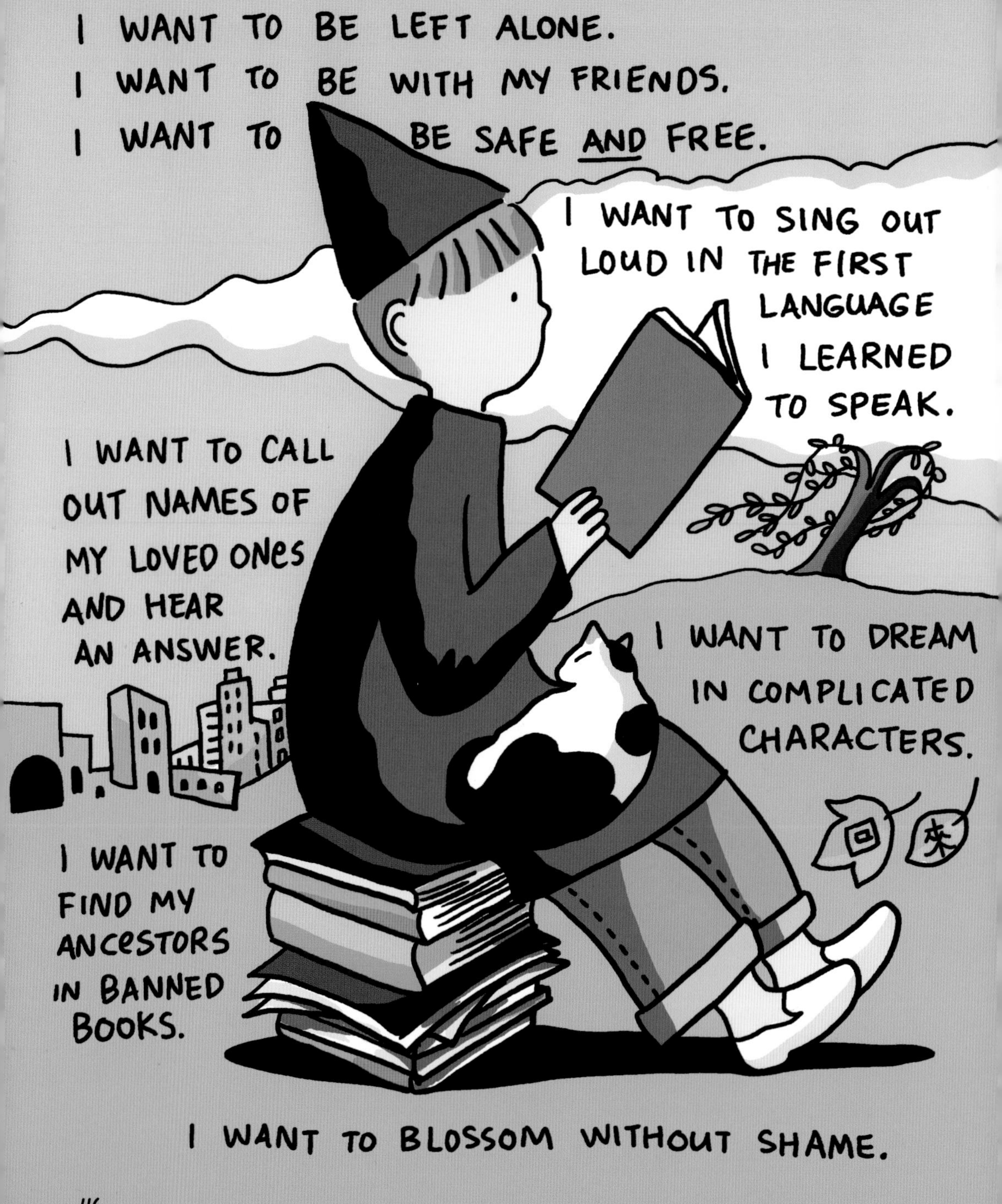
I WANT TO BE LEFT ALONE.
I WANT TO BE WITH MY FRIENDS.
I WANT TO BE SAFE AND FREE.
I WANT TO SING OUT LOUD IN THE FIRST LANGUAGE I LEARNED TO SPEAK.
I WANT TO CALL OUT NAMES OF MY LOVED ONES AND HEAR AN ANSWER.
I WANT TO DREAM IN COMPLICATED CHARACTERS.
回
來
I WANT TO FIND MY ANCESTORS IN BANNED BOOKS.
I WANT TO BLOSSOM WITHOUT SHAME.

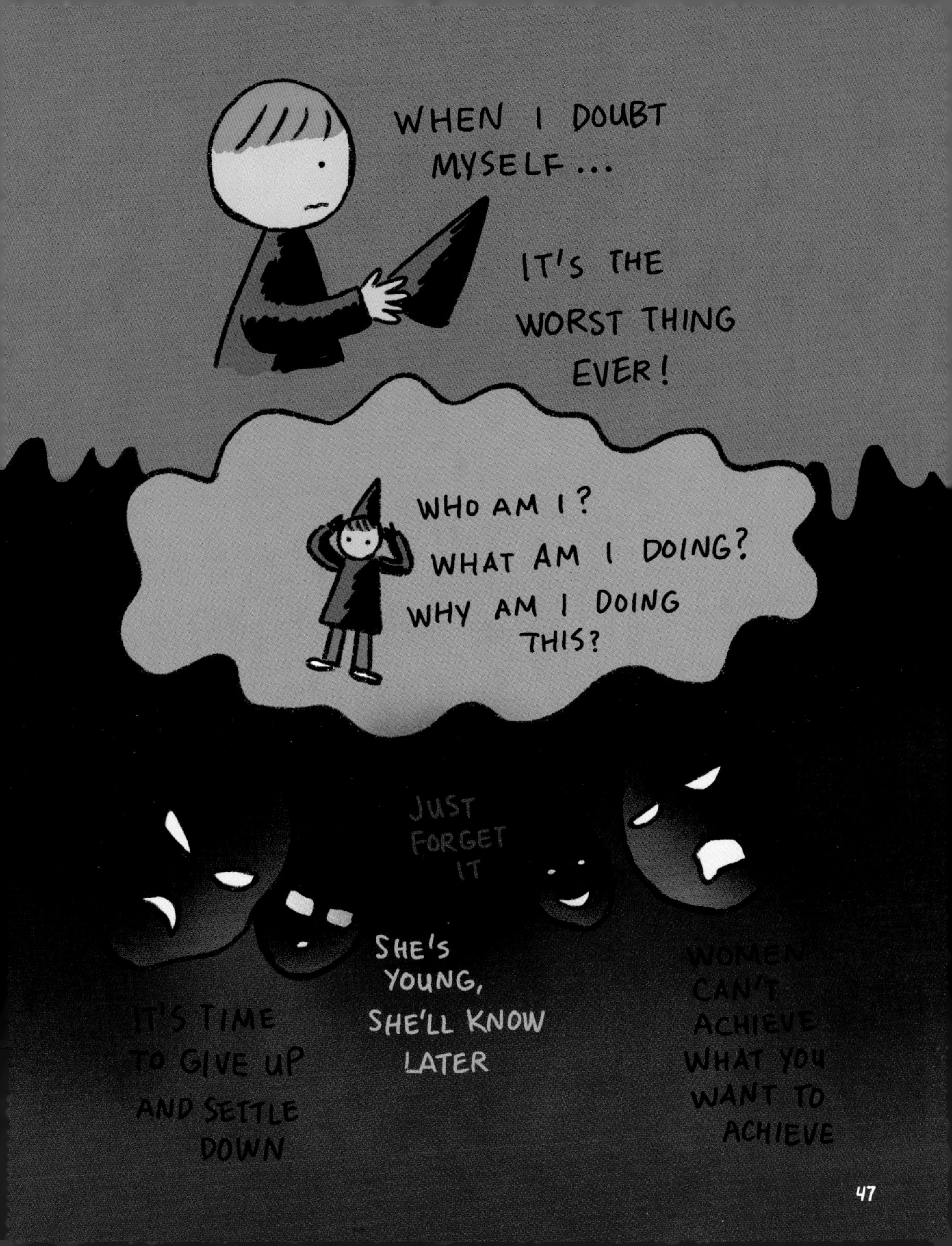
WHEN I DOUBT MYSELF...
IT'S THE WORST THING EVER!
WHO AM I?
WHAT AM I DOING?
WHY AM I DOING THIS?
JUST FORGET IT
IT'S TIME TO GIVE UP AND SETTLE DOWN
SHE'S YOUNG, SHE'LL KNOW LATER
WOMEN CAN'T ACHIEVE WHAT YOU WANT TO ACHIEVE

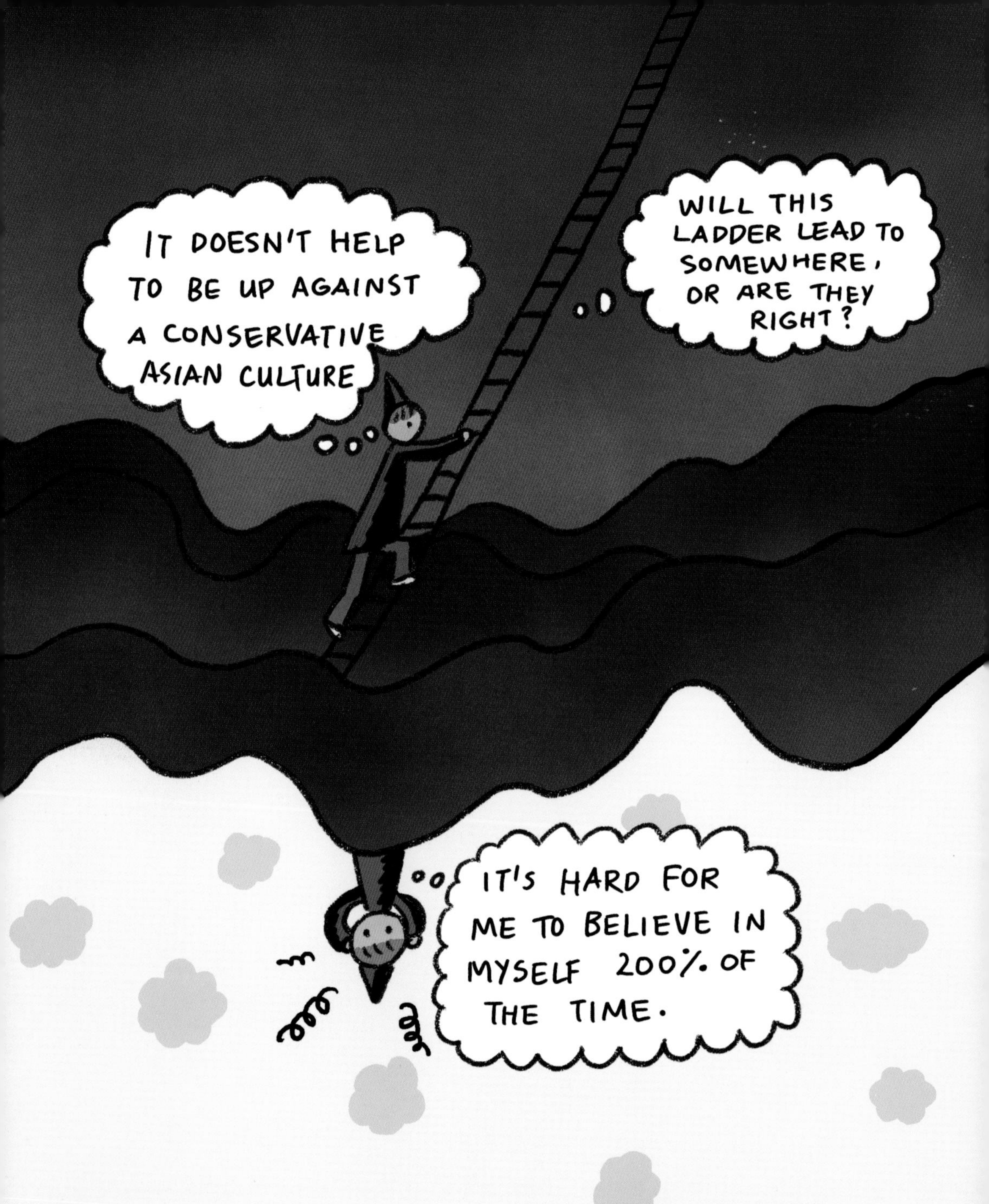
IT DOESN'T HELP TO BE UP AGAINST A CONSERVATIVE ASIAN CULTURE
WILL THIS LADDER LEAD TO SOMEWHERE, OR ARE THEY RIGHT?
IT'S HARD FOR ME TO BELIEVE IN MYSELF 200% OF THE TIME.

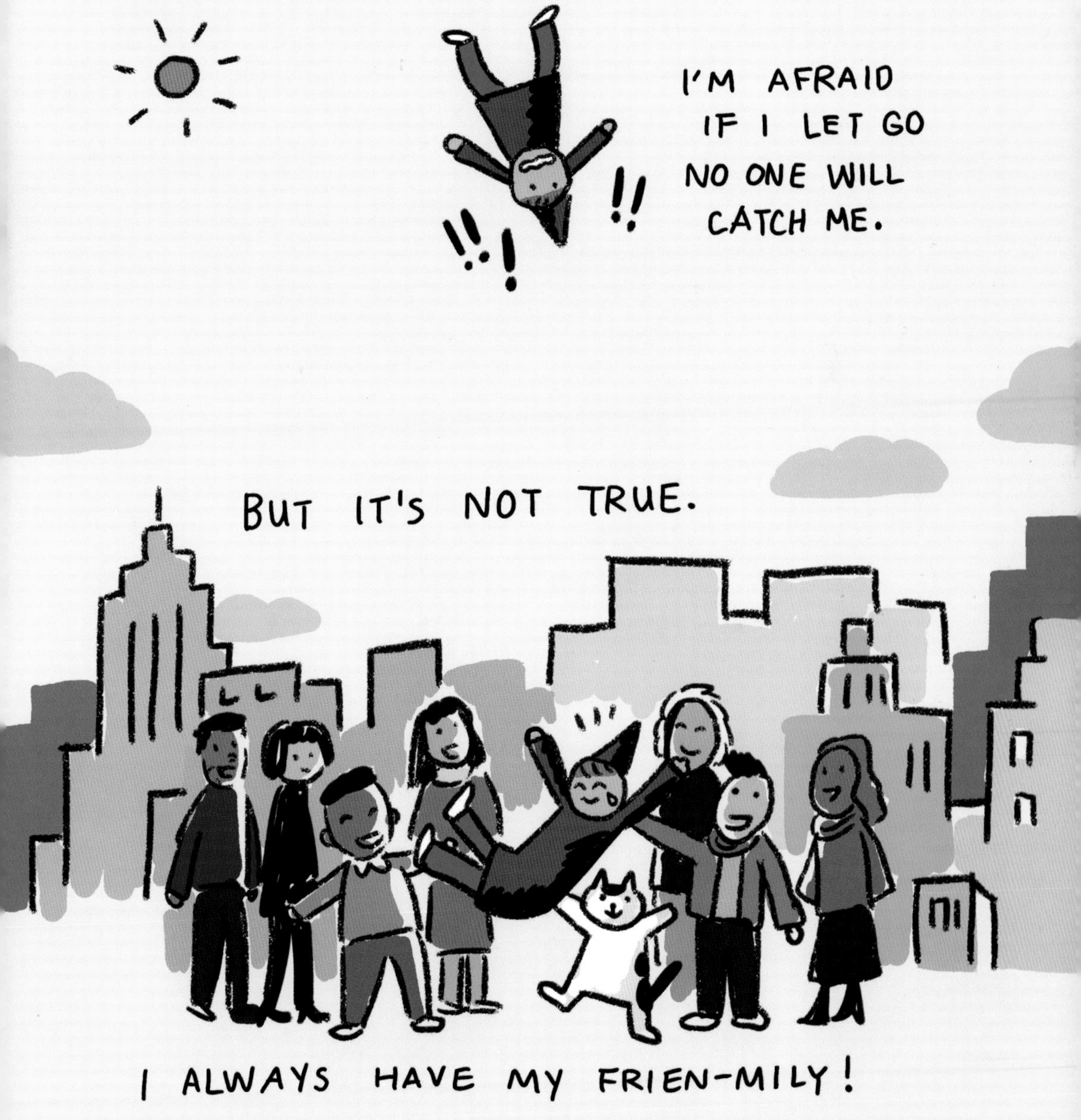
I'M AFRAID IF I LET GO NO ONE WILL CATCH ME.
!!
!!!
BUT IT'S NOT TRUE.
I ALWAYS HAVE MY FRIEN-MILY!

MY SELF-DOUBT

GOING TO Therapy

I'VE BEEN GOING TO THERAPY REGULARLY FOR 5 YEARS.

REALLY? YOU DON'T LOOK _____

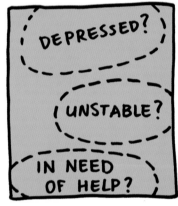

DEPRESSED?

UNSTABLE?

IN NEED OF HELP?

YOU CAN BE SEEING A THERAPIST WHEN YOU'RE "PERFECTLY FINE,"

WHATEVER THAT MEANS TO YOU.

INDEED, THERAPY IS SUITABLE FOR UNPACKING VERY DIFFICULT SUBJECTS.

I NEVER THOUGHT... I MEAN... IT'S JUST ...

SOMETIMES, HOWEVER, IT CAN BE LIKE TALKING TO A FRIEND OR A PARENT,

AND THEN I ATE LUNCH IN CENTRAL PARK...

ESPECIALLY IF THOSE RELATIONSHIPS ARE UNAVAILABLE.

I'M NOT ALONE.

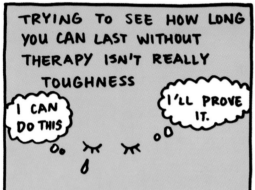

TRYING TO SEE HOW LONG YOU CAN LAST WITHOUT THERAPY ISN'T REALLY TOUGHNESS

I CAN DO THIS

I'LL PROVE IT.

WHILE SEEKING HELP DOES NOT IMPLY WEAKNESS.

BE STRONG!

I AM STRONG. I'M TAKING CARE OF MYSELF.

"TOUGH" AND "WEAK" ARE BINARIES THAT DON'T COVER THE DYNAMIC LAYERS OF HUMAN emotions, anyway.

"TOUGH"

"WEAK"

"WEAK"

"TOUGH"

THERAPY IS COSTLY; IT'S NOT AS ACCESSIBLE AS IT SHOULD BE FOR EVERYONE WHO NEEDS IT.

YOU SHOULD TAKE ADVANTAGE OF IT IF YOU CAN.

I SEE.

AND DON'T, FOR ANY REASON, SHAME SOMEBODY FOR SEEKING PROFESSIONAL CARE.

THEIR LIVES, AND NEEDS, MAY NOT ALWAYS BE WHAT YOU THINK.

GOING TO THERAPY

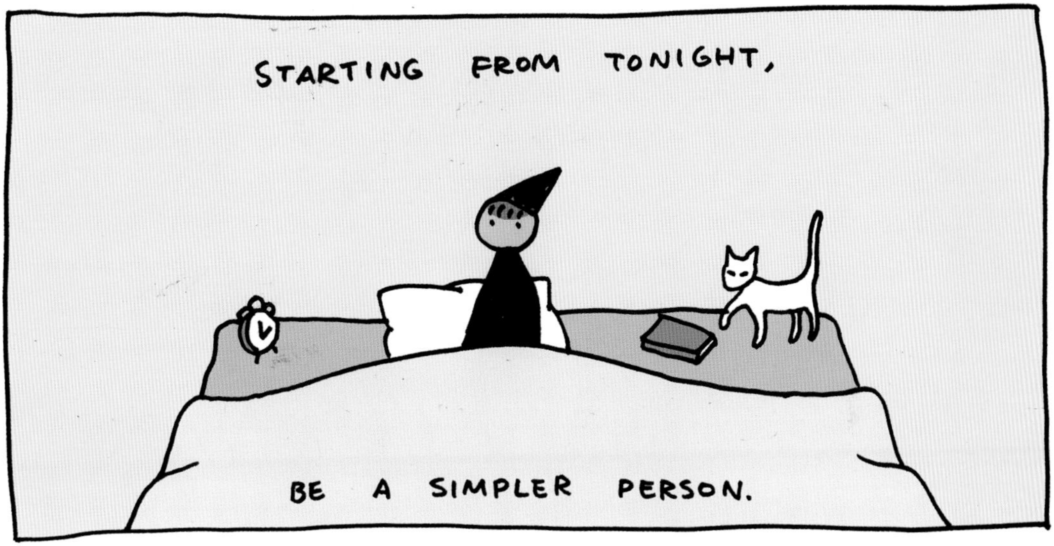
STARTING FROM TONIGHT,
BE A SIMPLER PERSON.

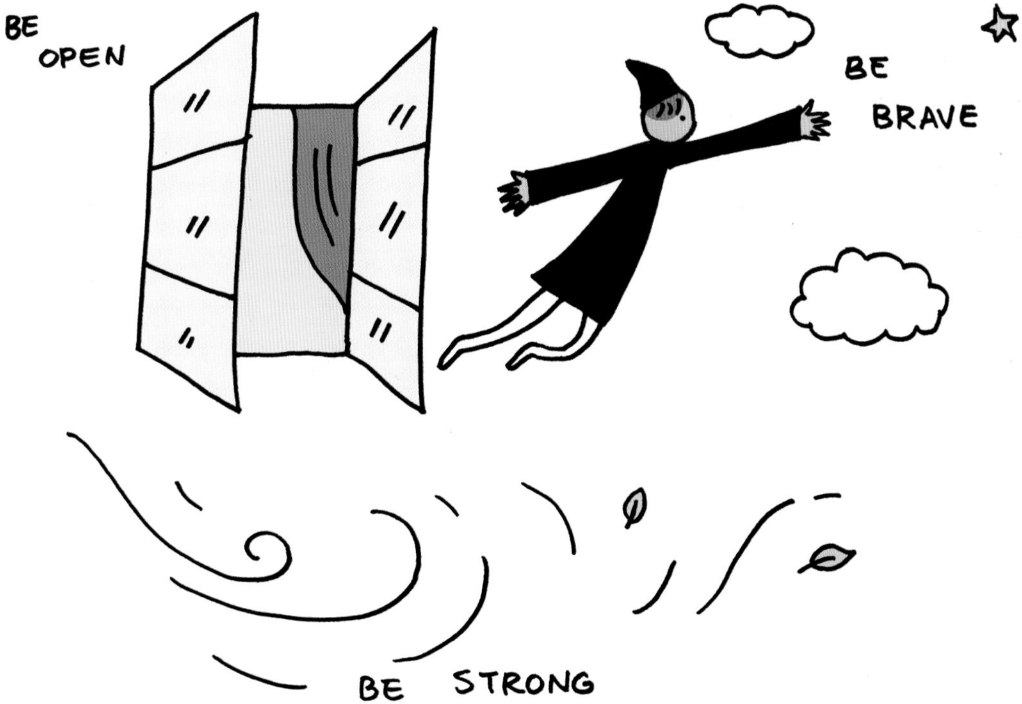
BE OPEN
BE BRAVE
BE STRONG

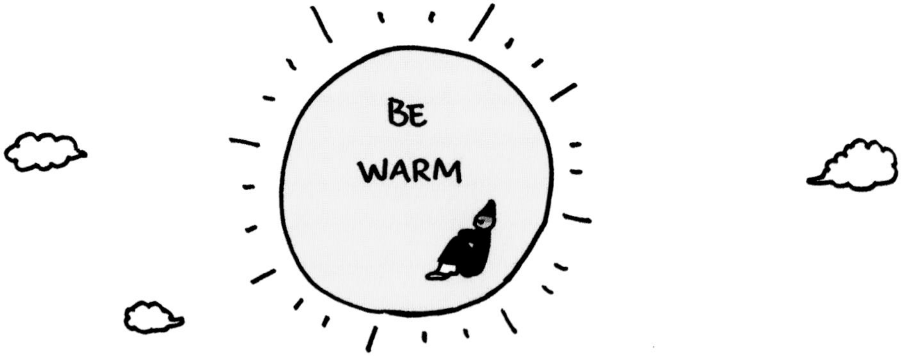
BE WARM

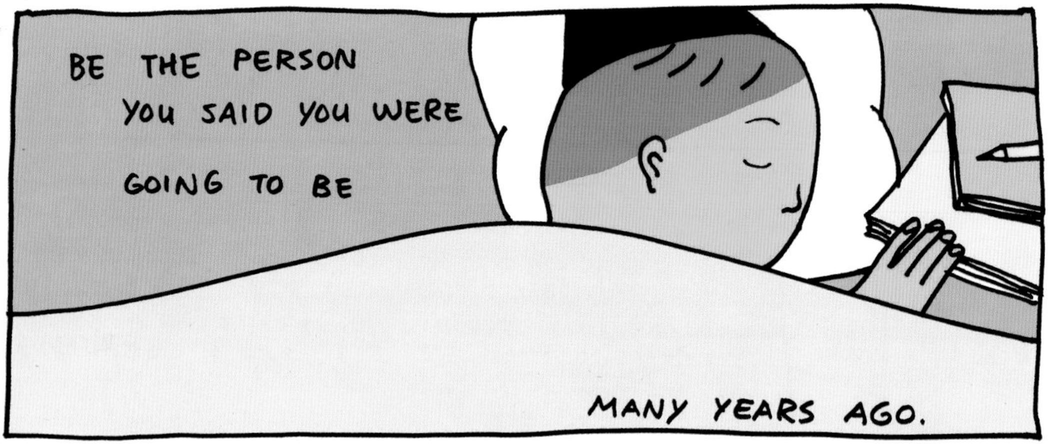
BE THE PERSON YOU SAID YOU WERE GOING TO BE
MANY YEARS AGO.

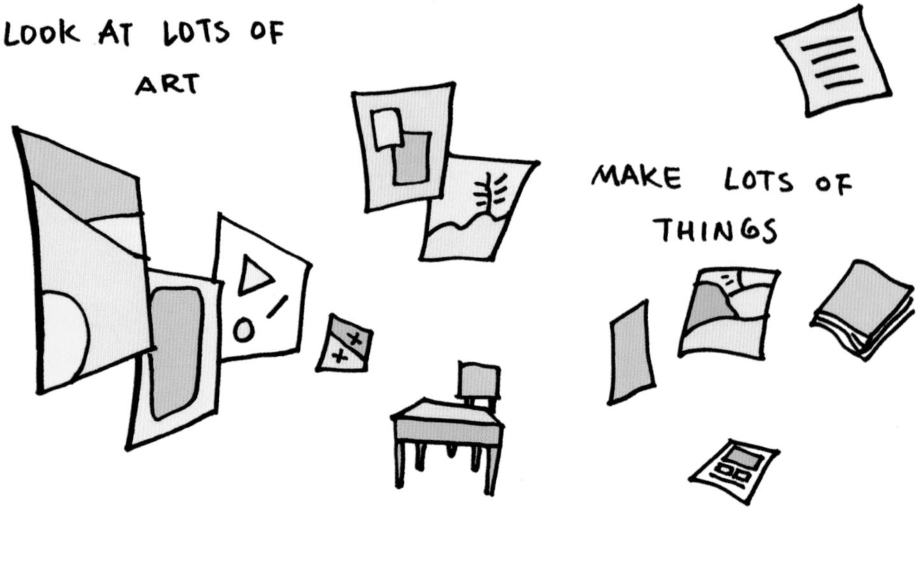
LOOK AT LOTS OF ART
MAKE LOTS OF THINGS

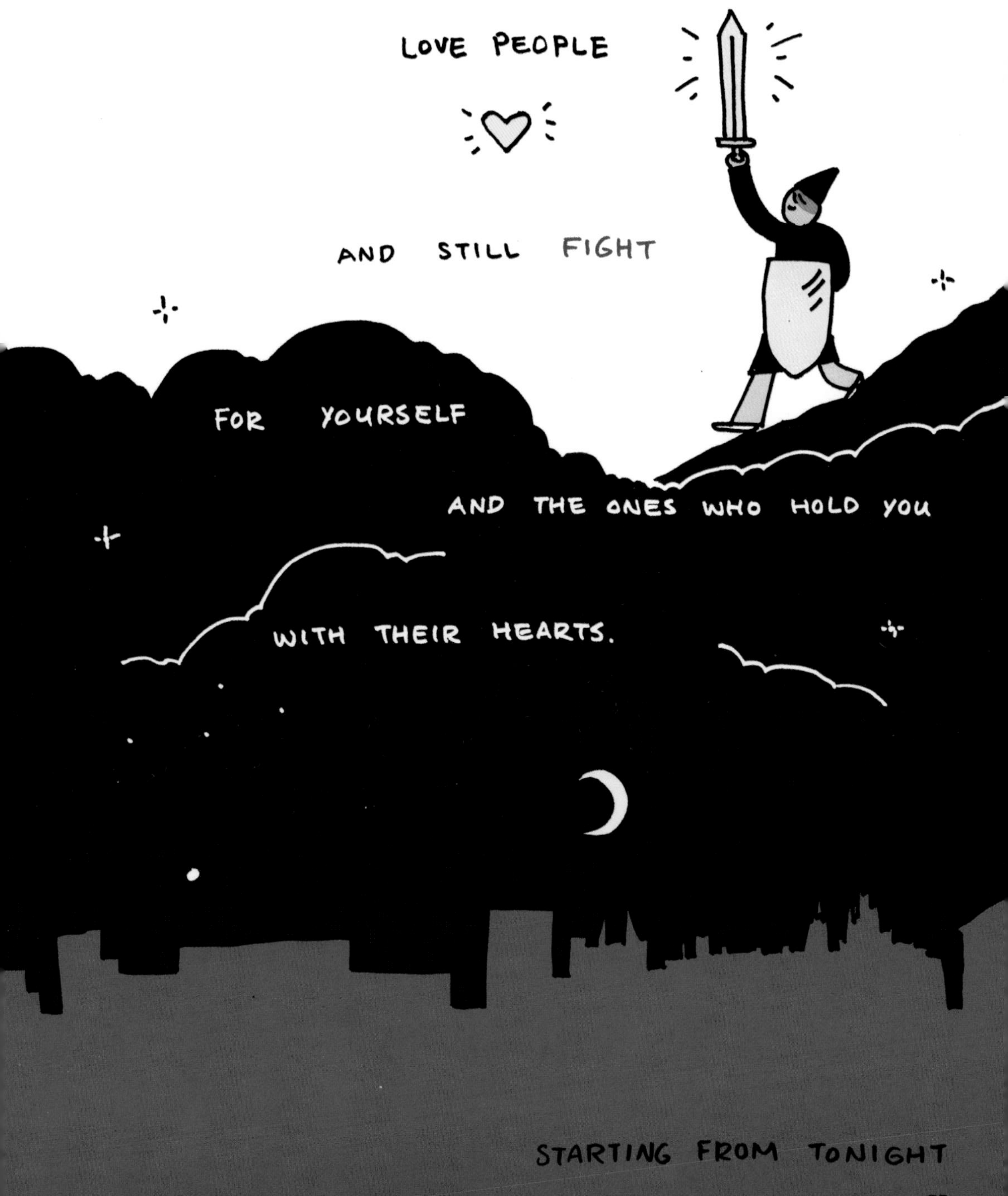
LOVE PEOPLE
AND STILL FIGHT
FOR YOURSELF
AND THE ONES WHO HOLD YOU
WITH THEIR HEARTS.
STARTING FROM TONIGHT

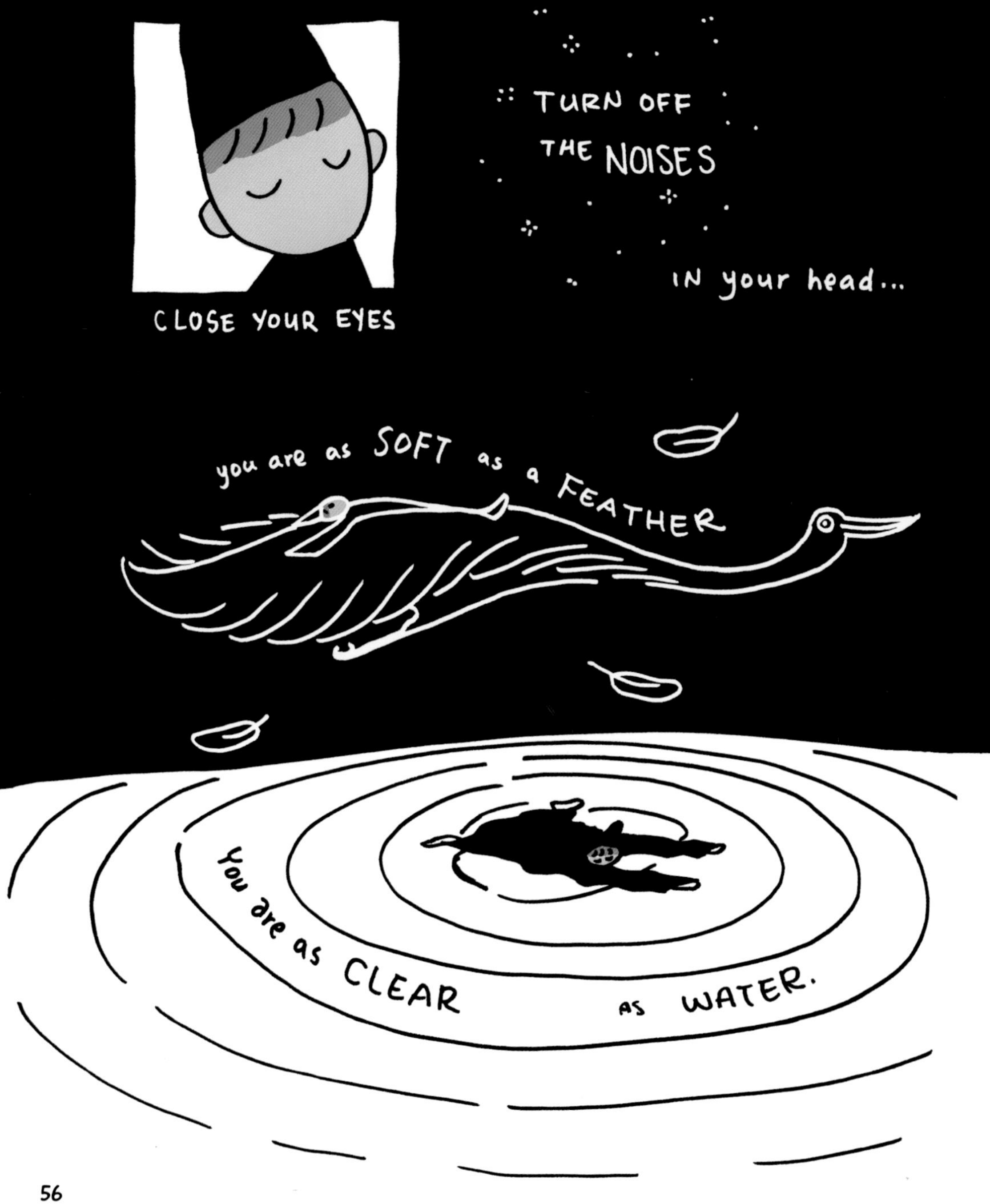
CLOSE YOUR EYES
TURN OFF THE NOISES
IN your head...
you are as SOFT as a FEATHER
You are as CLEAR as WATER.

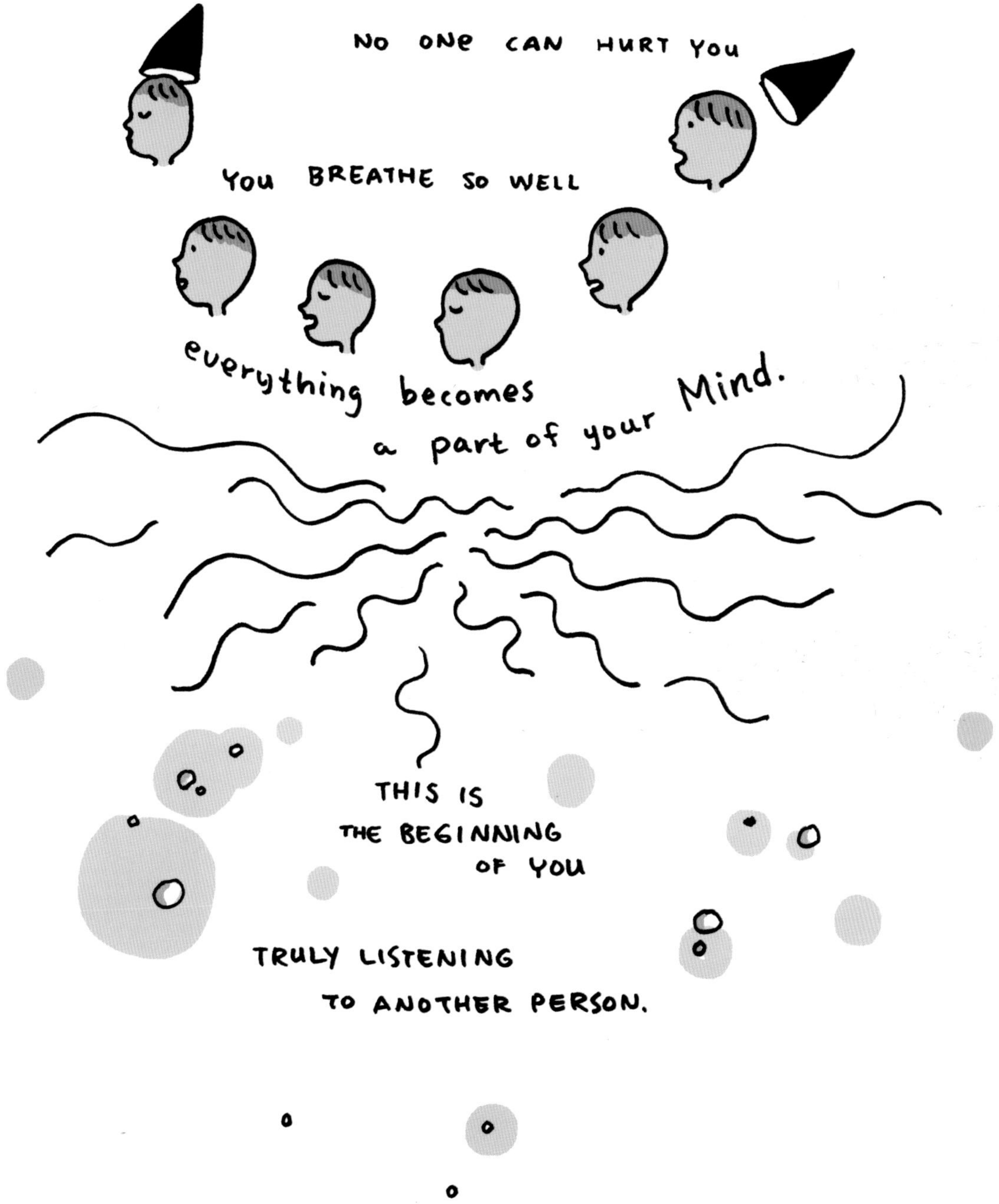
NO ONE CAN HURT YOU
YOU BREATHE SO WELL
everything becomes a part of your Mind.
THIS IS THE BEGINNING OF YOU
TRULY LISTENING TO ANOTHER PERSON.

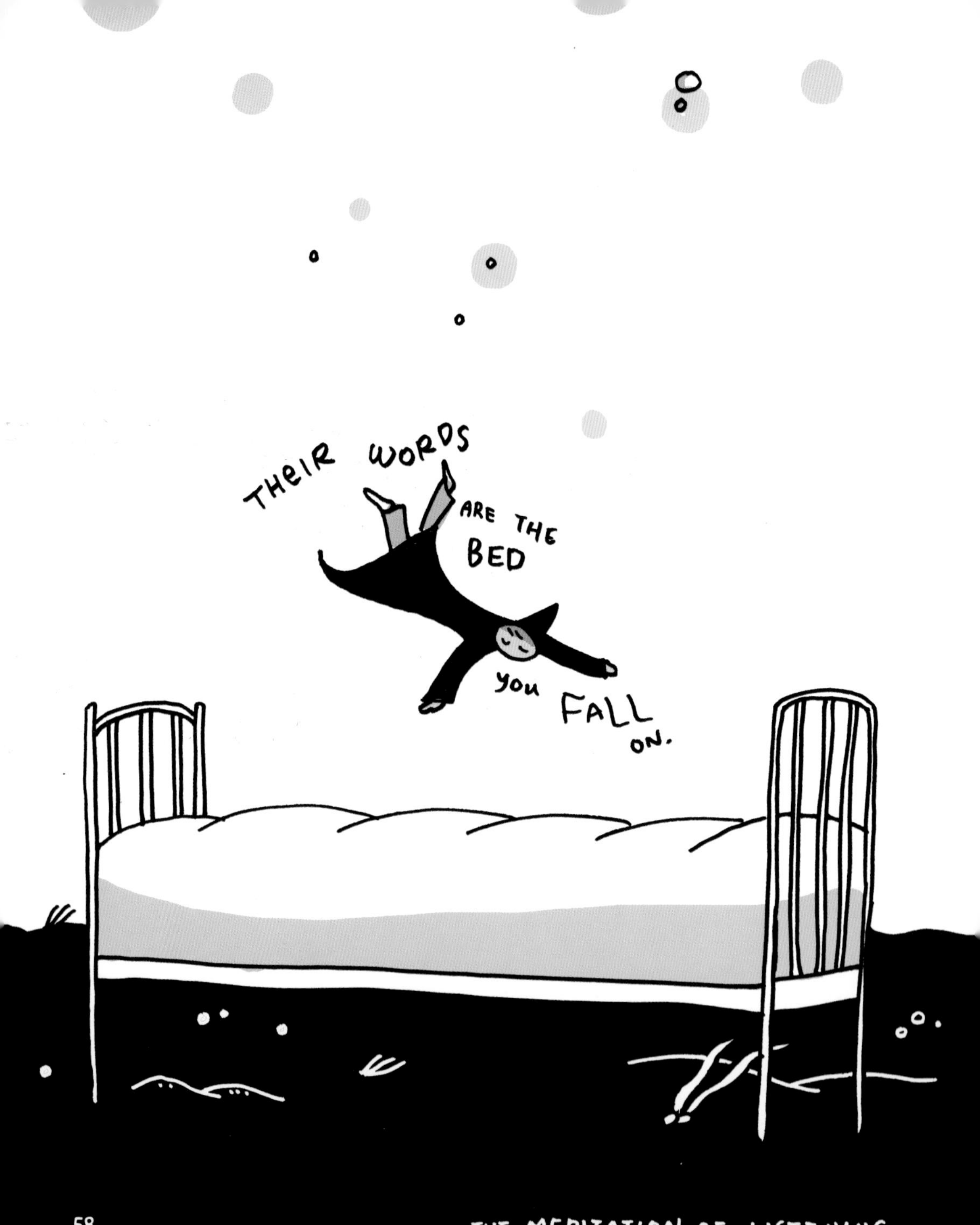
THEIR WORDS
ARE THE
BED
YOU FALL
ON.

WHAT THEY DON'T TELL YOU

WHEN THEY TELL STORIES

OF
GODS,

FAIRIES,

and
SHOOTING
STARS

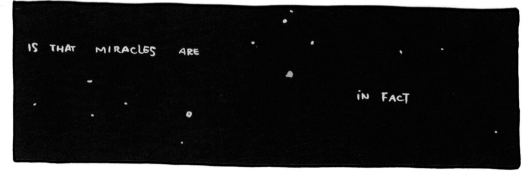

IS THAT MIRACLES ARE

IN FACT

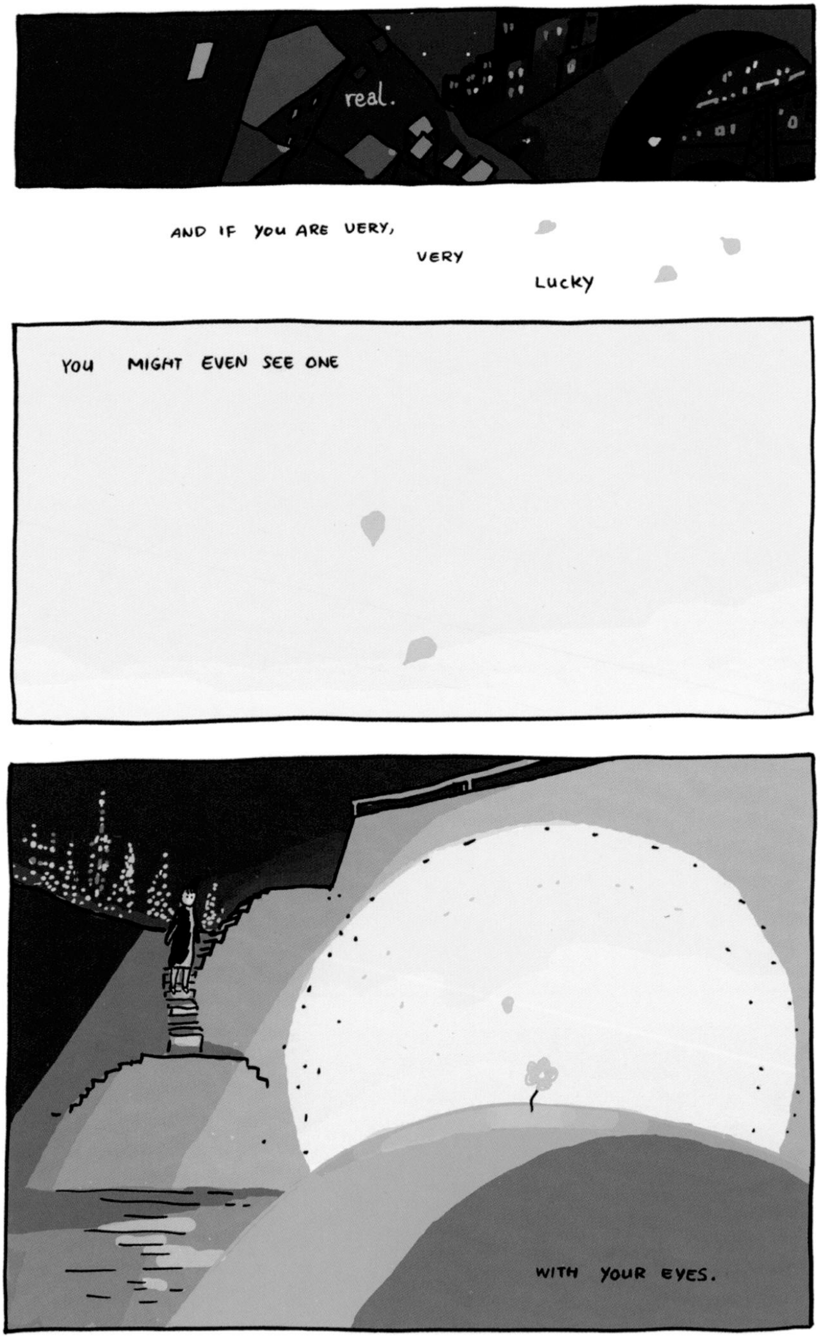
real.
AND IF YOU ARE VERY,
VERY
LUCKY
YOU MIGHT EVEN SEE ONE
WITH YOUR EYES.

WHAT THEY DON'T TELL YOU ABOUT MIRACLES

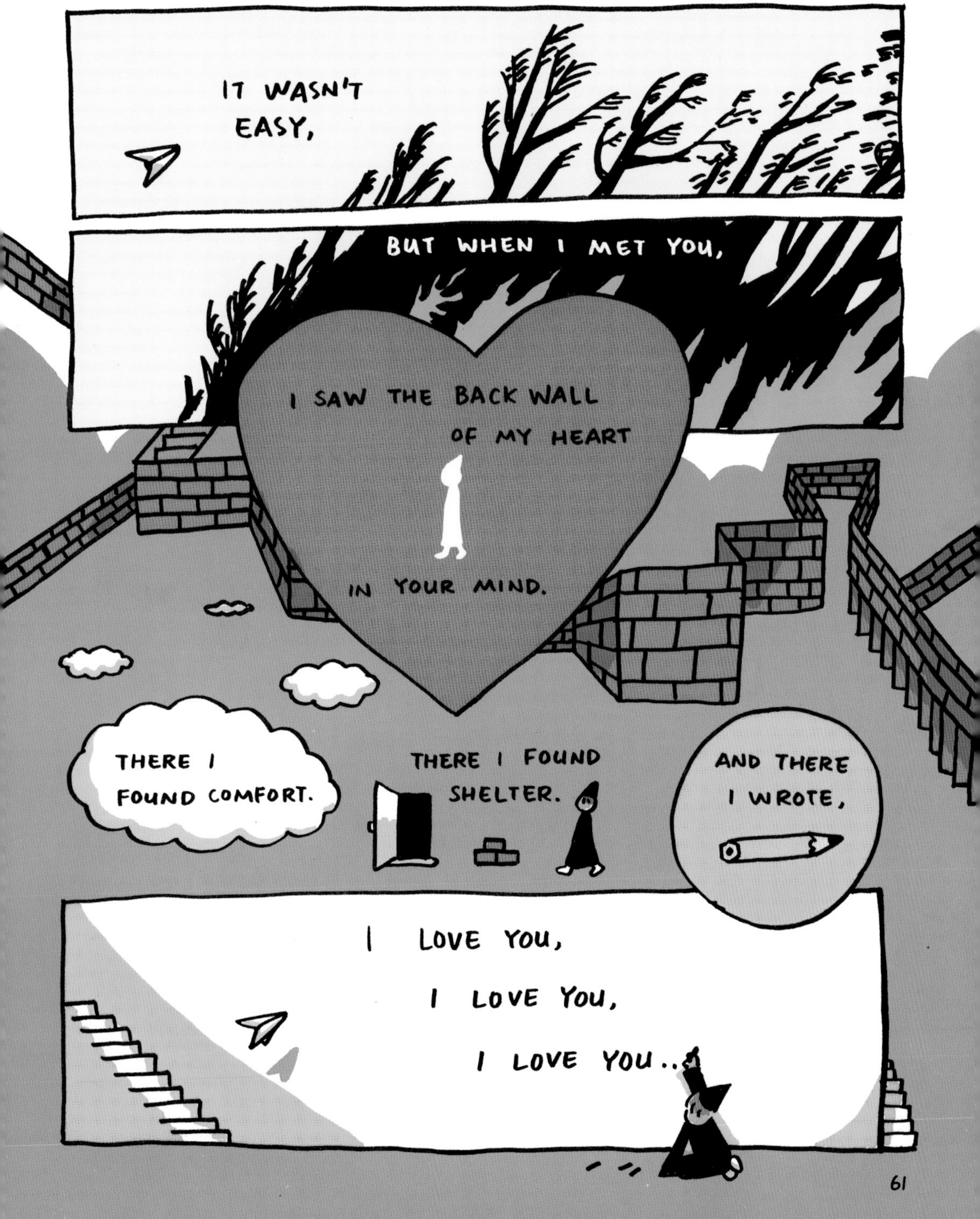
IT WASN'T EASY,
BUT WHEN I MET YOU,
I SAW THE BACK WALL OF MY HEART
IN YOUR MIND.
THERE I FOUND COMFORT.
THERE I FOUND SHELTER.
AND THERE I WROTE,
I LOVE YOU,
I LOVE YOU,
I LOVE YOU..

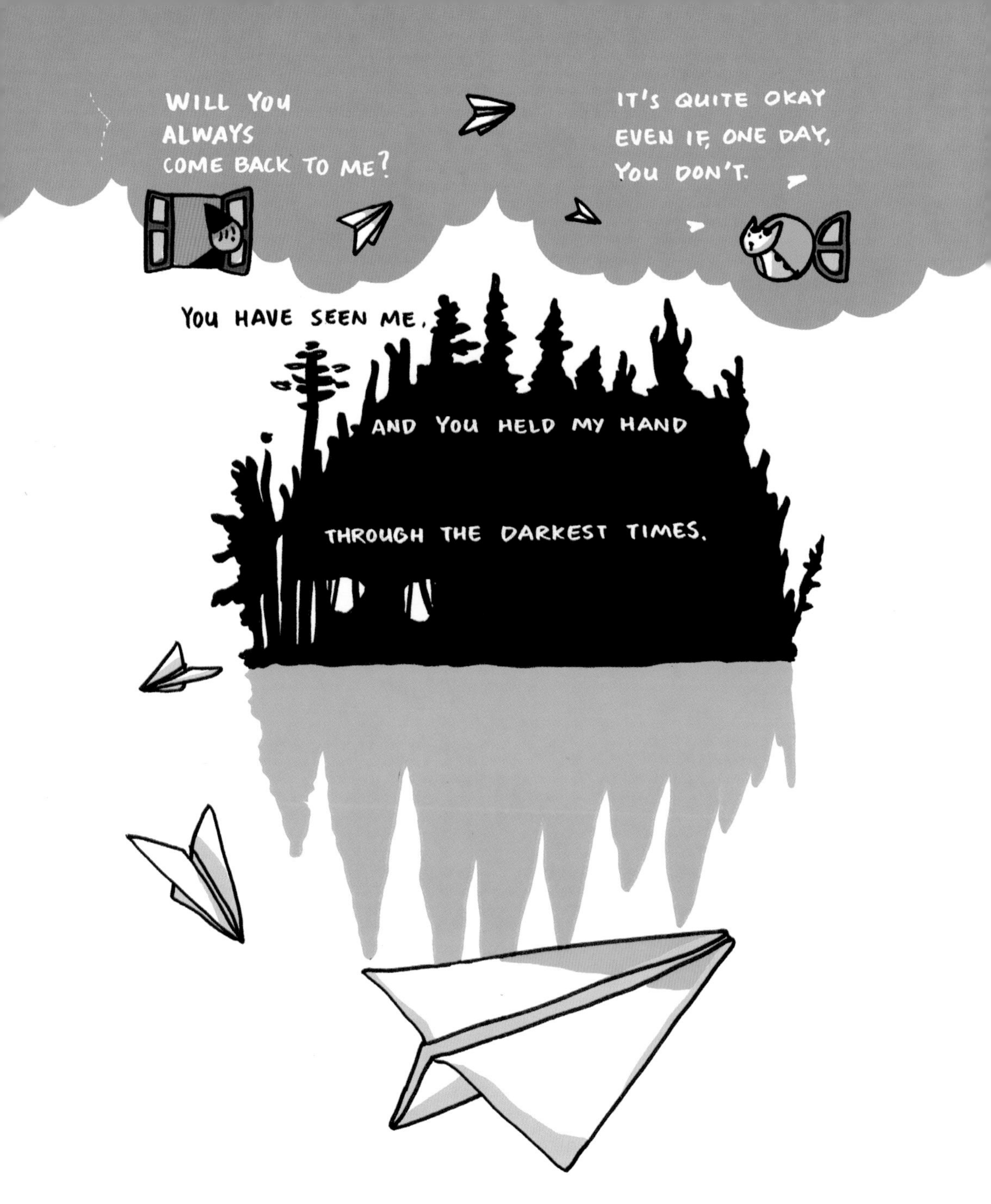
WILL YOU ALWAYS COME BACK TO ME?
IT'S QUITE OKAY EVEN IF, ONE DAY, YOU DON'T.
YOU HAVE SEEN ME,
AND YOU HELD MY HAND
THROUGH THE DARKEST TIMES.

A SECRET LOVE LETTER

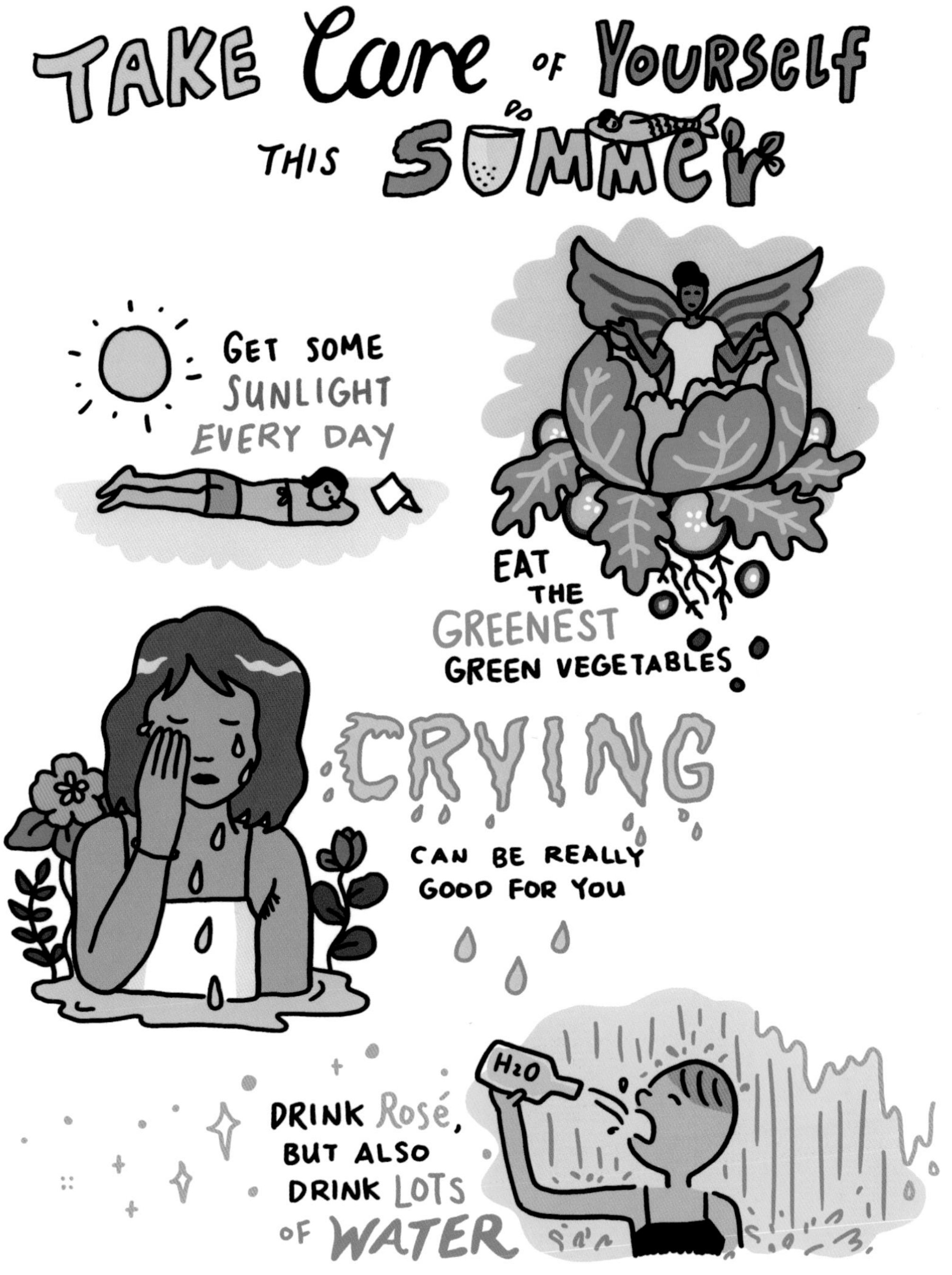
TAKE Care OF YOURSELF
THIS SUMMER
GET SOME SUNLIGHT EVERY DAY
EAT THE GREENEST GREEN VEGETABLES
CRYING CAN BE REALLY GOOD FOR YOU
H2O
DRINK Rosé, BUT ALSO DRINK LOTS OF WATER

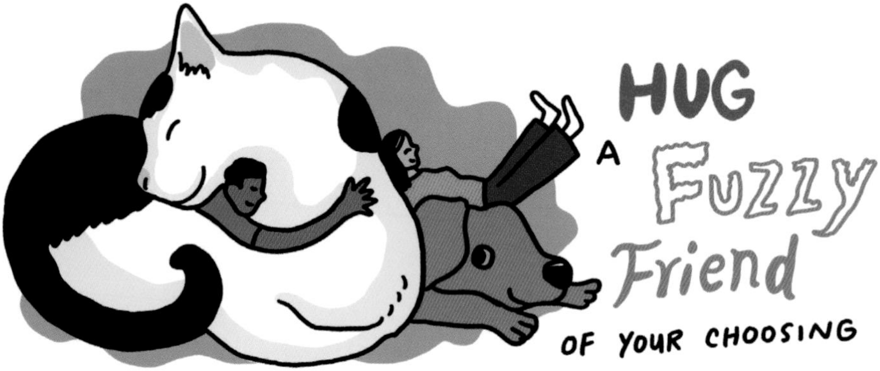
HUG A Fuzzy Friend
OF YOUR CHOOSING

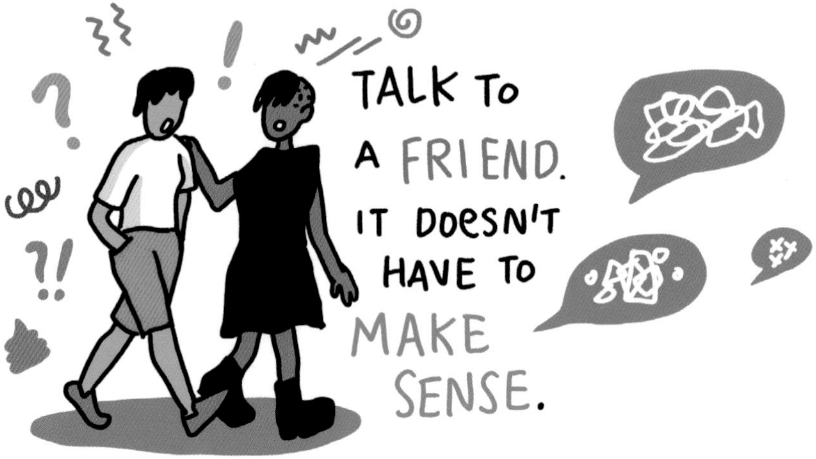
TALK TO A FRIEND. IT DOESN'T HAVE TO MAKE SENSE.

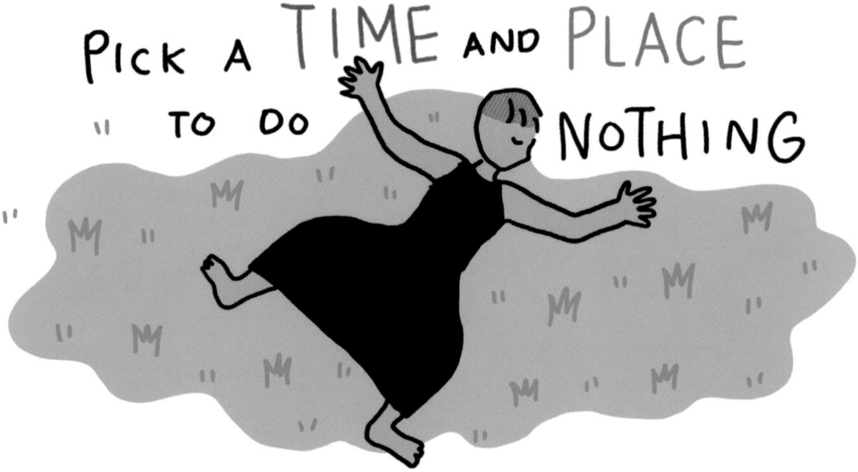
PICK A TIME AND PLACE
TO DO NOTHING

I'VE BEEN SUSTAINING MY LIVELIHOOD ON A NONIMMIGRANT VISA FOR MORE THAN 10 YEARS.

PEOPLE ASSUME I'M "AMERICAN" OR INSIST I'M AMERICANIZED.

BUT HAVE A CLOSER LOOK AT MY LIFE...

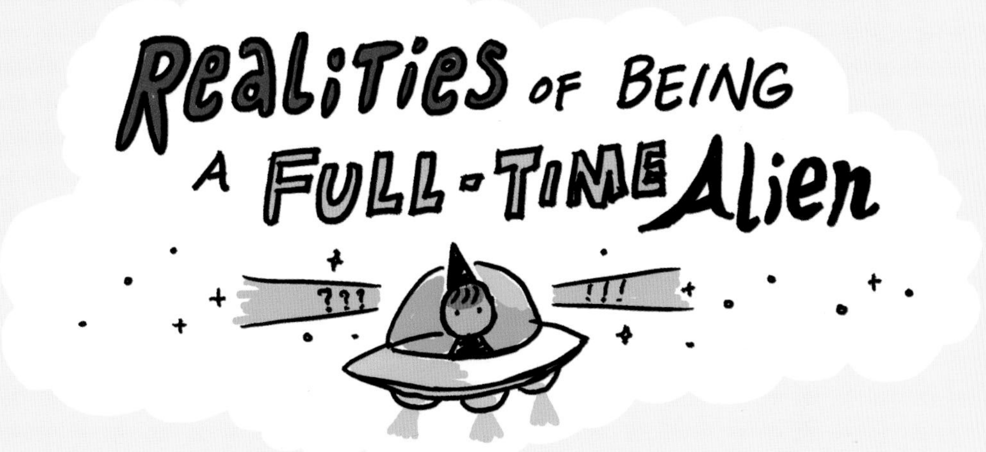
Realities of BEING A FULL-TIME Alien
???
!!!

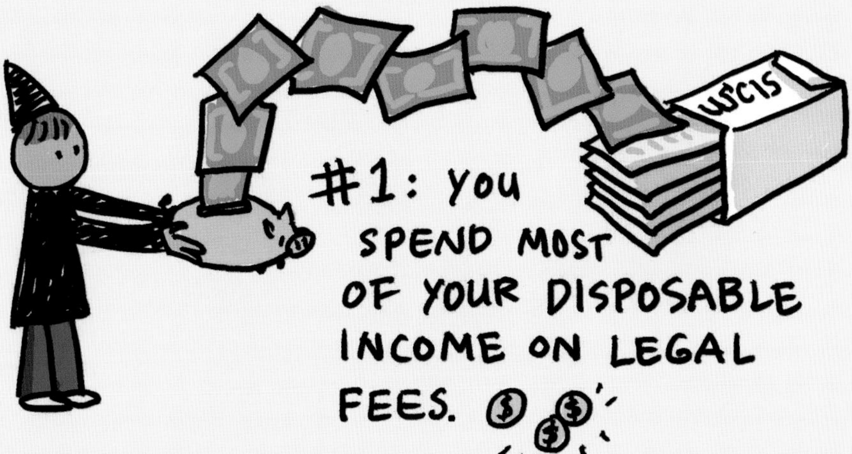
USCIS
#1: you SPEND MOST OF YOUR DISPOSABLE INCOME ON LEGAL FEES.

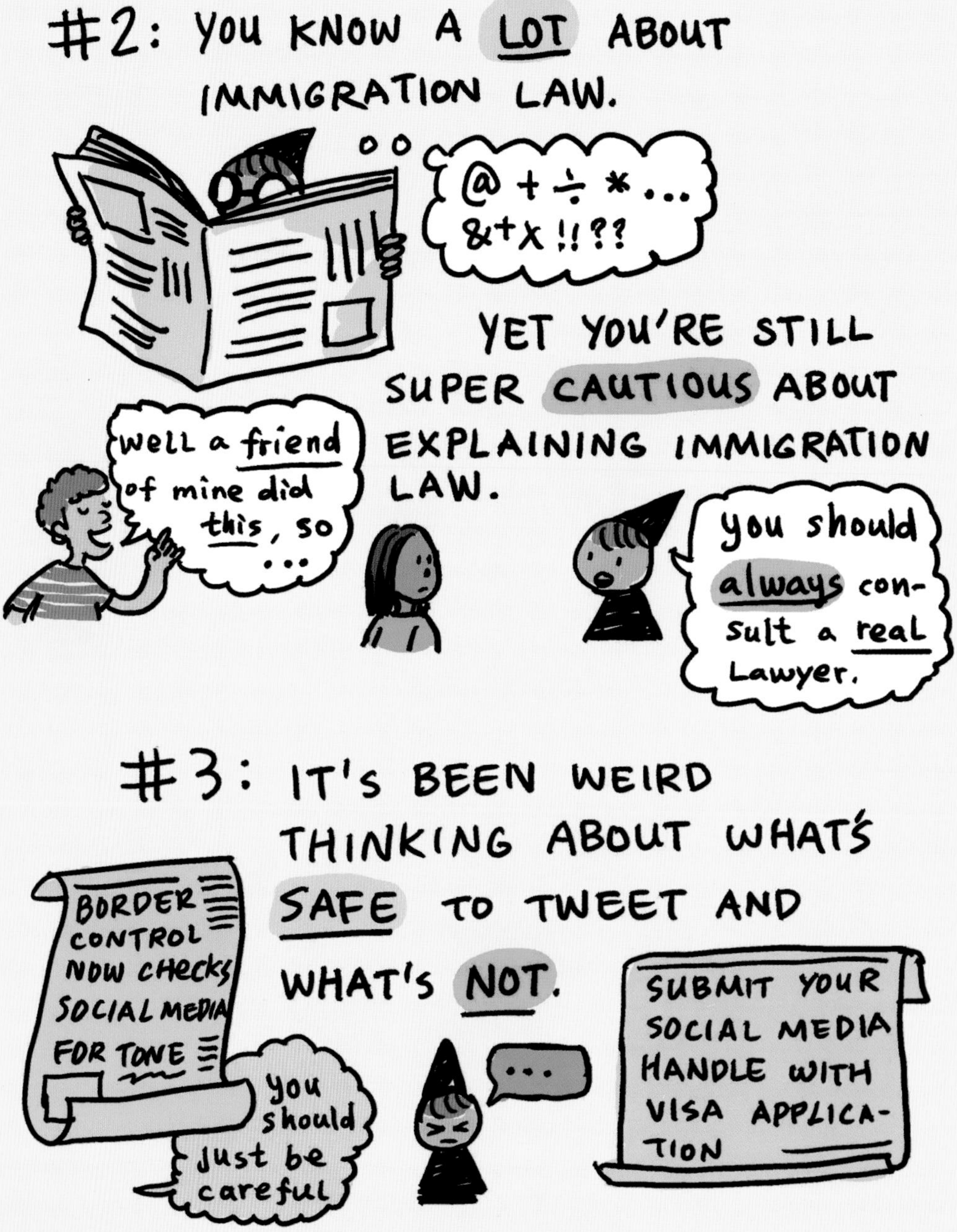
#2: YOU KNOW A LOT ABOUT IMMIGRATION LAW.
@ + ÷ * ... &+x !!??
YET YOU'RE STILL SUPER CAUTIOUS ABOUT EXPLAINING IMMIGRATION LAW.
well a friend of mine did this, so ...
you should always con-sult a real Lawyer.
#3: IT'S BEEN WEIRD THINKING ABOUT WHAT'S SAFE TO TWEET AND WHAT'S NOT.
BORDER CONTROL NOW CHECKS SOCIAL MEDIA FOR TONE
you should just be careful
...
SUBMIT YOUR SOCIAL MEDIA HANDLE WITH VISA APPLICA-TION

#4: YOU WATCH YOUR FRIENDS LEAVE—SOMETIMES DISAPPEAR—AND WONDER IF YOU'RE REALLY DOING SOMETHING WRONG.

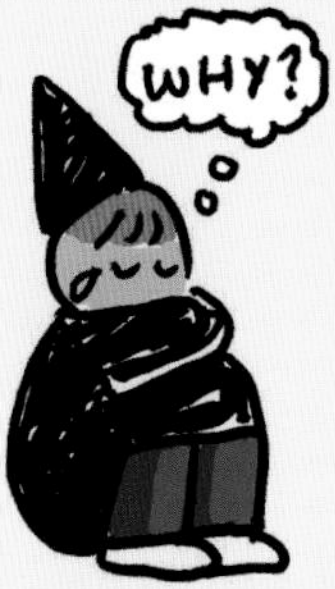
WHY?

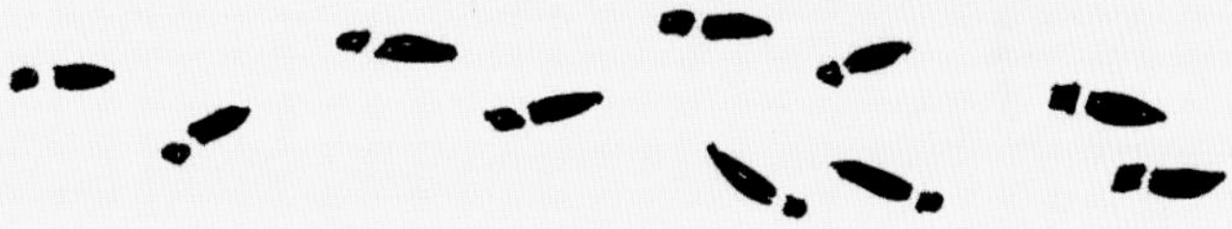

#5: YOU GROW APART FROM YOUR FAMILY BECAUSE THEY CAN'T AFFORD TO LIVE / BE (ALLOWED ENTRY) IN THE PLACE YOU CALL HOME.

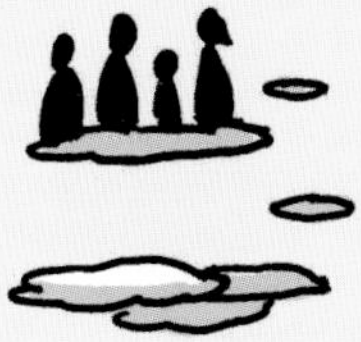

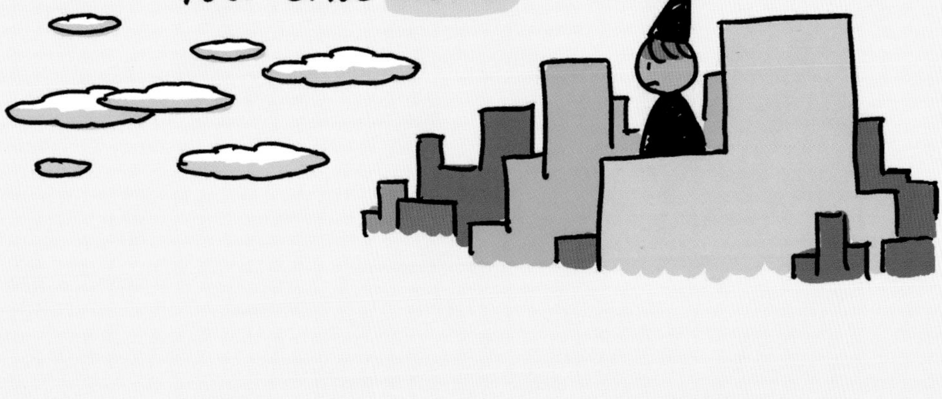

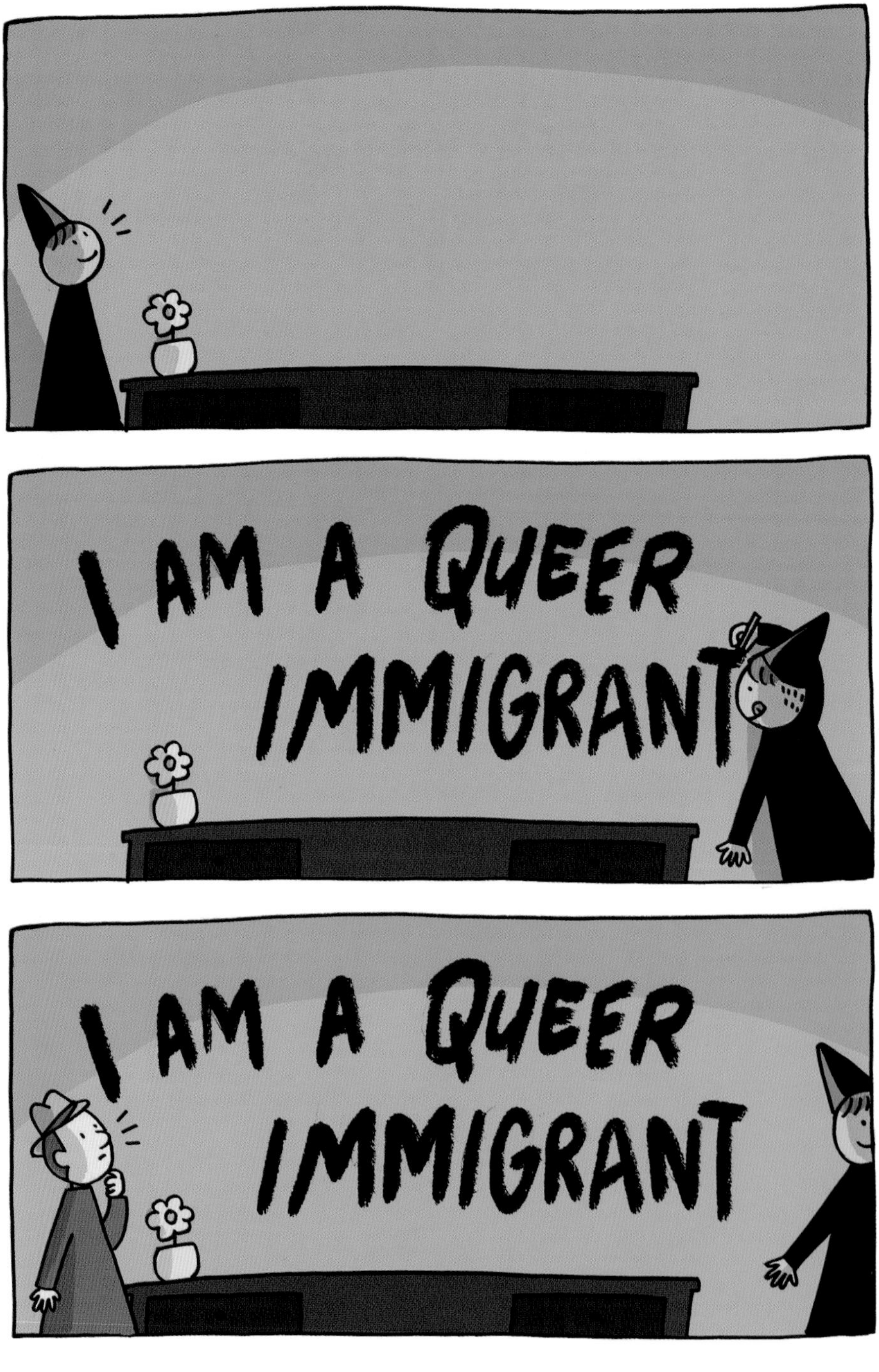
I AM A QUEER IMMIGRANT
I AM A QUEER IMMIGRANT

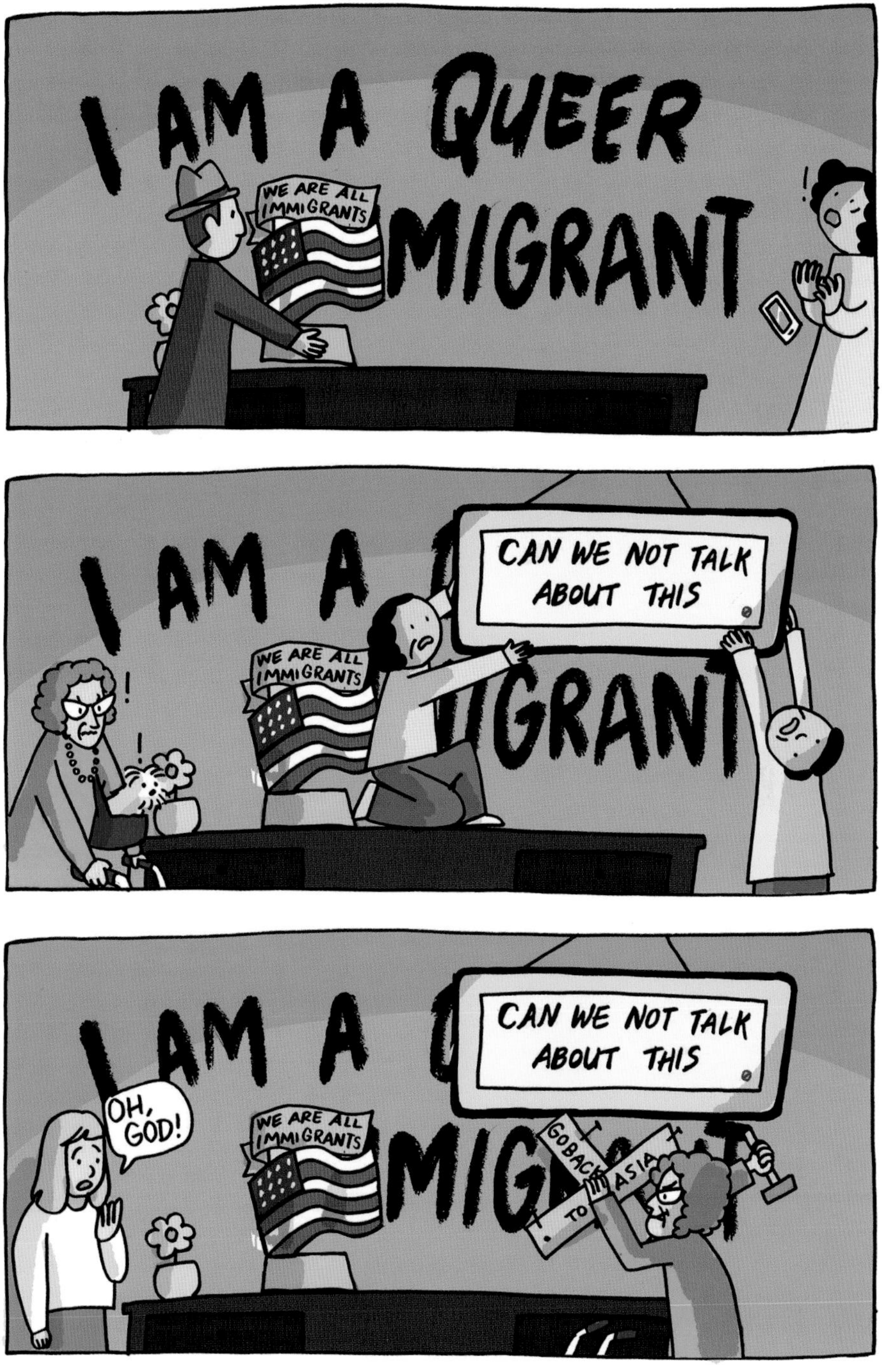
I AM A QUEER MIGRANT
WE ARE ALL IMMIGRANTS
!
I AM A
IGRANT
CAN WE NOT TALK ABOUT THIS
WE ARE ALL IMMIGRANTS
!
!
I AM A
MIG
CAN WE NOT TALK ABOUT THIS
OH, GOD!
WE ARE ALL IMMIGRANTS
GO BACK TO ASIA

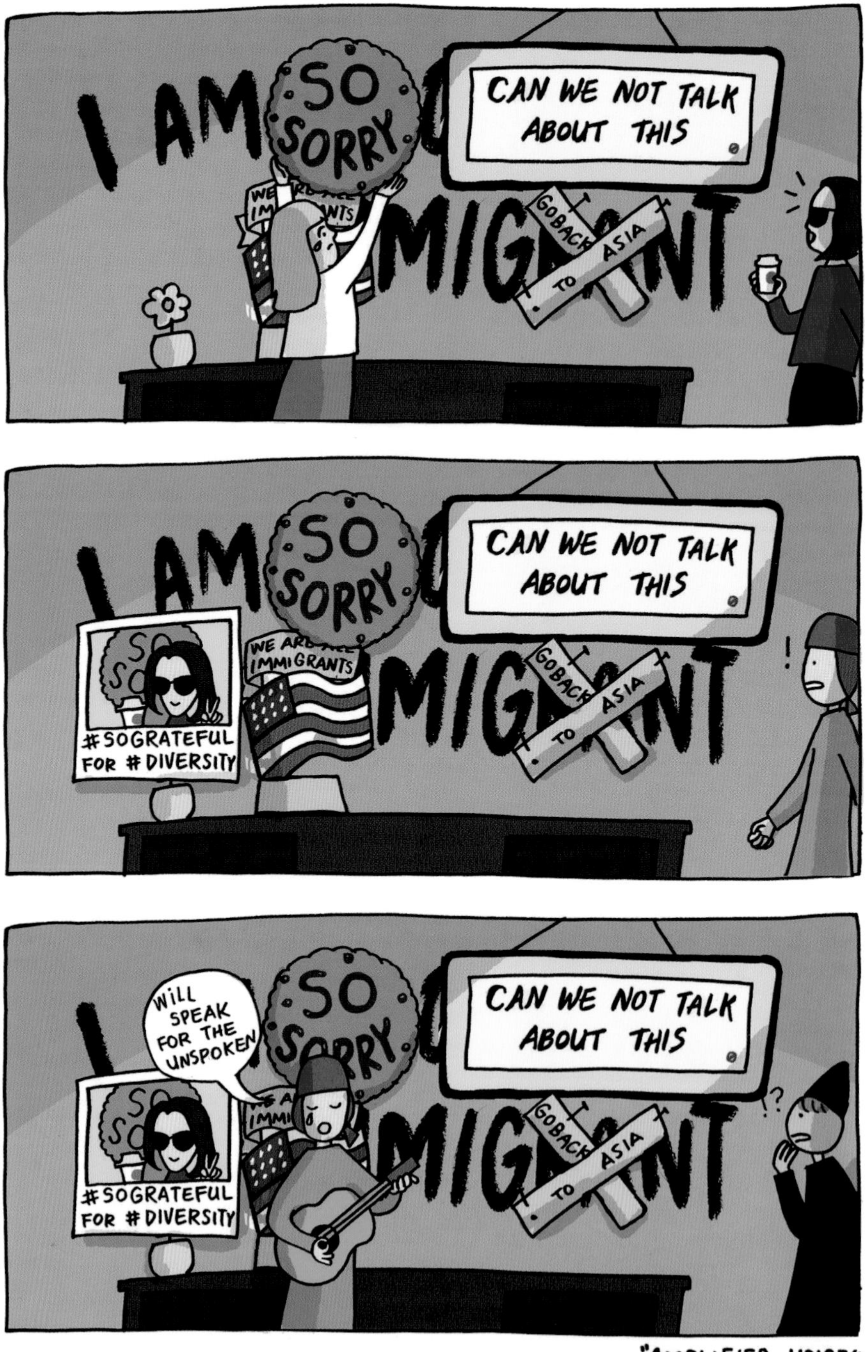
I AM
SO SORRY
CAN WE NOT TALK ABOUT THIS
GO BACK TO ASIA
CAN WE NOT TALK ABOUT THIS
WE ARE ALL IMMIGRANTS
#SOGRATEFUL FOR #DIVERSITY
GO BACK TO ASIA
WILL SPEAK FOR THE UNSPOKEN
CAN WE NOT TALK ABOUT THIS
#SOGRATEFUL FOR #DIVERSITY
GO BACK TO ASIA

"AMPLIFIED VOICE"

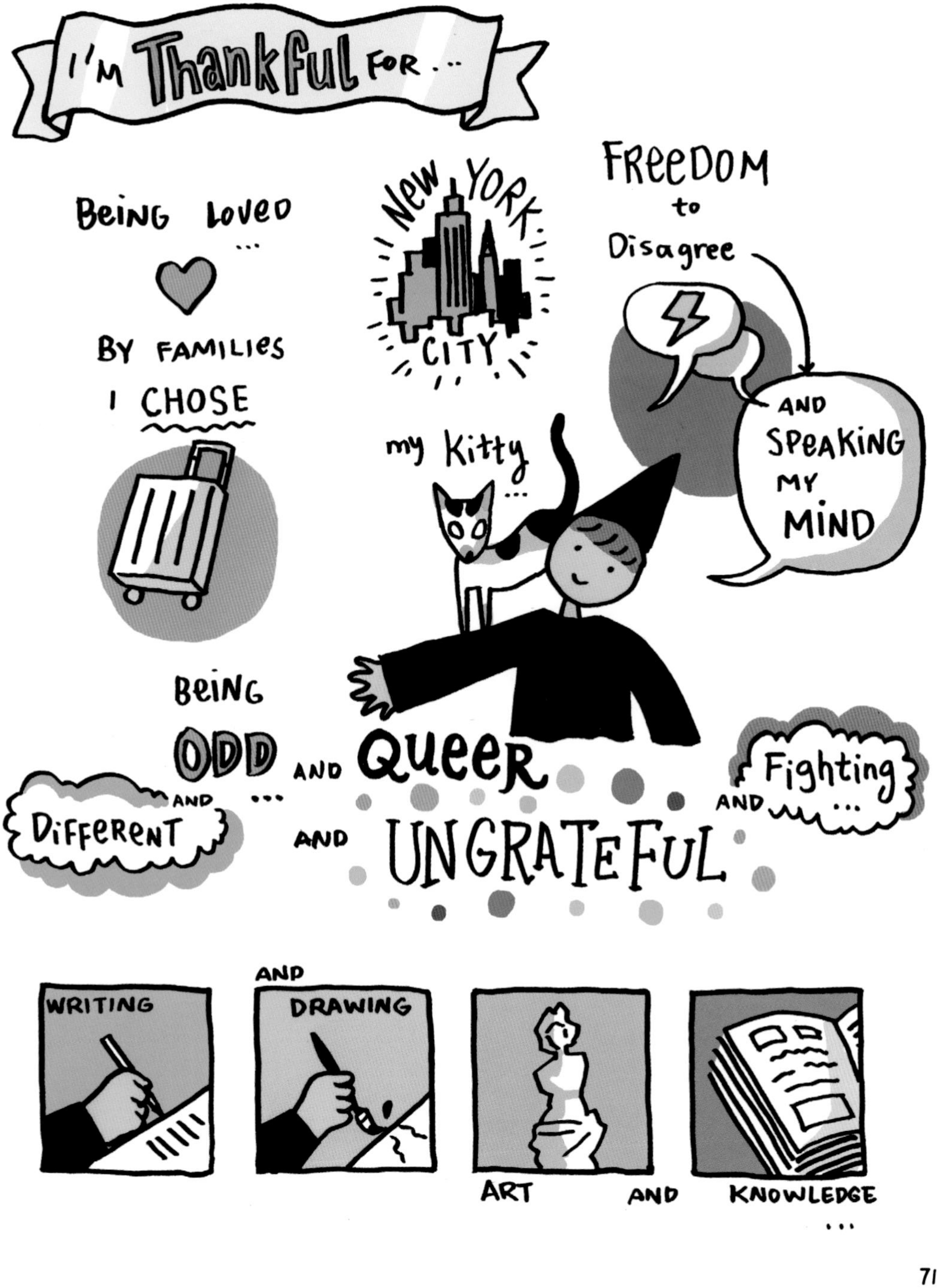

I'M Thankful FOR...
Being Loved ...
BY FAMILIES I CHOSE
NEW YORK CITY
FREEDOM to Disagree
AND SPEAKING MY MIND
my Kitty ...
Being ODD AND Queer AND Different ... AND UNGRATEFUL AND Fighting ...
WRITING
AND DRAWING
ART AND KNOWLEDGE ...

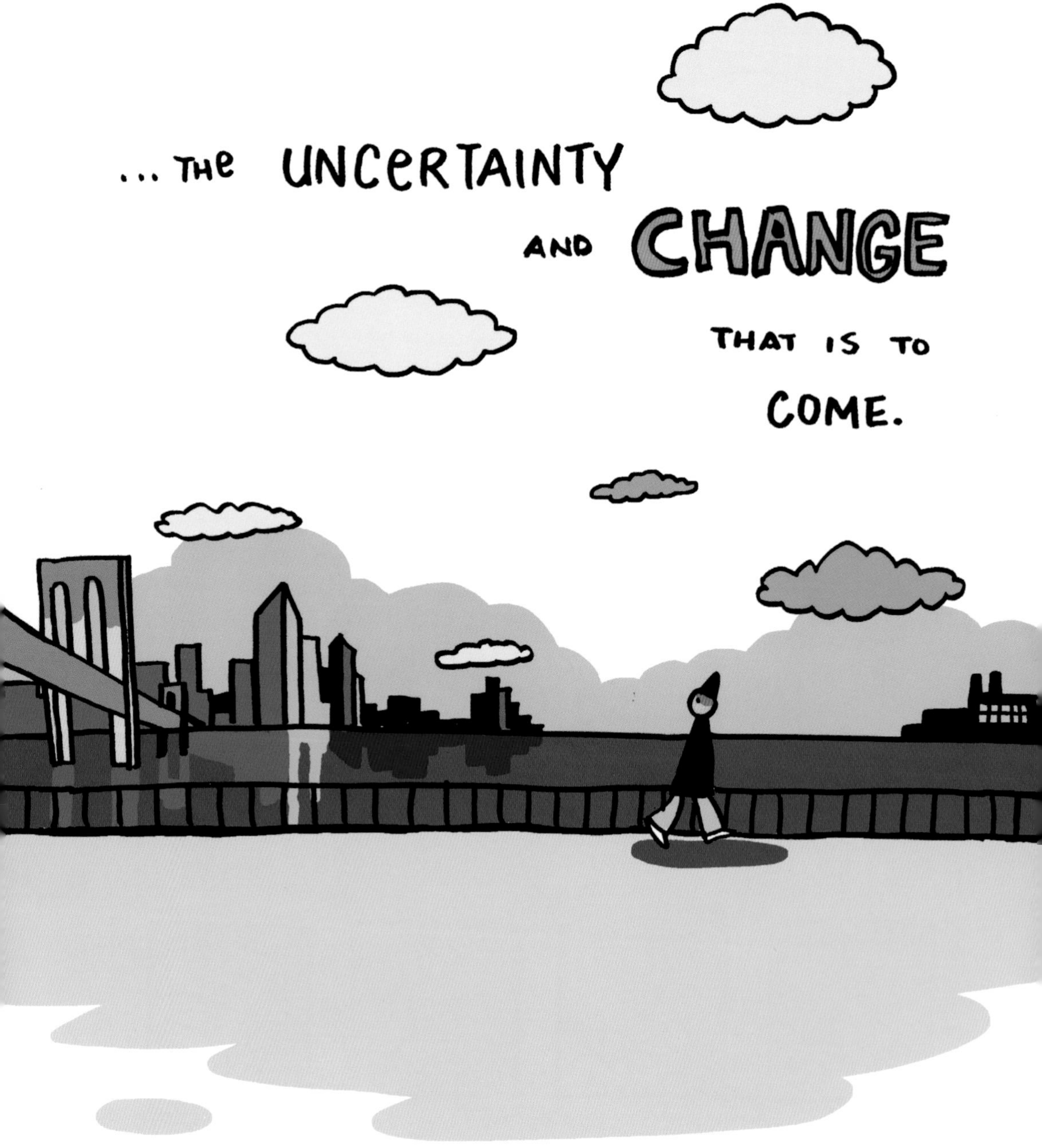
... THE UNCERTAINTY
AND CHANGE
THAT IS TO
COME.

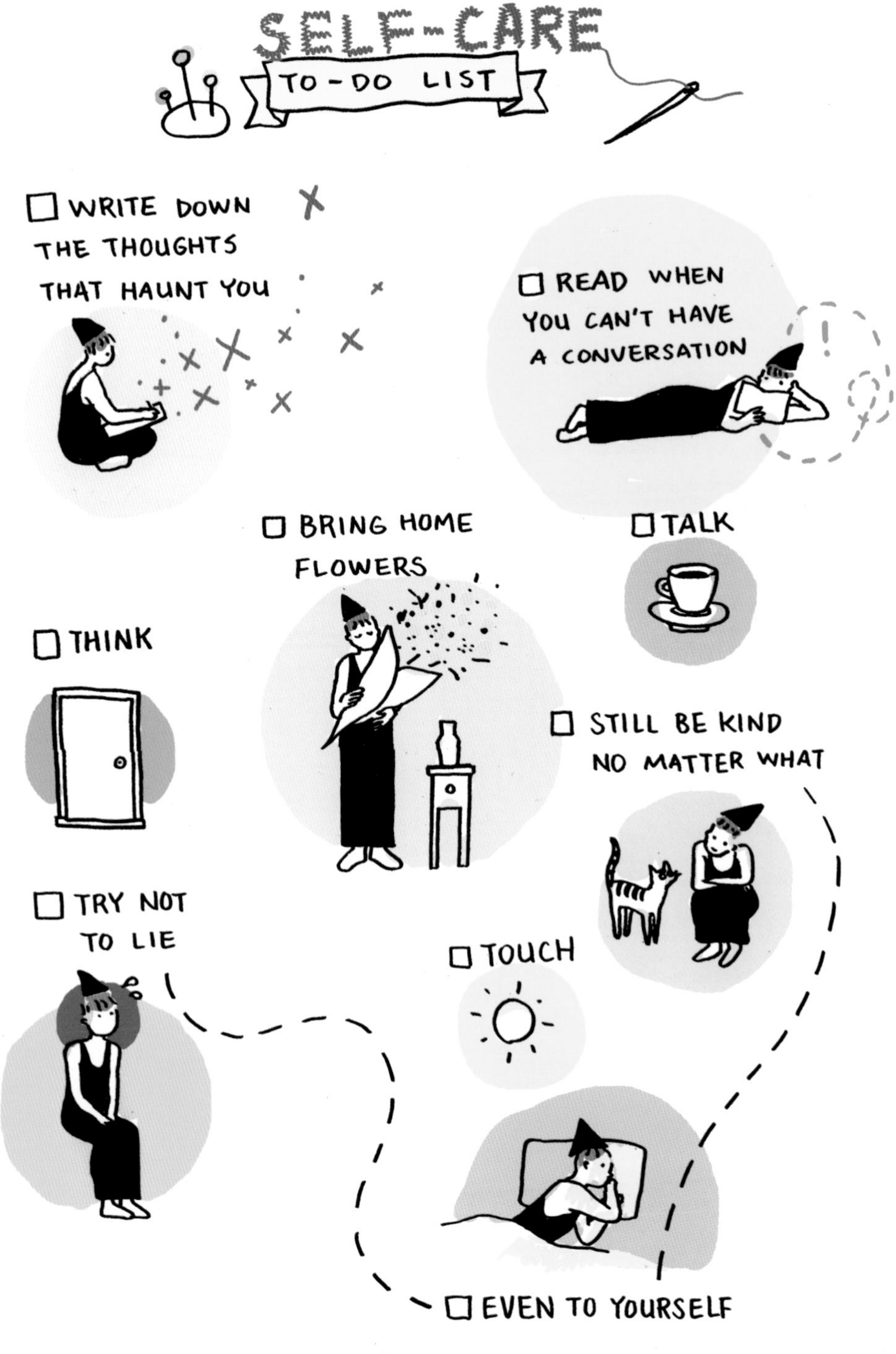
SELF-CARE
TO-DO LIST
☐ WRITE DOWN THE THOUGHTS THAT HAUNT YOU
☐ READ WHEN YOU CAN'T HAVE A CONVERSATION
☐ BRING HOME FLOWERS
☐ TALK
☐ THINK
☐ STILL BE KIND NO MATTER WHAT
☐ TRY NOT TO LIE
☐ TOUCH
☐ EVEN TO YOURSELF

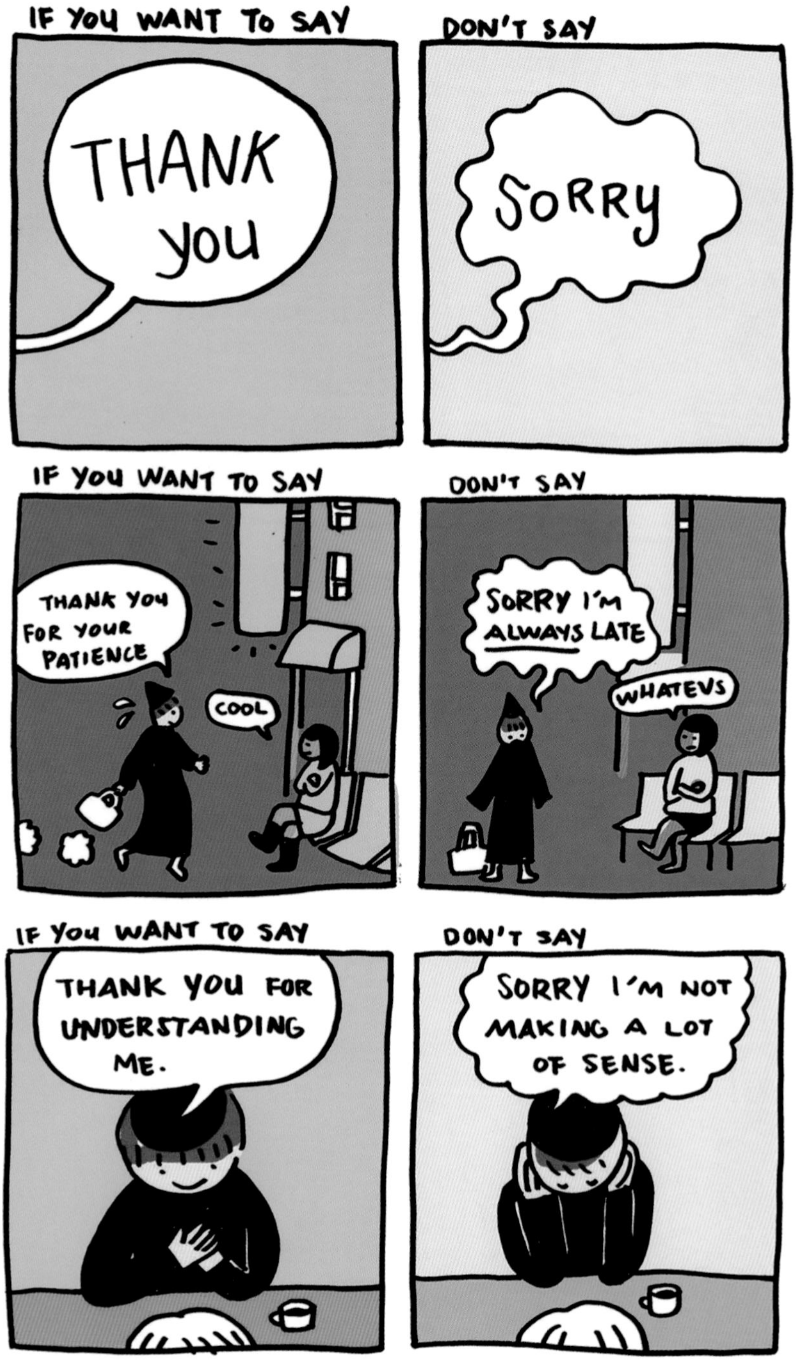
IF YOU WANT TO SAY
THANK YOU
DON'T SAY
SORRY
IF YOU WANT TO SAY
THANK YOU FOR YOUR PATIENCE
COOL
DON'T SAY
SORRY I'M ALWAYS LATE
WHATEVS
IF YOU WANT TO SAY
THANK YOU FOR UNDERSTANDING ME.
DON'T SAY
SORRY I'M NOT MAKING A LOT OF SENSE.

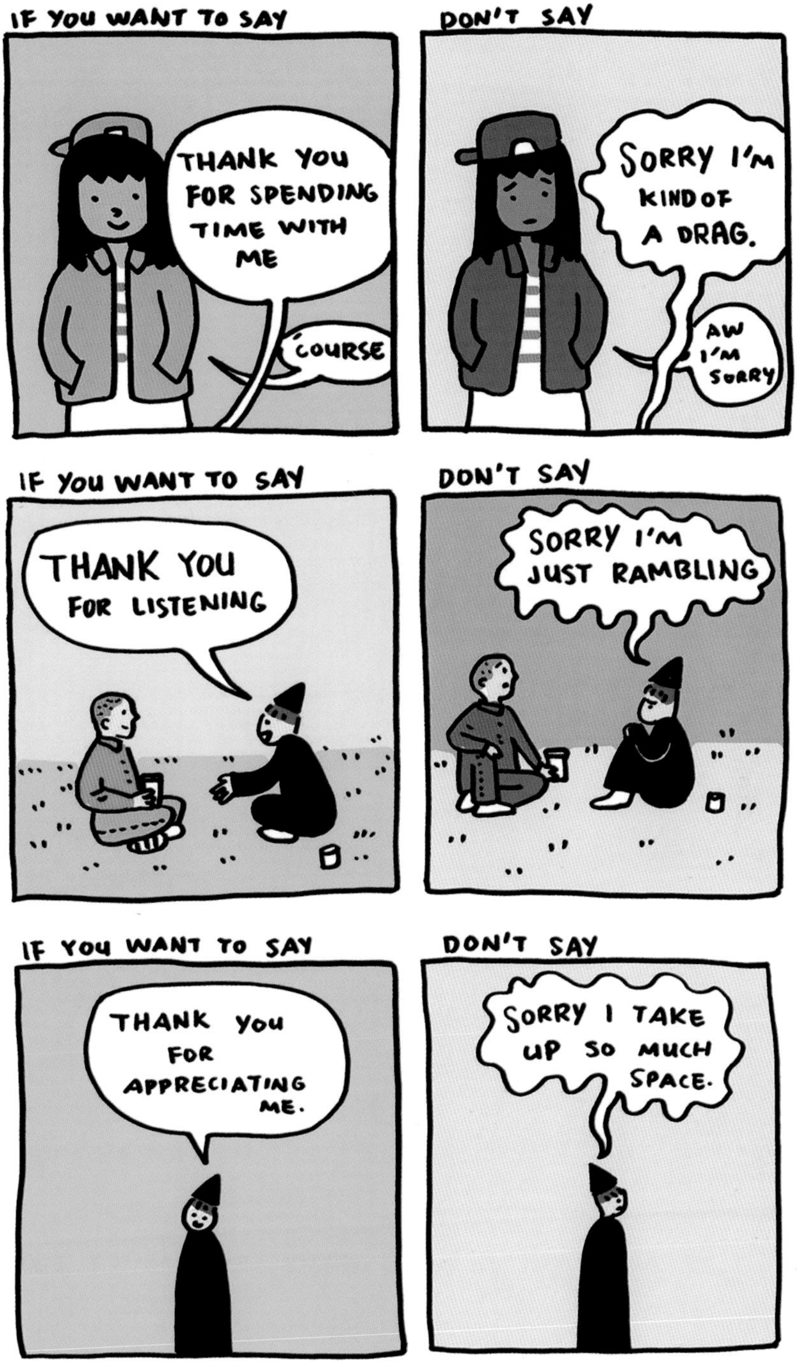
IF YOU WANT TO SAY
THANK YOU FOR SPENDING TIME WITH ME
COURSE
DON'T SAY
SORRY I'M KIND OF A DRAG.
AW I'M SORRY
IF YOU WANT TO SAY
THANK YOU FOR LISTENING
DON'T SAY
SORRY I'M JUST RAMBLING
IF YOU WANT TO SAY
THANK YOU FOR APPRECIATING ME.
DON'T SAY
SORRY I TAKE UP SO MUCH SPACE.

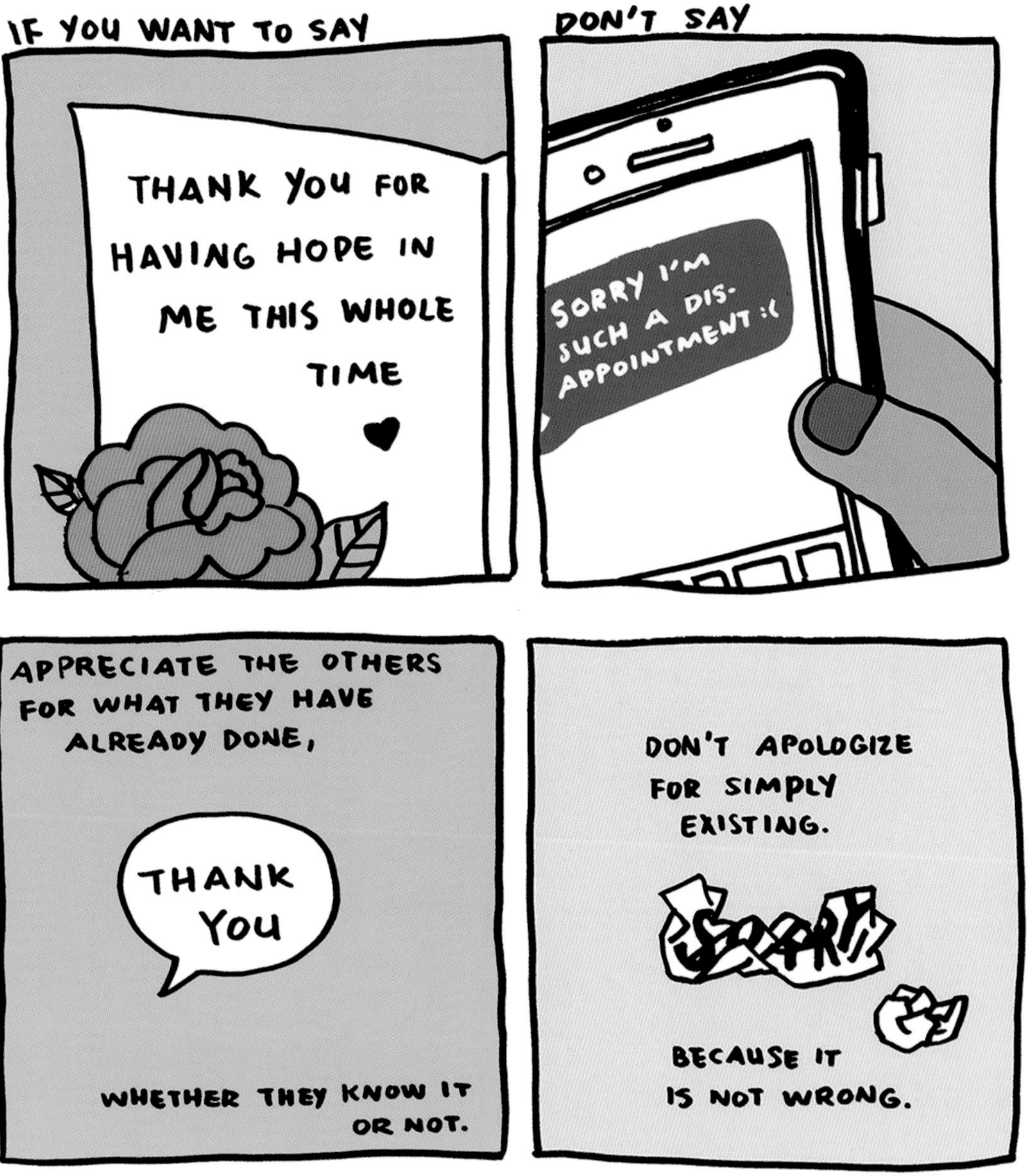
IF YOU WANT TO SAY
THANK YOU FOR HAVING HOPE IN ME THIS WHOLE TIME
DON'T SAY
SORRY I'M SUCH A DIS-APPOINTMENT :(
APPRECIATE THE OTHERS FOR WHAT THEY HAVE ALREADY DONE,
THANK YOU
WHETHER THEY KNOW IT OR NOT.
DON'T APOLOGIZE FOR SIMPLY EXISTING.
SORRY
BECAUSE IT IS NOT WRONG.

IF YOU WANT TO SAY "THANK YOU," DON'T SAY "SORRY"

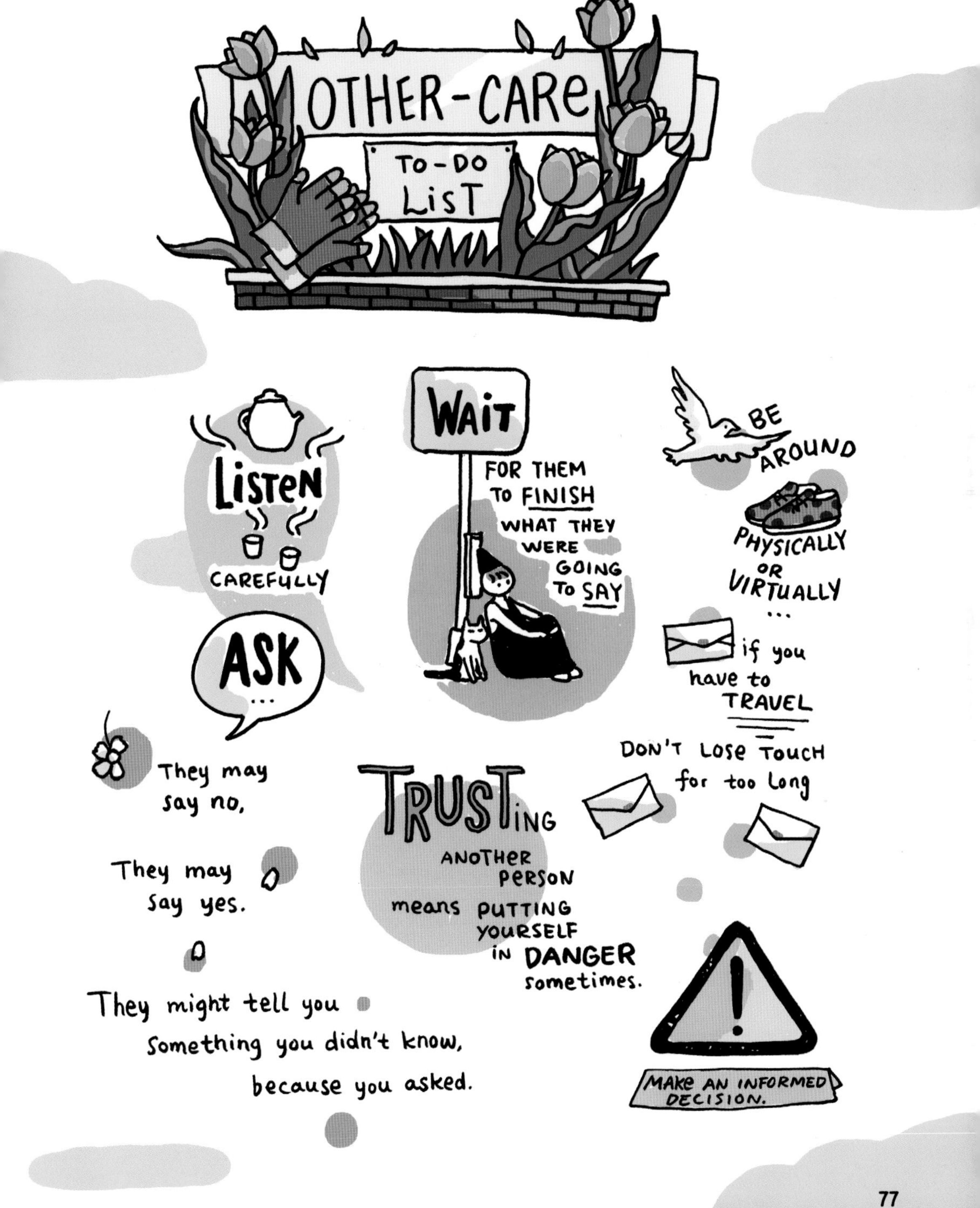
OTHER-CARE
TO-DO LIST
LISTEN CAREFULLY
ASK ...
They may say no,
They may say yes.
They might tell you something you didn't know, because you asked.
WAIT
FOR THEM TO FINISH WHAT THEY WERE GOING TO SAY
TRUSTING ANOTHER PERSON means PUTTING YOURSELF IN DANGER sometimes.
BE AROUND
PHYSICALLY OR VIRTUALLY ...
if you have to TRAVEL
DON'T LOSE TOUCH for too long
MAKE AN INFORMED DECISION.

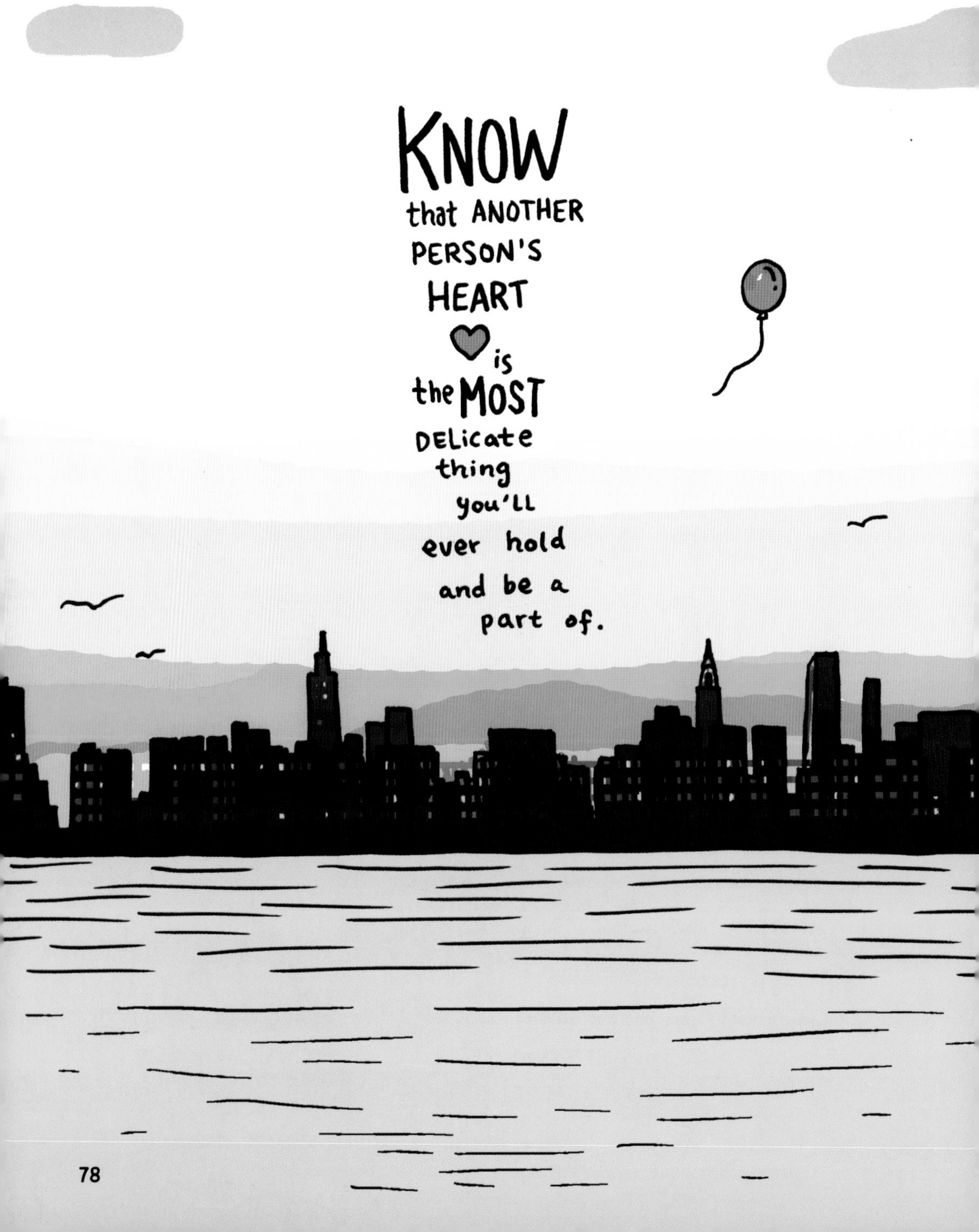
KNOW
that ANOTHER PERSON'S HEART
is the MOST DELicate thing you'll ever hold and be a part of.

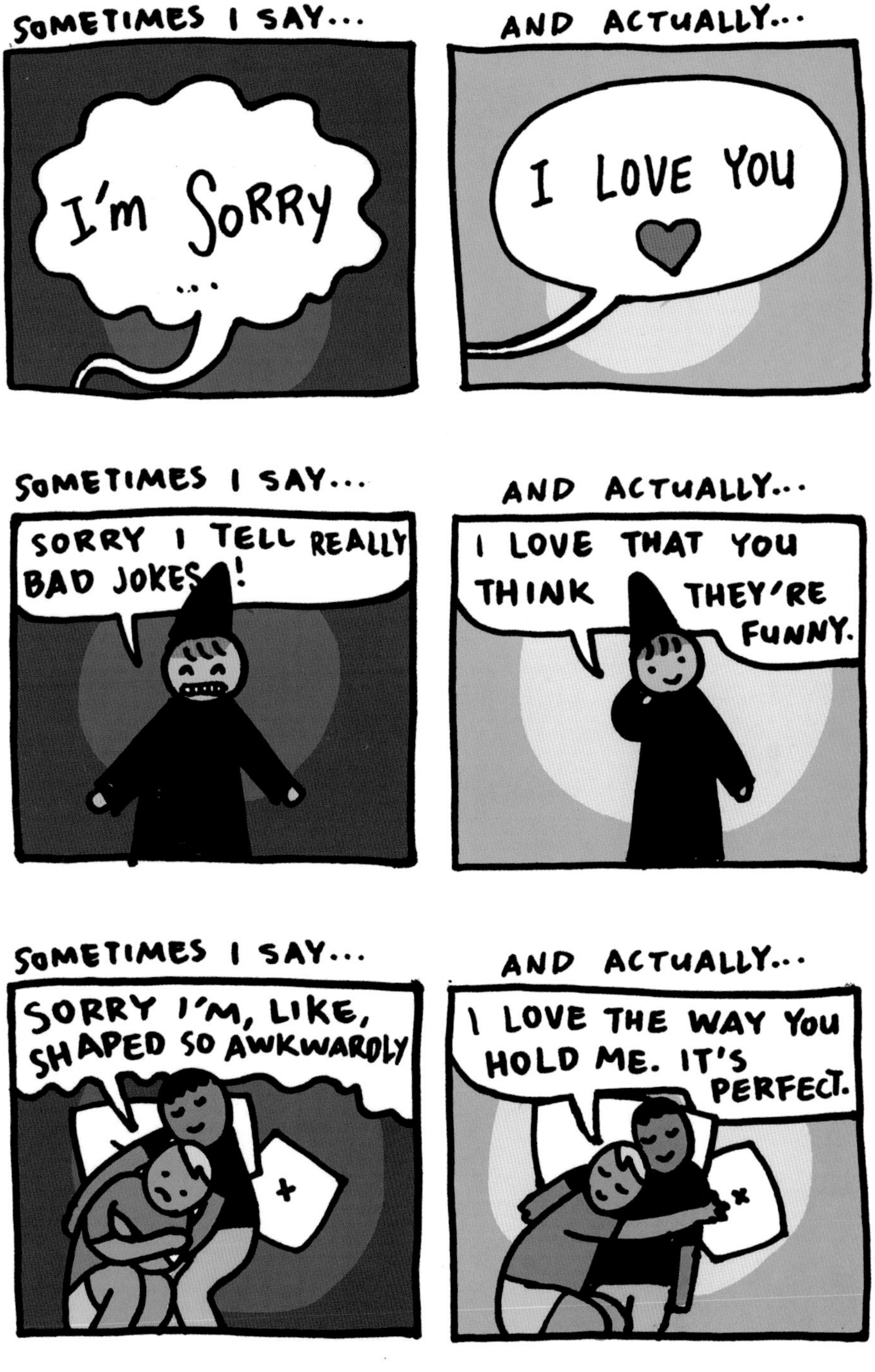
SOMETIMES I SAY...
I'M SORRY
...
AND ACTUALLY...
I LOVE YOU
SOMETIMES I SAY...
SORRY I TELL REALLY BAD JOKES!
AND ACTUALLY...
I LOVE THAT YOU THINK THEY'RE FUNNY.
SOMETIMES I SAY...
SORRY I'M, LIKE, SHAPED SO AWKWARDLY
AND ACTUALLY...
I LOVE THE WAY YOU HOLD ME. IT'S PERFECT.

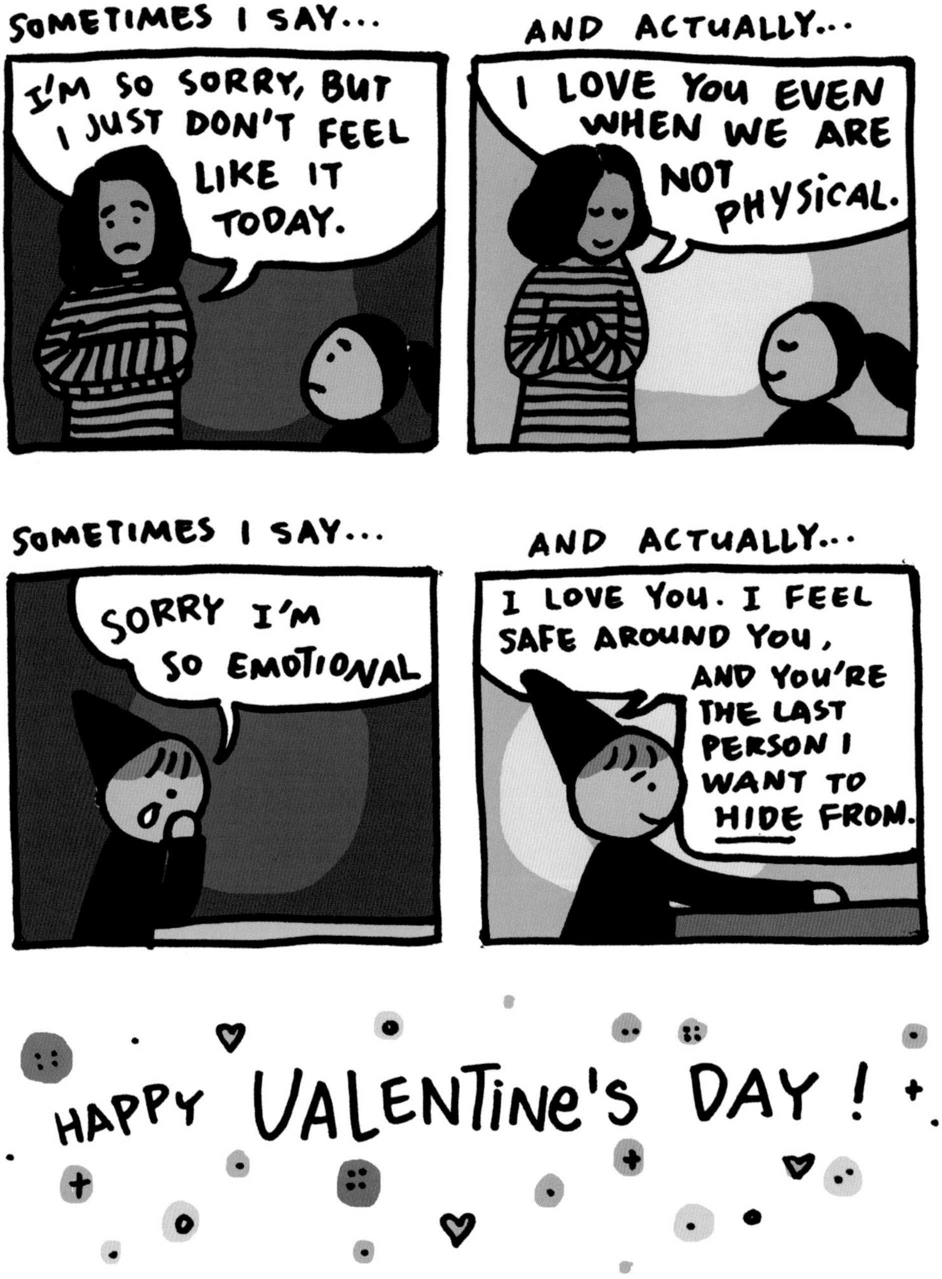
SOMETIMES I SAY...
I'M SO SORRY, BUT I JUST DON'T FEEL LIKE IT TODAY.
AND ACTUALLY...
I LOVE YOU EVEN WHEN WE ARE NOT PHYSICAL.
SOMETIMES I SAY...
SORRY I'M SO EMOTIONAL
AND ACTUALLY...
I LOVE YOU. I FEEL SAFE AROUND YOU,
AND YOU'RE THE LAST PERSON I WANT TO HIDE FROM.
HAPPY VALENTINE'S DAY!

ACTUALLY, I LOVE YOU

SHORTS ...

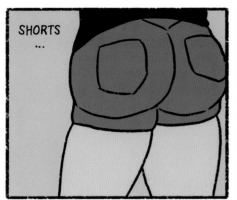

SHOWING MY ARMS...

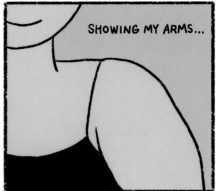

SUMMER is ALMOST Here!

... so is Asian Body Shaming.

WHOA! I'M **FAT** LIKE YOU, AND I CAN NEVER SHOW SO MUCH SKIN.

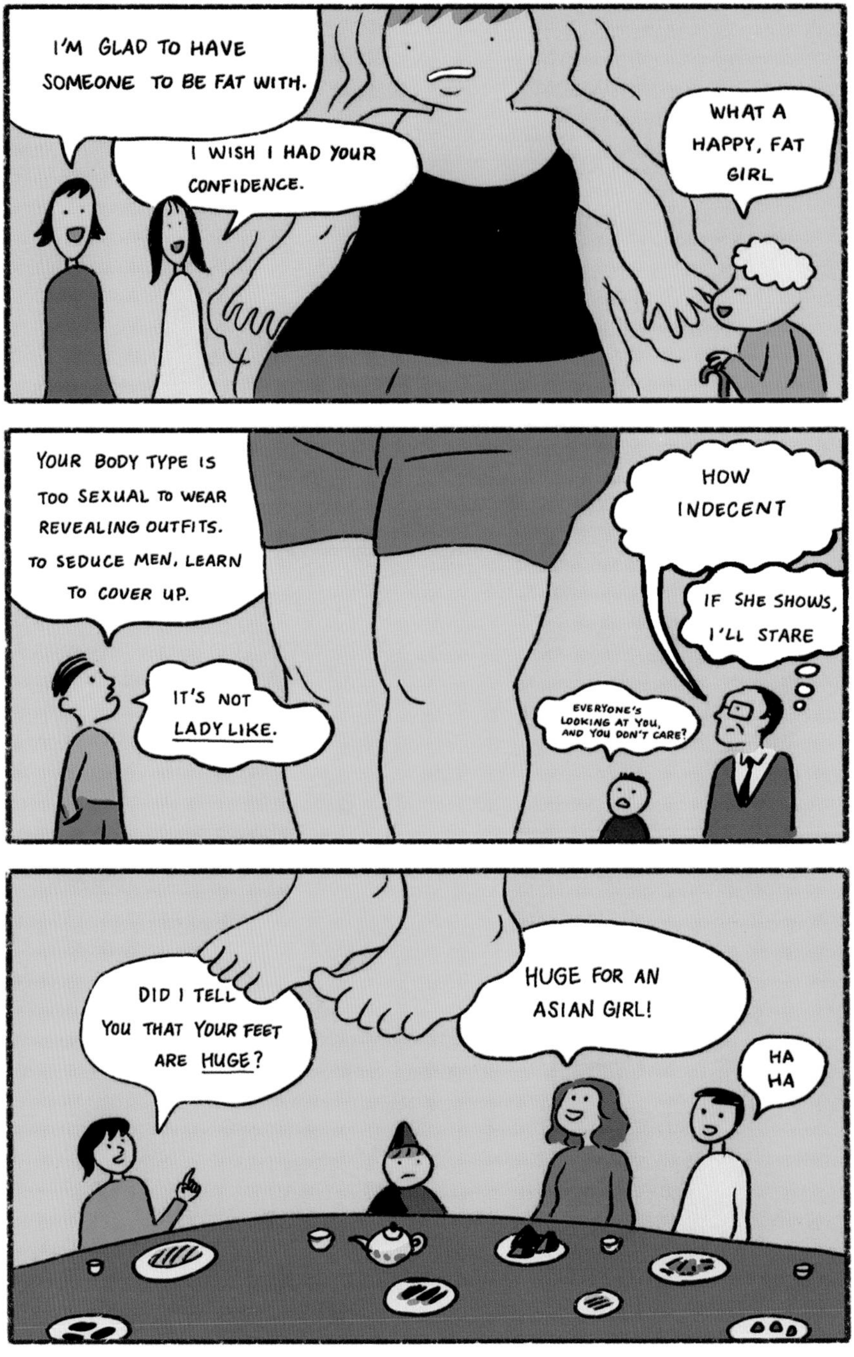
I'M GLAD TO HAVE SOMEONE TO BE FAT WITH.
I WISH I HAD YOUR CONFIDENCE.
WHAT A HAPPY, FAT GIRL
YOUR BODY TYPE IS TOO SEXUAL TO WEAR REVEALING OUTFITS. TO SEDUCE MEN, LEARN TO COVER UP.
IT'S NOT LADY LIKE.
HOW INDECENT
IF SHE SHOWS, I'LL STARE
EVERYONE'S LOOKING AT YOU, AND YOU DON'T CARE?
DID I TELL YOU THAT YOUR FEET ARE HUGE?
HUGE FOR AN ASIAN GIRL!
HA HA

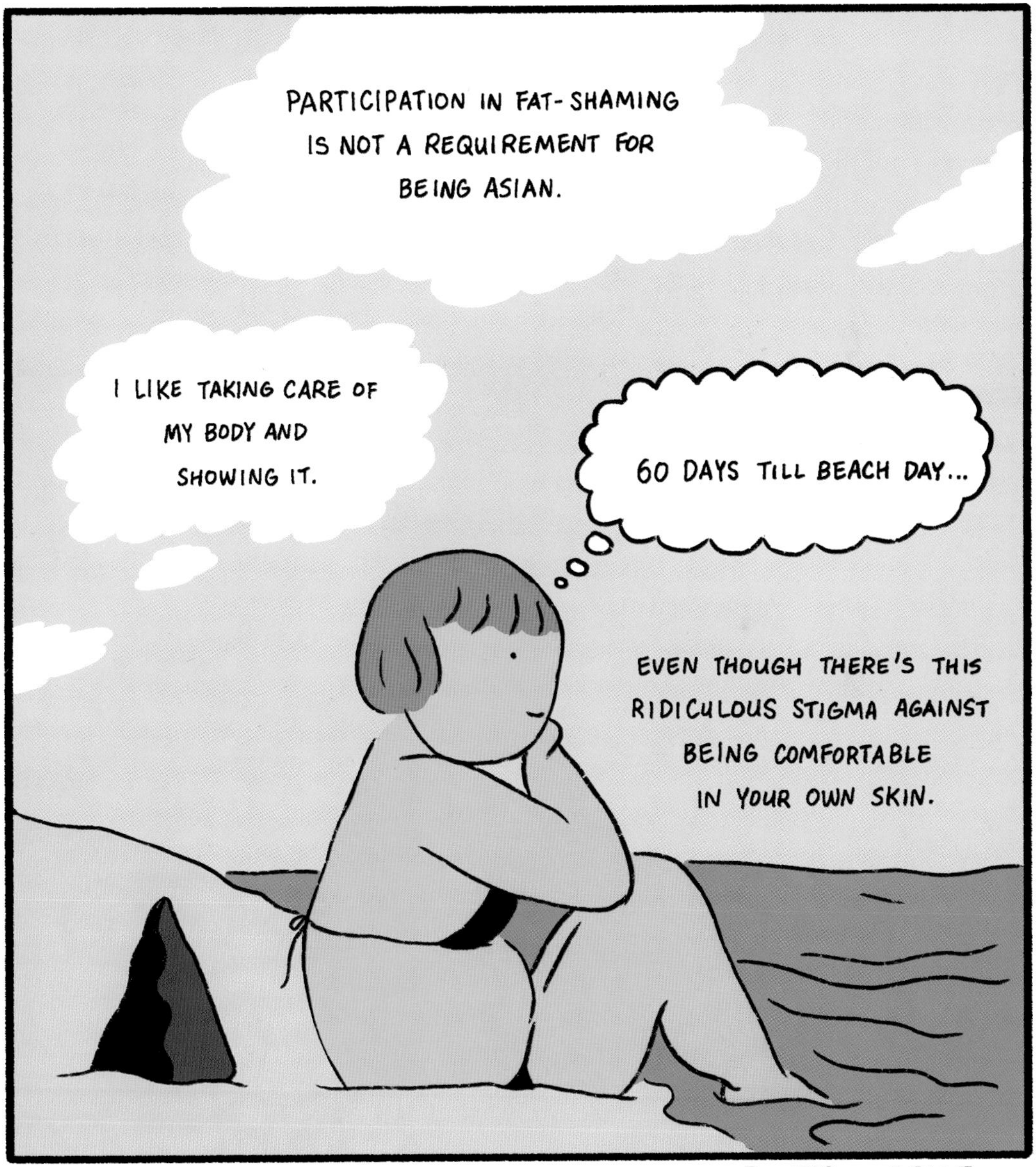
PARTICIPATION IN FAT-SHAMING IS NOT A REQUIREMENT FOR BEING ASIAN.
I LIKE TAKING CARE OF MY BODY AND SHOWING IT.
60 DAYS TILL BEACH DAY...
EVEN THOUGH THERE'S THIS RIDICULOUS STIGMA AGAINST BEING COMFORTABLE IN YOUR OWN SKIN.

BODY ISSUE

HOW NOT TO TALK TO A GIRL
(BLAH BLAH BLAH) (JUST STOP)

GROWING UP IN CHINA IN THE 1990s, I REBELLED AGAINST HABITUAL GENDER STEREOTYPES IN THE LANGUAGE OF ADULTS.

you'll be SOOO PRETTY WHEN YOU GROW UP!

I, like, literally just peed my pants, and I have no hair.

You want to be an ASTRONAUT! How cute. But that's no job for a girl — How will you raise children if you are in space?

......what ??

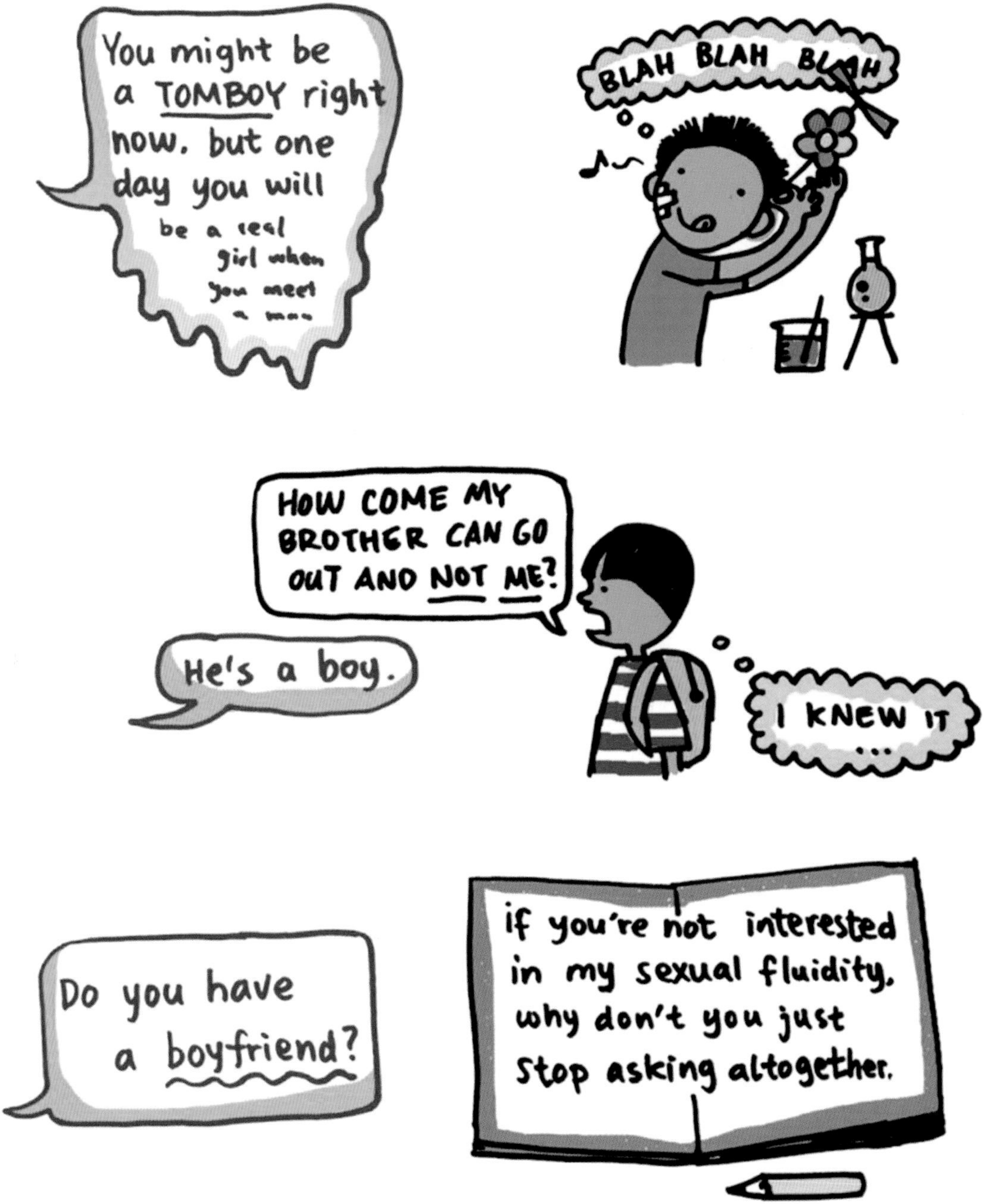
You might be a TOMBOY right now, but one day you will
be a real girl when you meet
BLAH BLAH BLAH
HOW COME MY BROTHER CAN GO OUT AND NOT ME?
He's a boy.
I KNEW IT ...
Do you have a boyfriend?
if you're not interested in my sexual fluidity, why don't you just stop asking altogether.

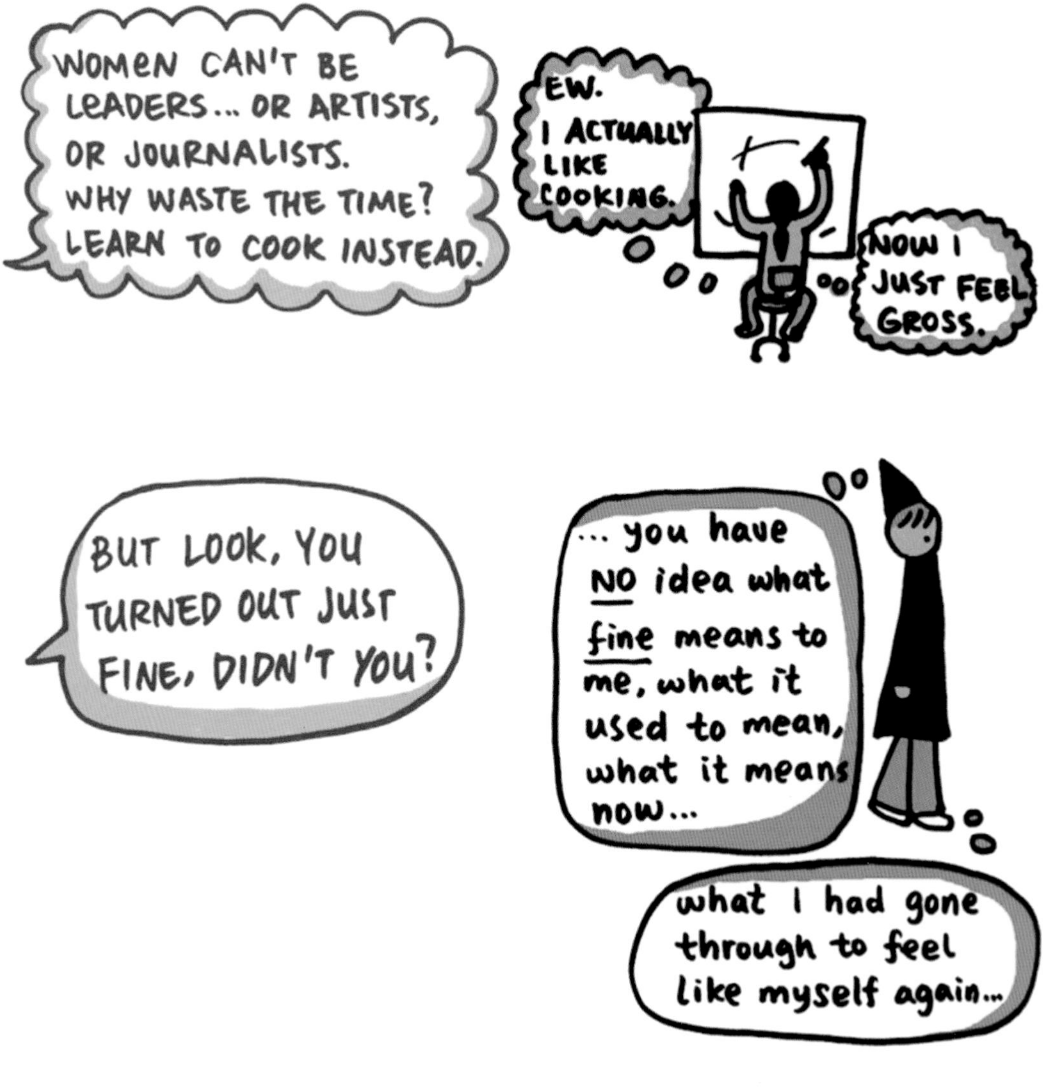
WOMEN CAN'T BE LEADERS... OR ARTISTS, OR JOURNALISTS. WHY WASTE THE TIME? LEARN TO COOK INSTEAD.
EW. I ACTUALLY LIKE COOKING.
NOW I JUST FEEL GROSS.
BUT LOOK, YOU TURNED OUT JUST FINE, DIDN'T YOU?
... you have NO idea what fine means to me, what it used to mean, what it means now...
what I had gone through to feel like myself again...

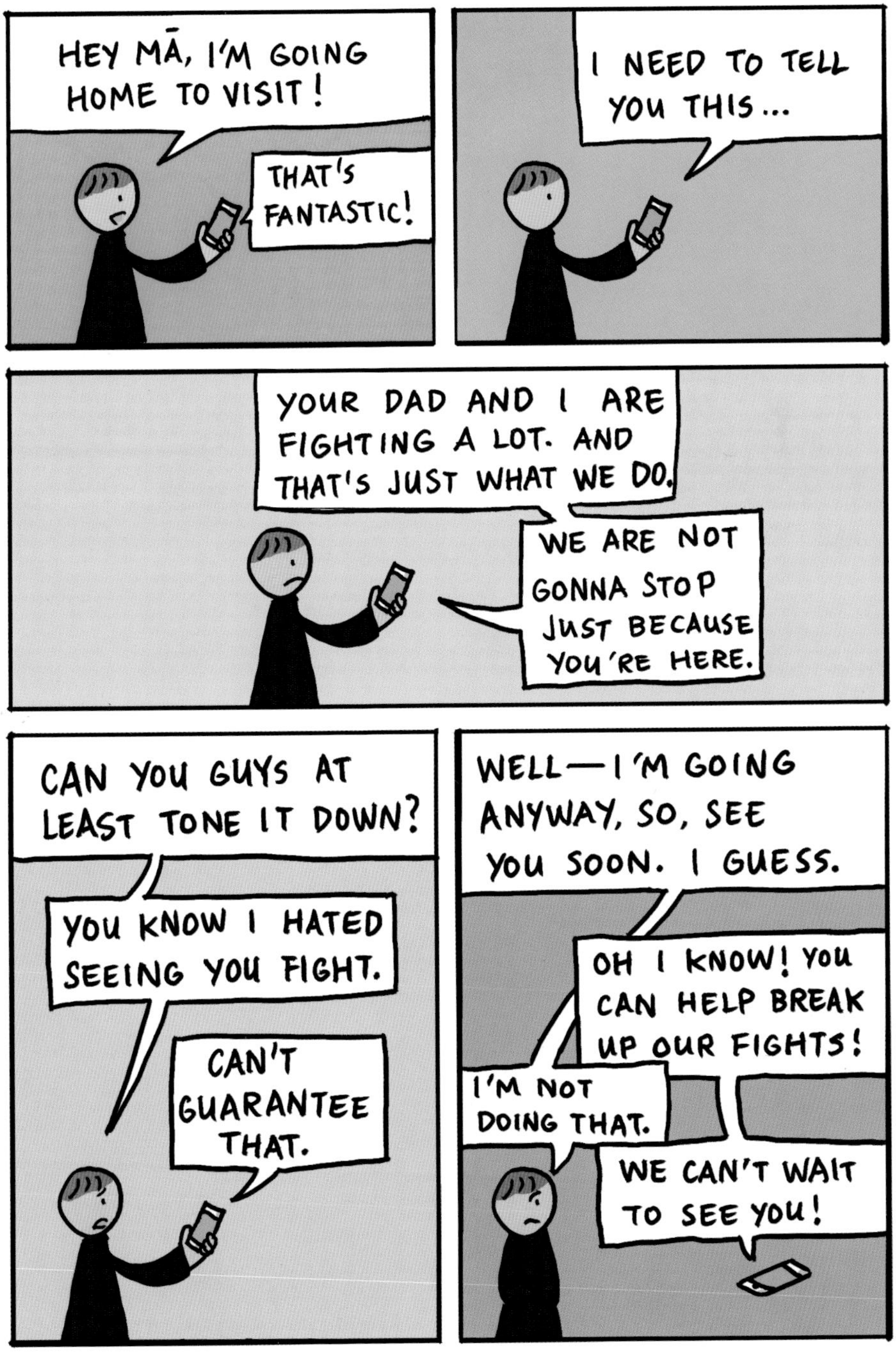
HEY MĀ, I'M GOING HOME TO VISIT!
THAT'S FANTASTIC!
I NEED TO TELL YOU THIS...
YOUR DAD AND I ARE FIGHTING A LOT. AND THAT'S JUST WHAT WE DO.
WE ARE NOT GONNA STOP JUST BECAUSE YOU'RE HERE.
CAN YOU GUYS AT LEAST TONE IT DOWN?
YOU KNOW I HATED SEEING YOU FIGHT.
CAN'T GUARANTEE THAT.
WELL—I'M GOING ANYWAY, SO, SEE YOU SOON. I GUESS.
OH I KNOW! YOU CAN HELP BREAK UP OUR FIGHTS!
I'M NOT DOING THAT.
WE CAN'T WAIT TO SEE YOU!

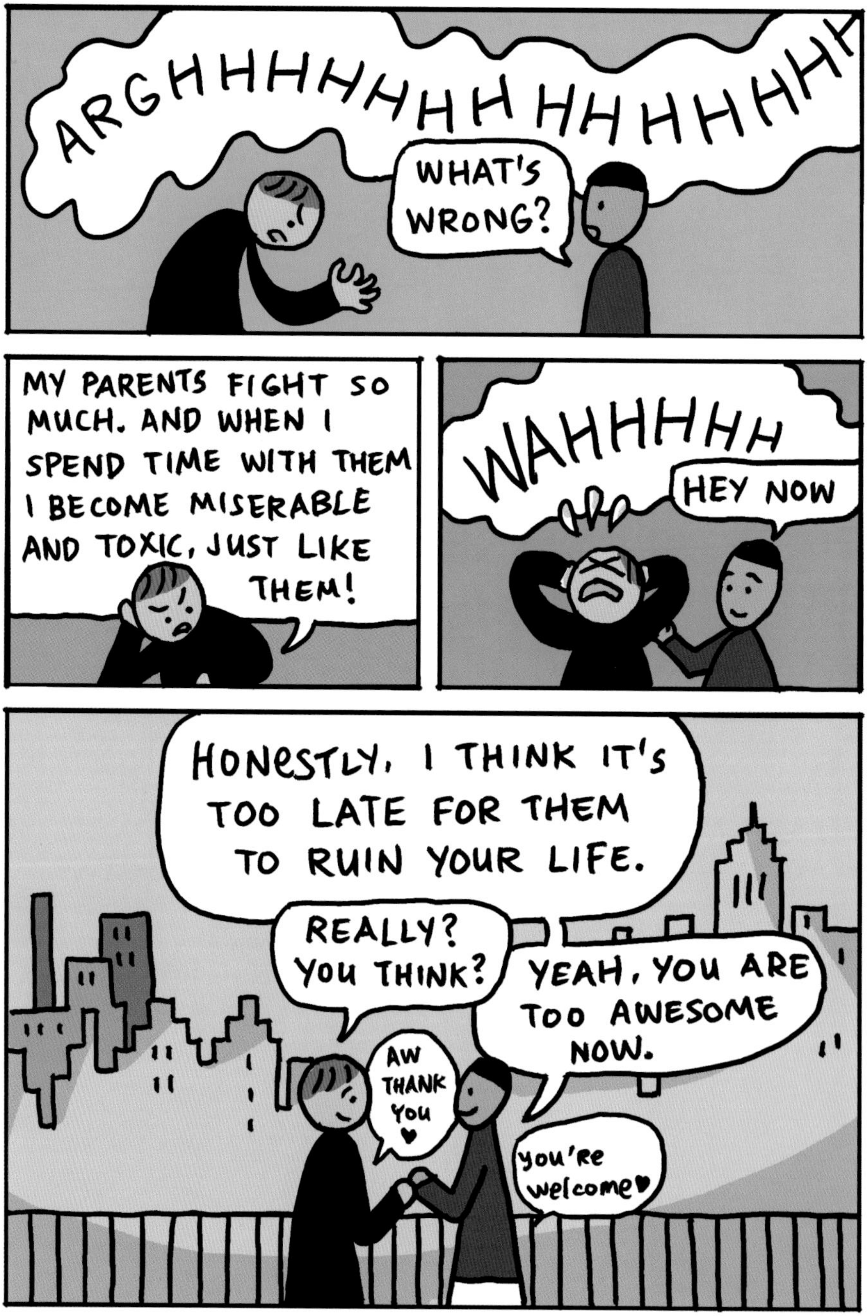
ARGHHHHHHHHHHHHHHH
WHAT'S WRONG?
MY PARENTS FIGHT SO MUCH. AND WHEN I SPEND TIME WITH THEM I BECOME MISERABLE AND TOXIC, JUST LIKE THEM!
WAHHHHH
HEY NOW
HONESTLY, I THINK IT'S TOO LATE FOR THEM TO RUIN YOUR LIFE.
REALLY? YOU THINK?
YEAH, YOU ARE TOO AWESOME NOW.
AW THANK YOU ♥
you're welcome♥

TOO AWESOME FOR MOM AND DAD

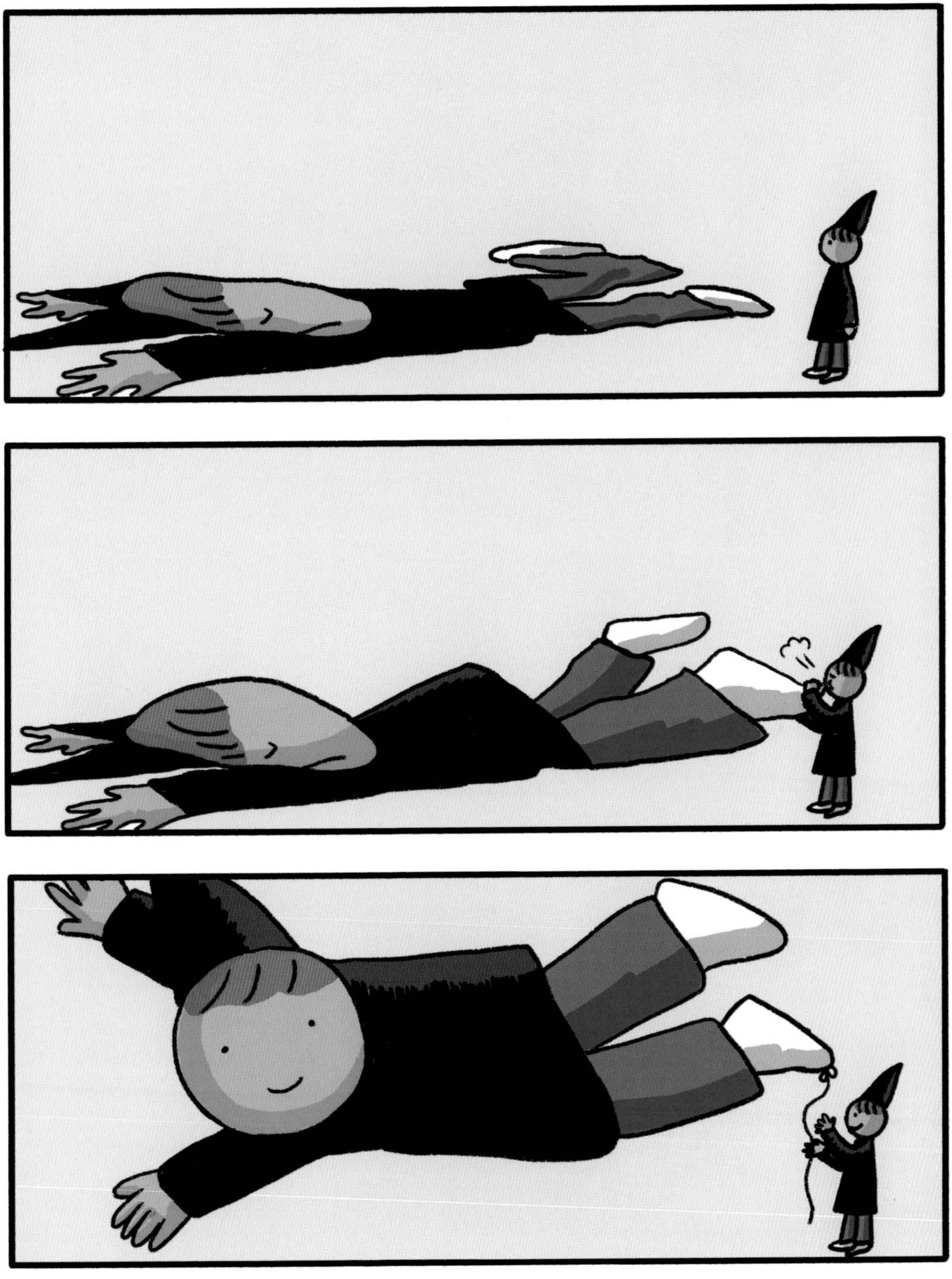

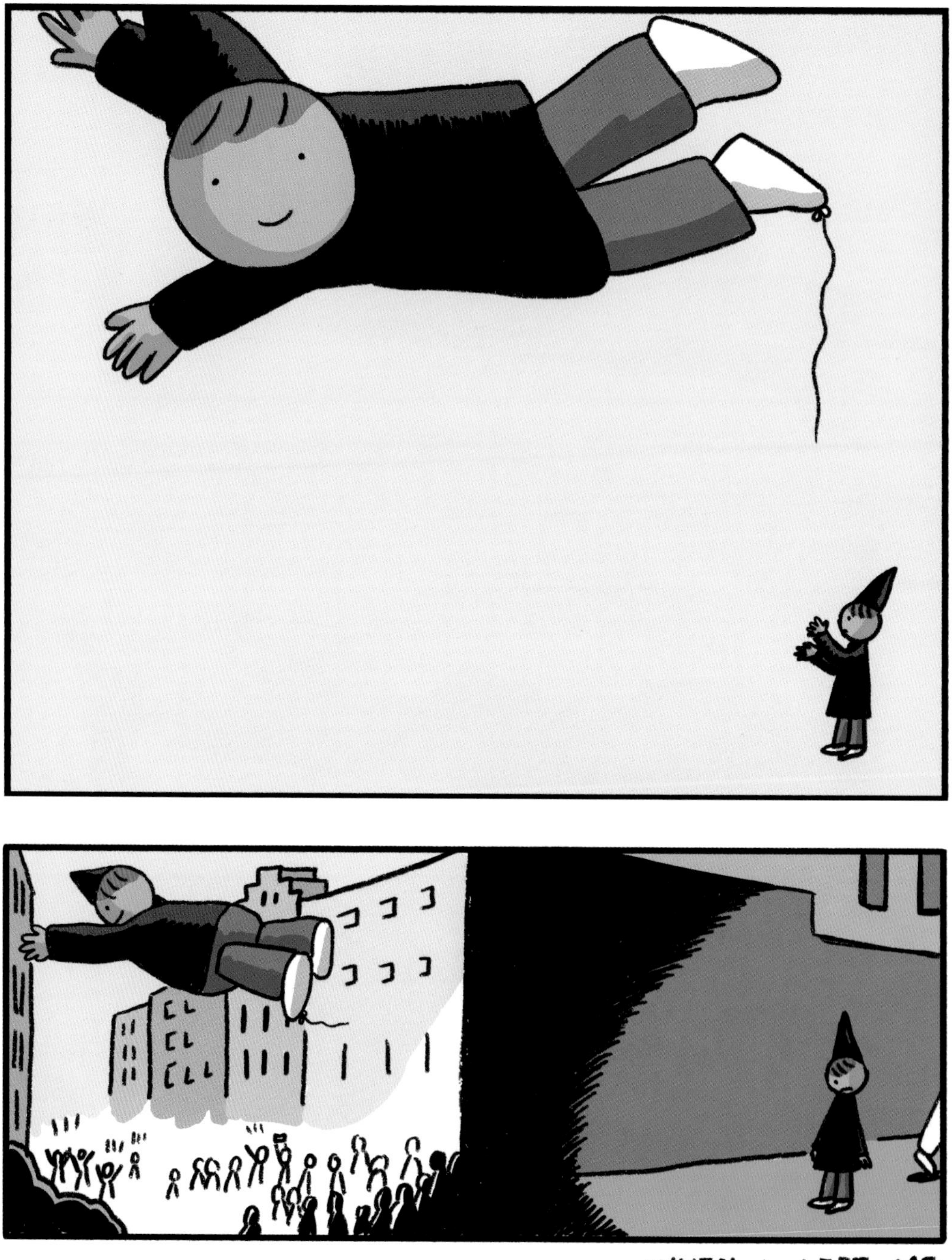

WHEN I LEFT ME

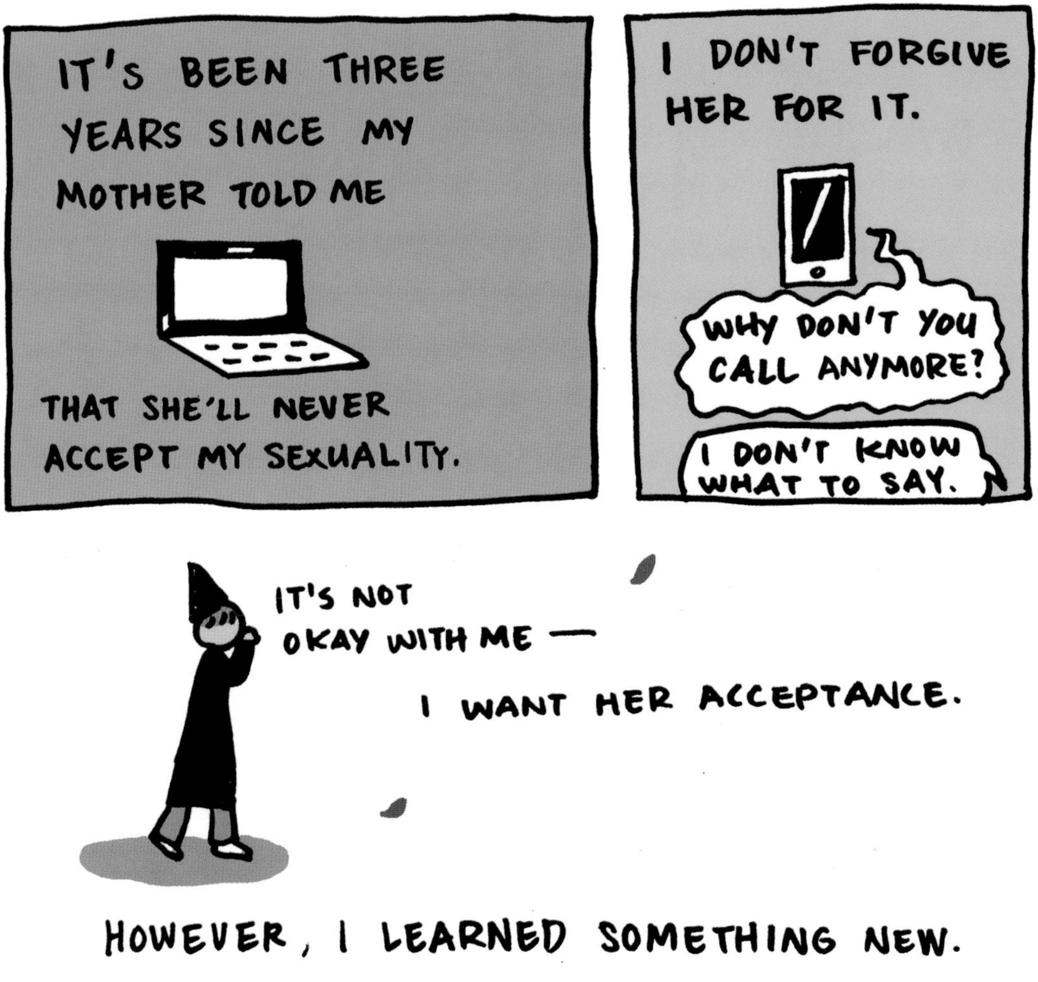
IT'S BEEN THREE YEARS SINCE MY MOTHER TOLD ME
THAT SHE'LL NEVER ACCEPT MY SEXUALITY.
I DON'T FORGIVE HER FOR IT.
WHY DON'T YOU CALL ANYMORE?
I DON'T KNOW WHAT TO SAY.
IT'S NOT OKAY WITH ME —
I WANT HER ACCEPTANCE.
HOWEVER, I LEARNED SOMETHING NEW.

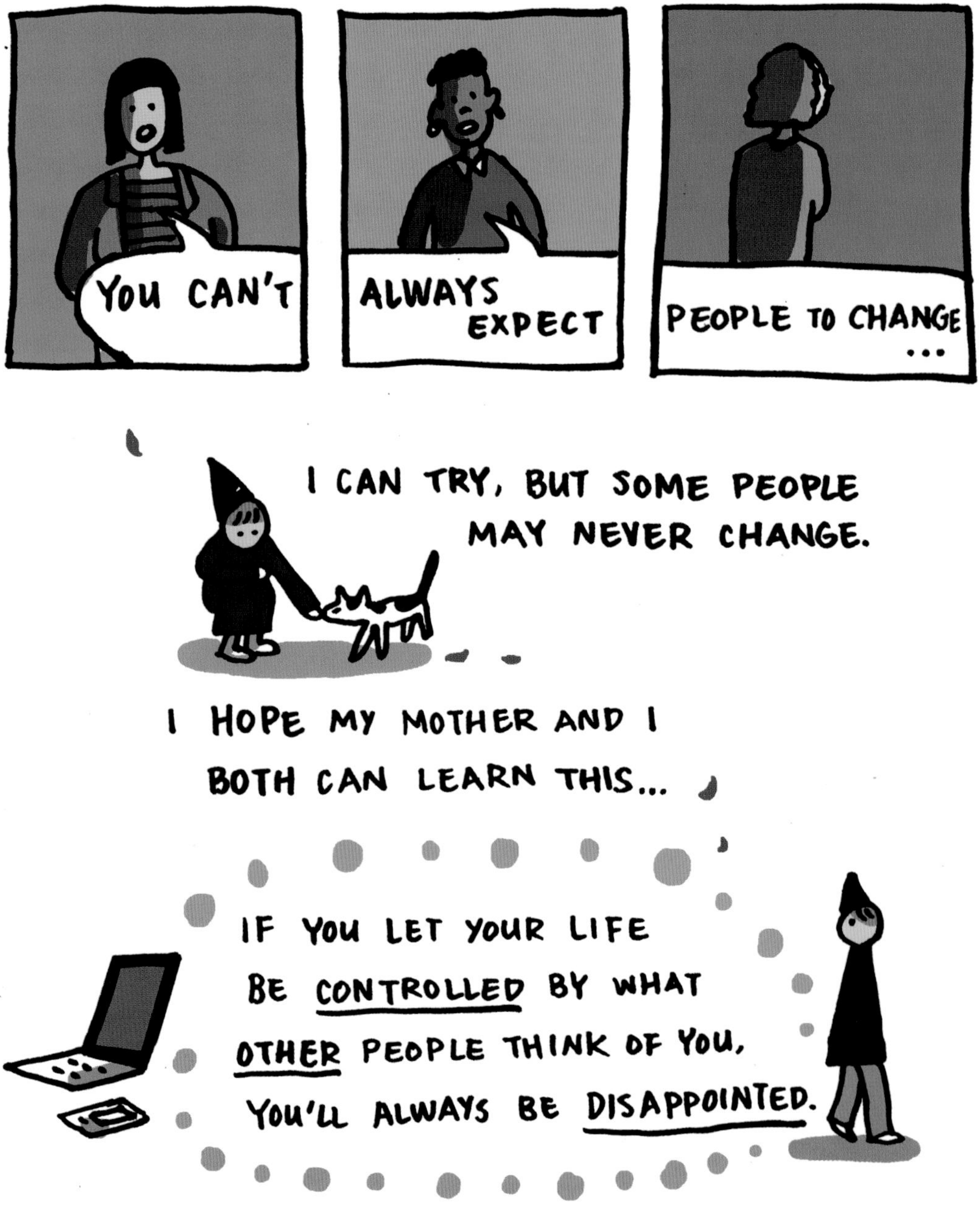
YOU CAN'T
ALWAYS EXPECT
PEOPLE TO CHANGE...
I CAN TRY, BUT SOME PEOPLE MAY NEVER CHANGE.
I HOPE MY MOTHER AND I BOTH CAN LEARN THIS...
IF YOU LET YOUR LIFE BE CONTROLLED BY WHAT OTHER PEOPLE THINK OF YOU, YOU'LL ALWAYS BE DISAPPOINTED.

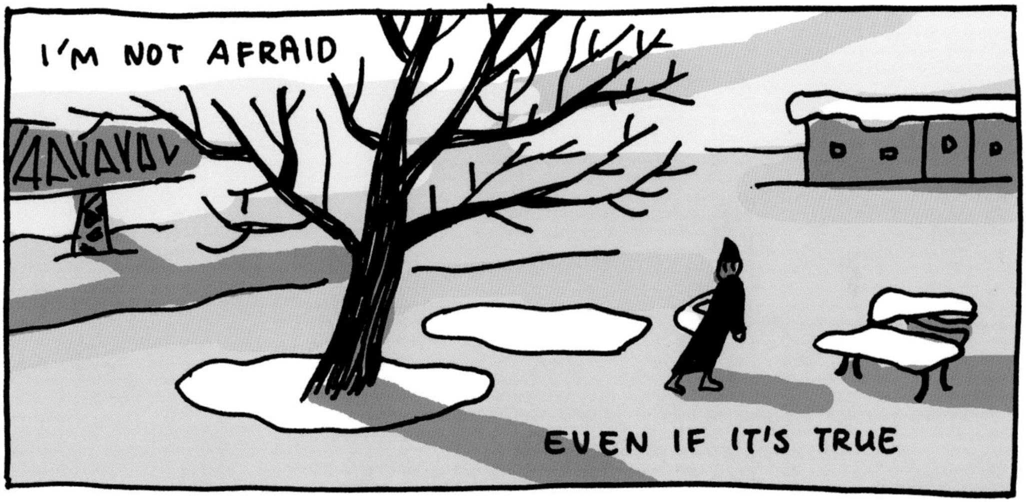
I'M NOT AFRAID
EVEN IF IT'S TRUE

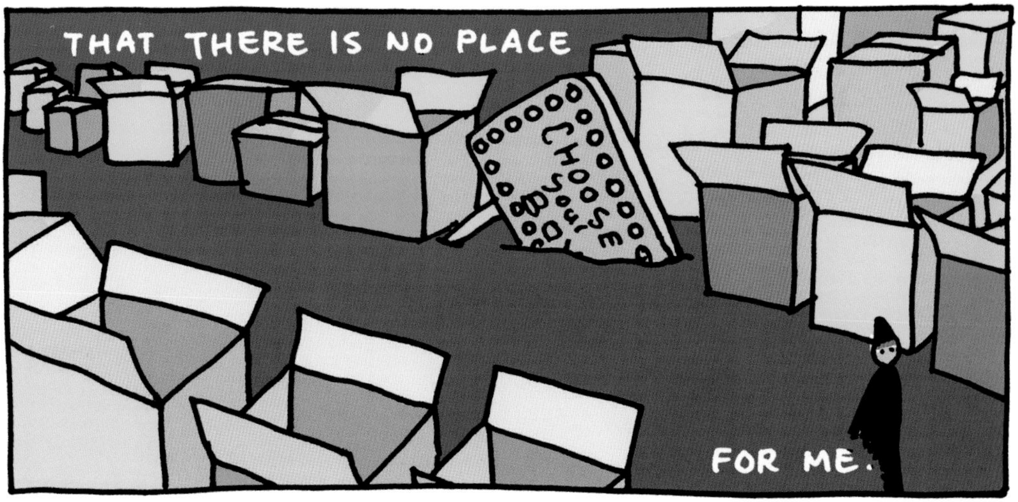
THAT THERE IS NO PLACE
CHOOSE
FOR ME.

MY HOME
IS
IN
MY HEART
AND IN THE HANDS
OF ALL OF MY FRIENDS.

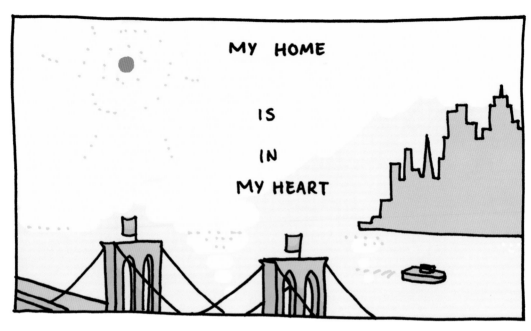

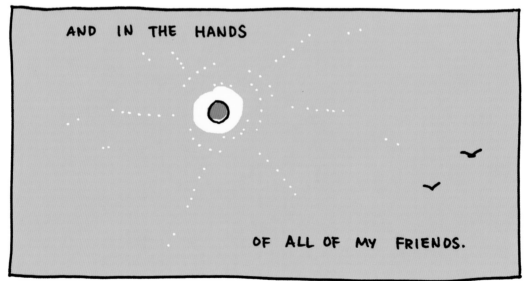

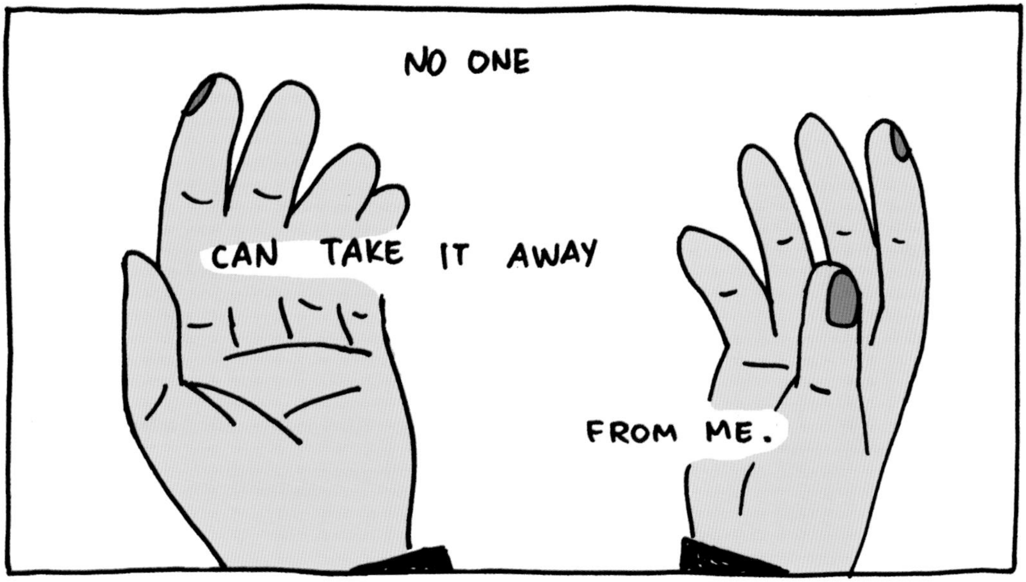
NO ONE
CAN TAKE IT AWAY
FROM ME.

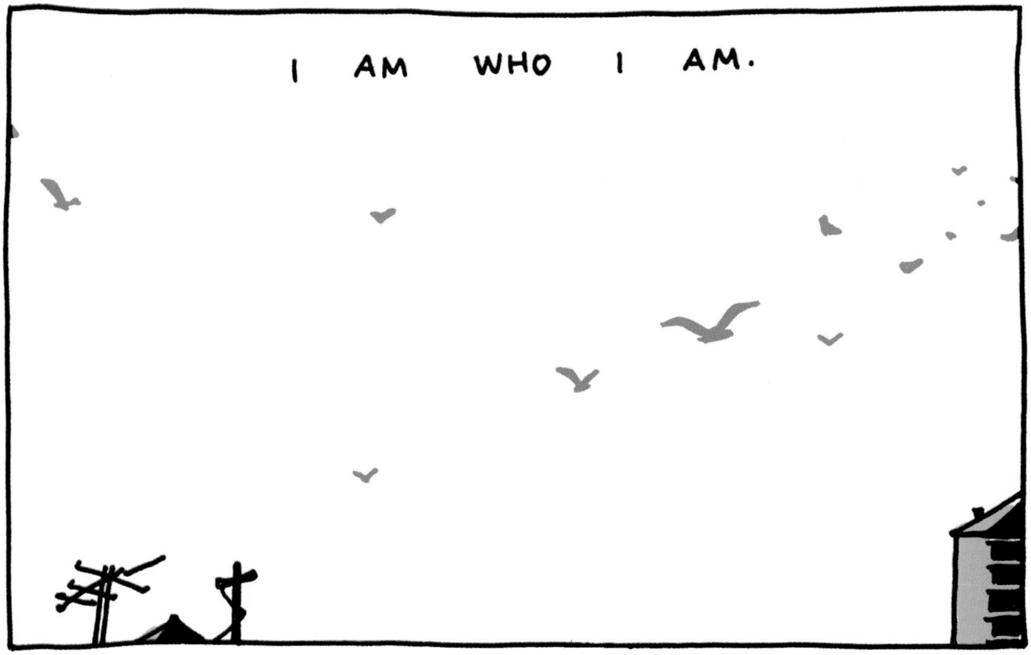
I AM WHO I AM.

MY HOME IS IN MY HEART

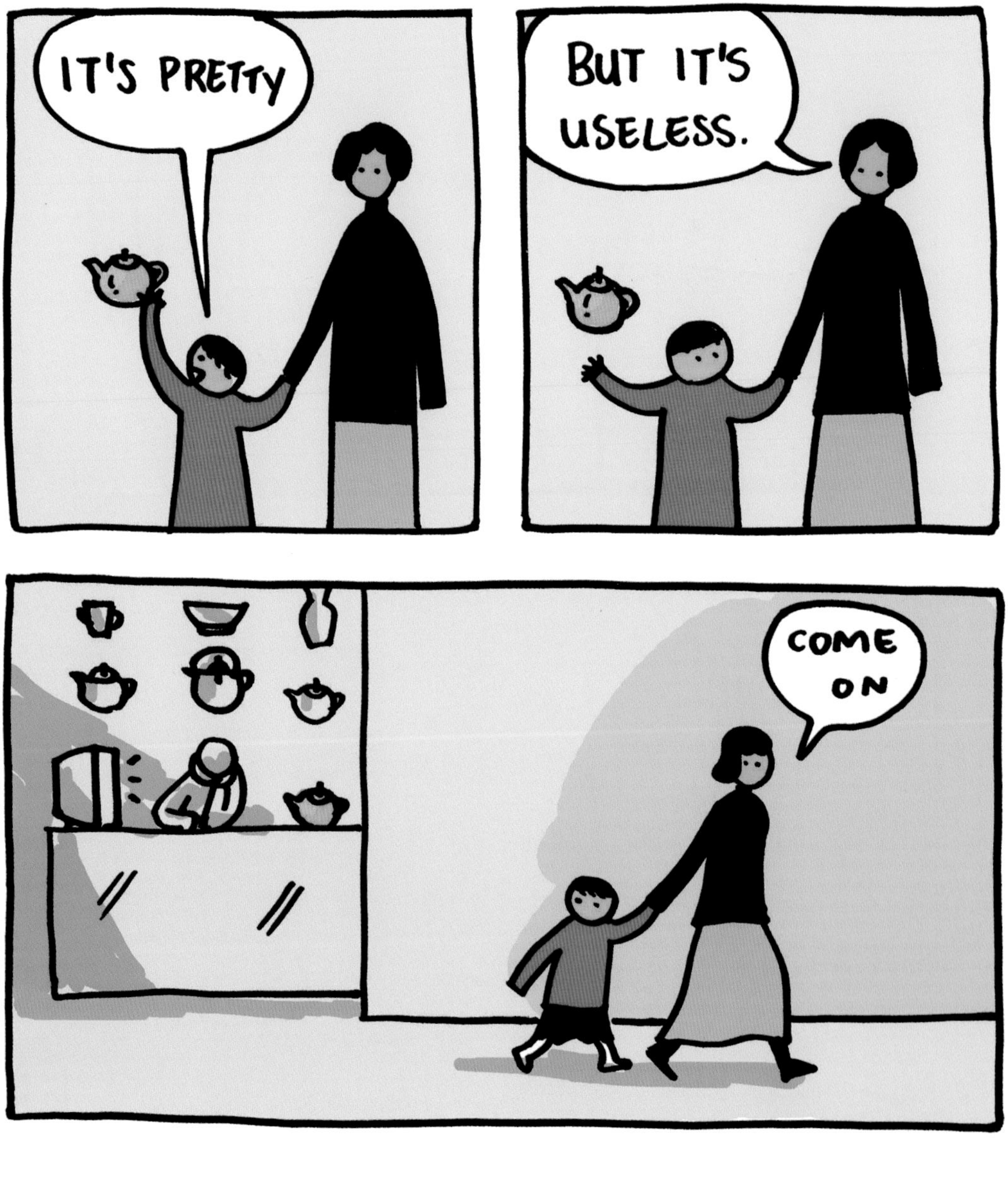
IT'S PRETTY
BUT IT'S USELESS.
COME ON

... 20 YEARS ...

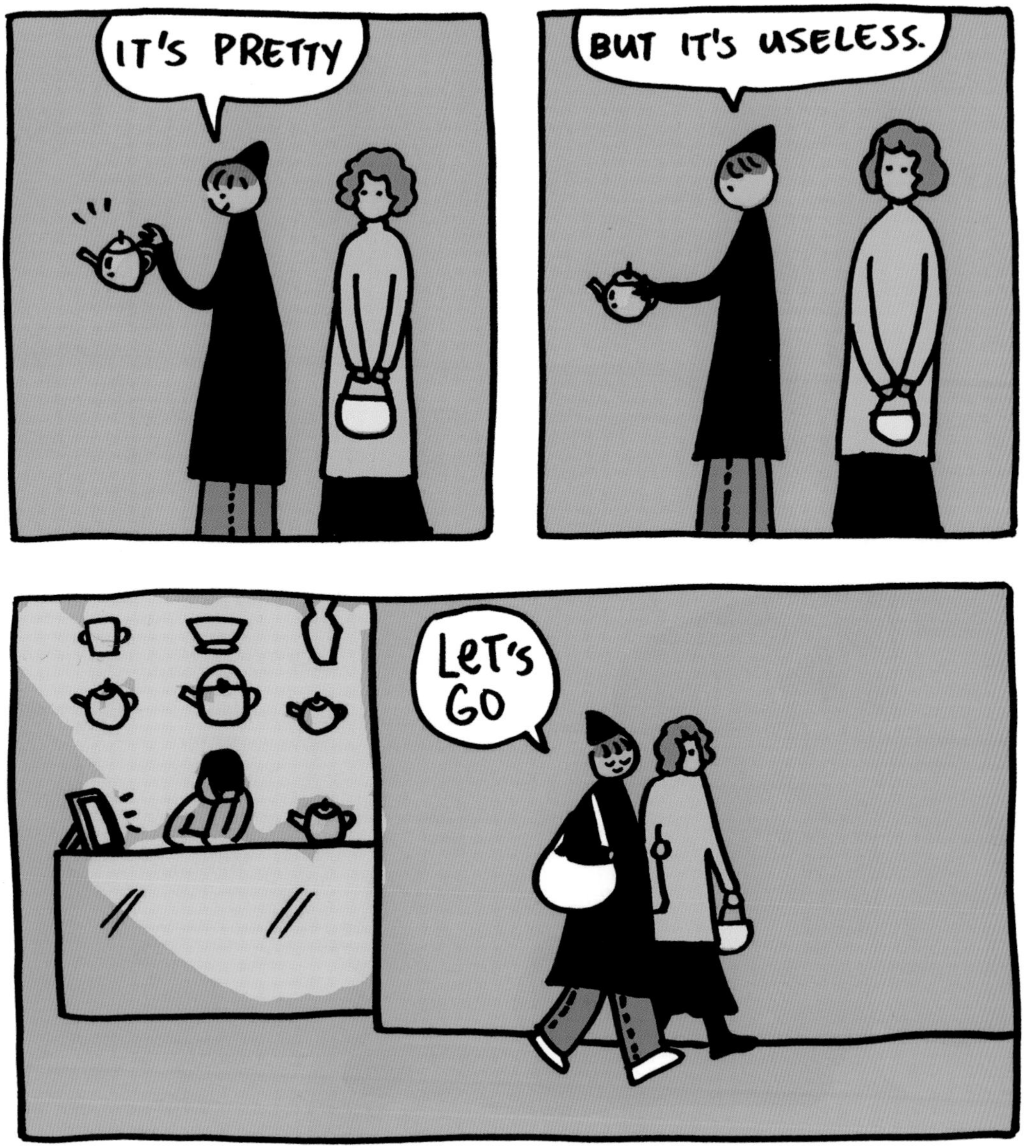
IT'S PRETTY
BUT IT'S USELESS.
LET'S GO

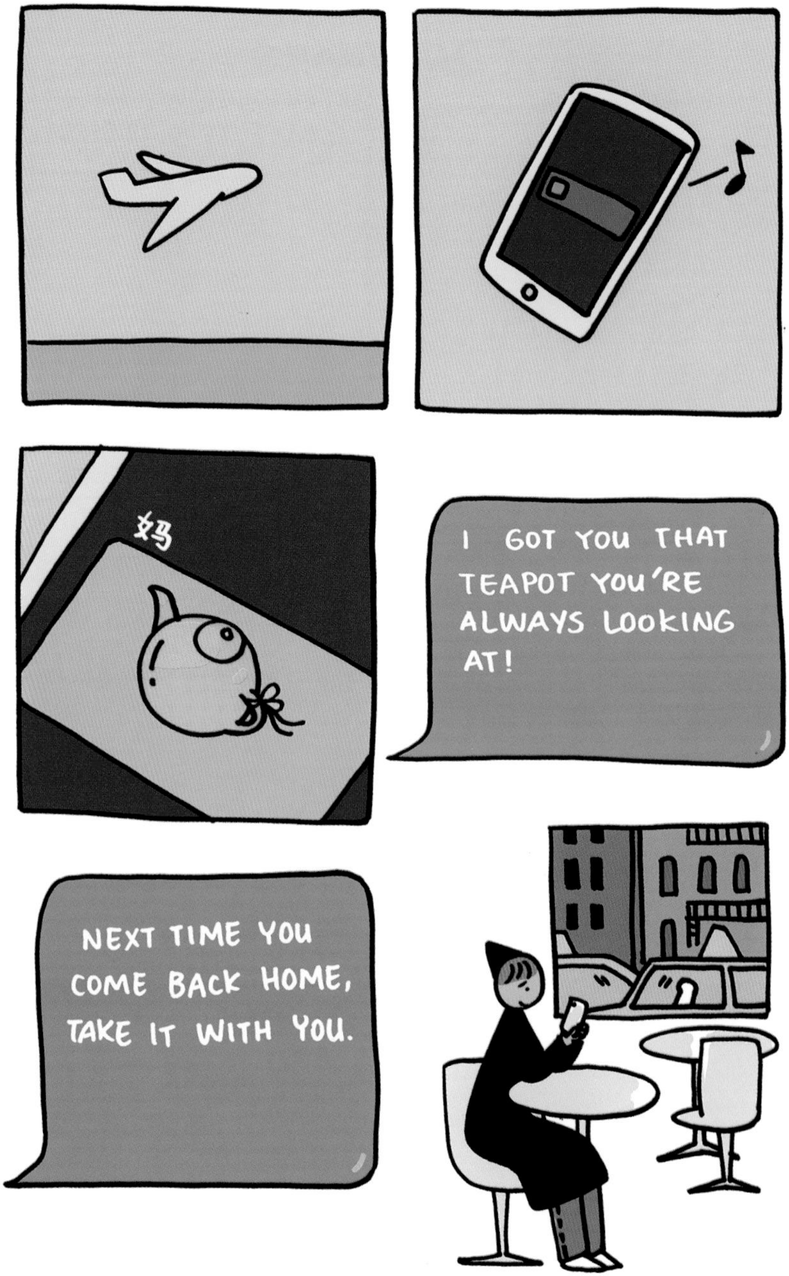
妈
I GOT YOU THAT TEAPOT YOU'RE ALWAYS LOOKING AT!
NEXT TIME YOU COME BACK HOME, TAKE IT WITH YOU.

PRETTY THINGS

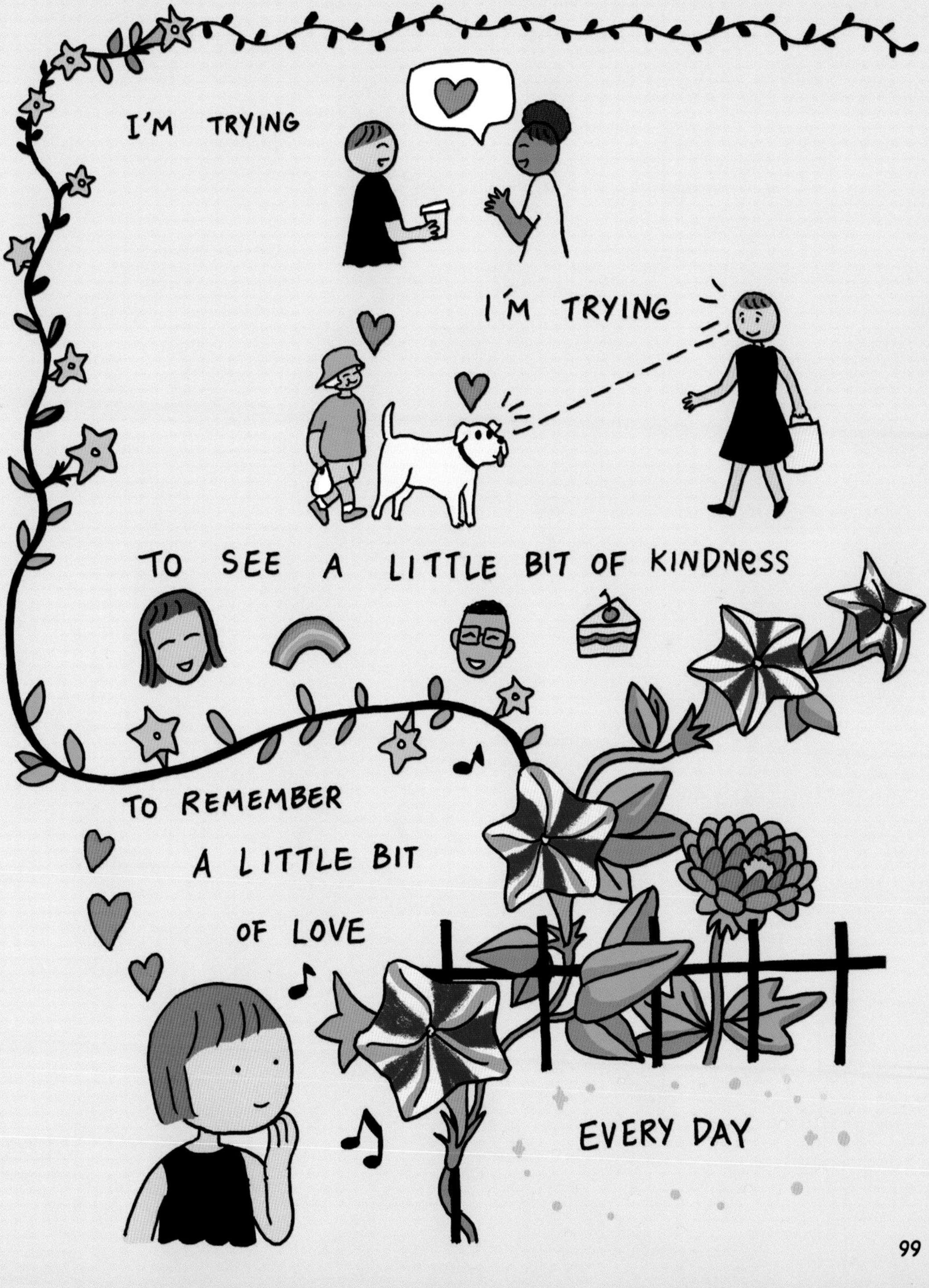
I'M TRYING
I'M TRYING
TO SEE A LITTLE BIT OF KINDNESS
TO REMEMBER
A LITTLE BIT
OF LOVE
EVERY DAY

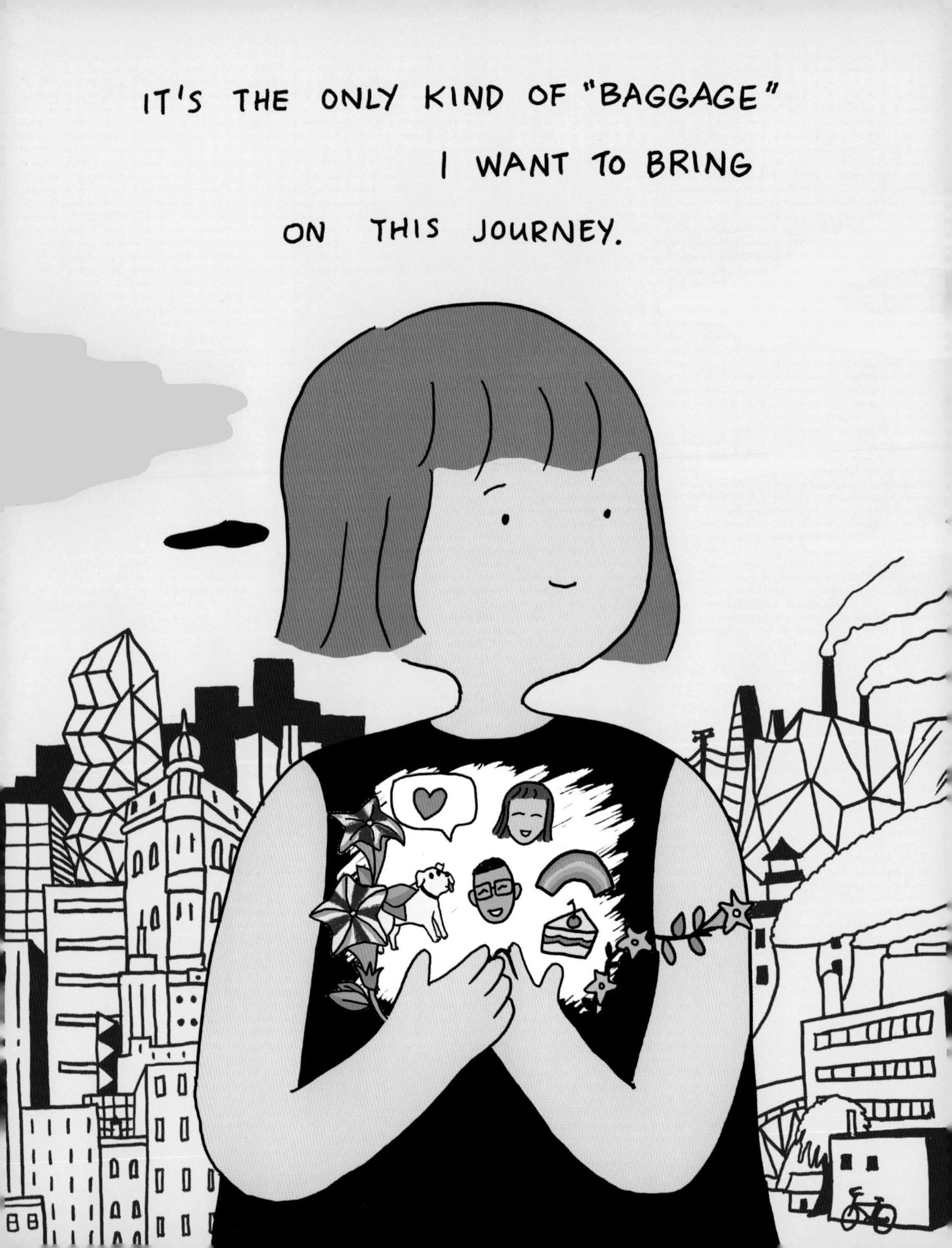
IT'S THE ONLY KIND OF "BAGGAGE"
I WANT TO BRING
ON THIS JOURNEY.

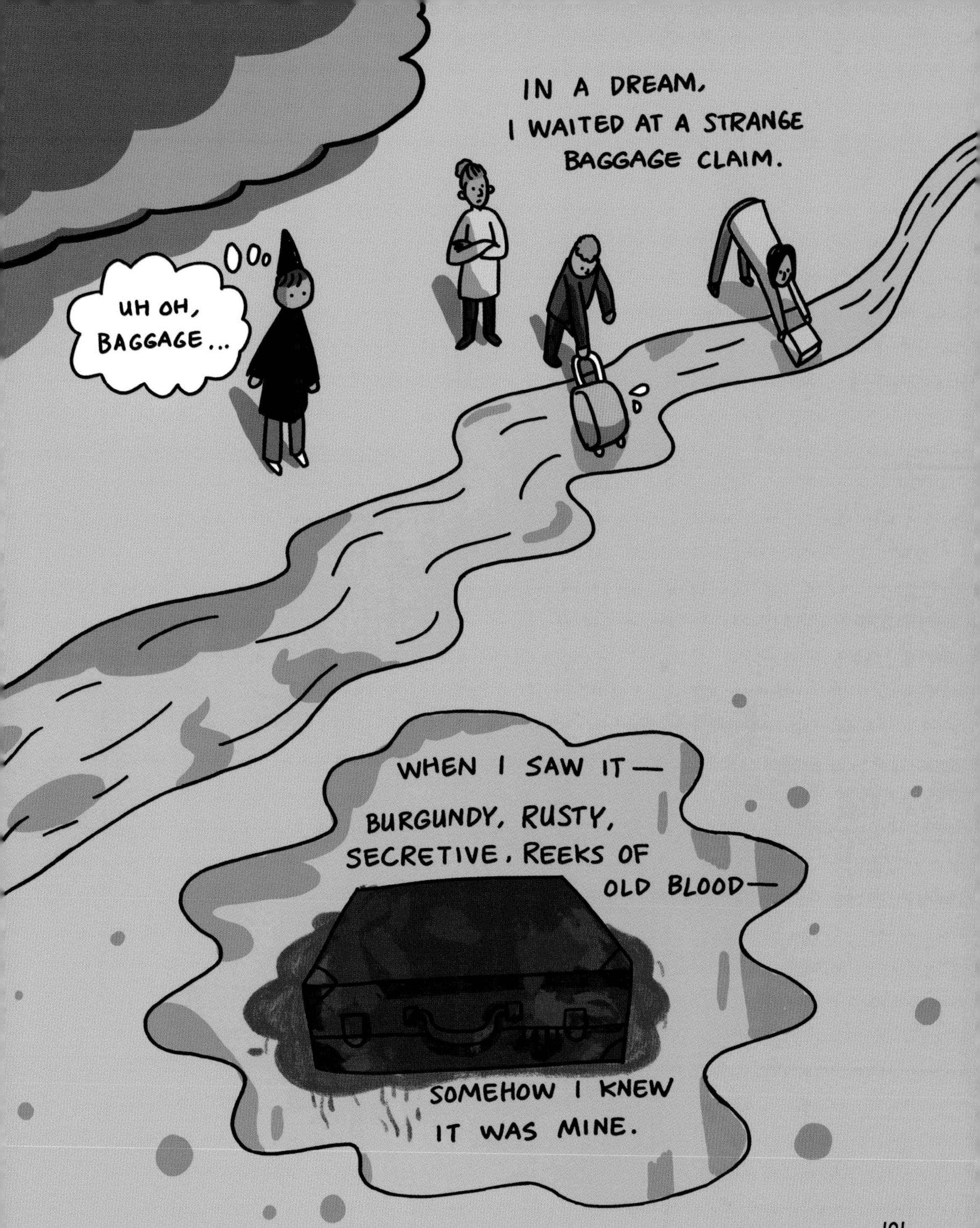
IN A DREAM, I WAITED AT A STRANGE BAGGAGE CLAIM.
UH OH, BAGGAGE...
WHEN I SAW IT—
BURGUNDY, RUSTY, SECRETIVE, REEKS OF OLD BLOOD—
SOMEHOW I KNEW IT WAS MINE.

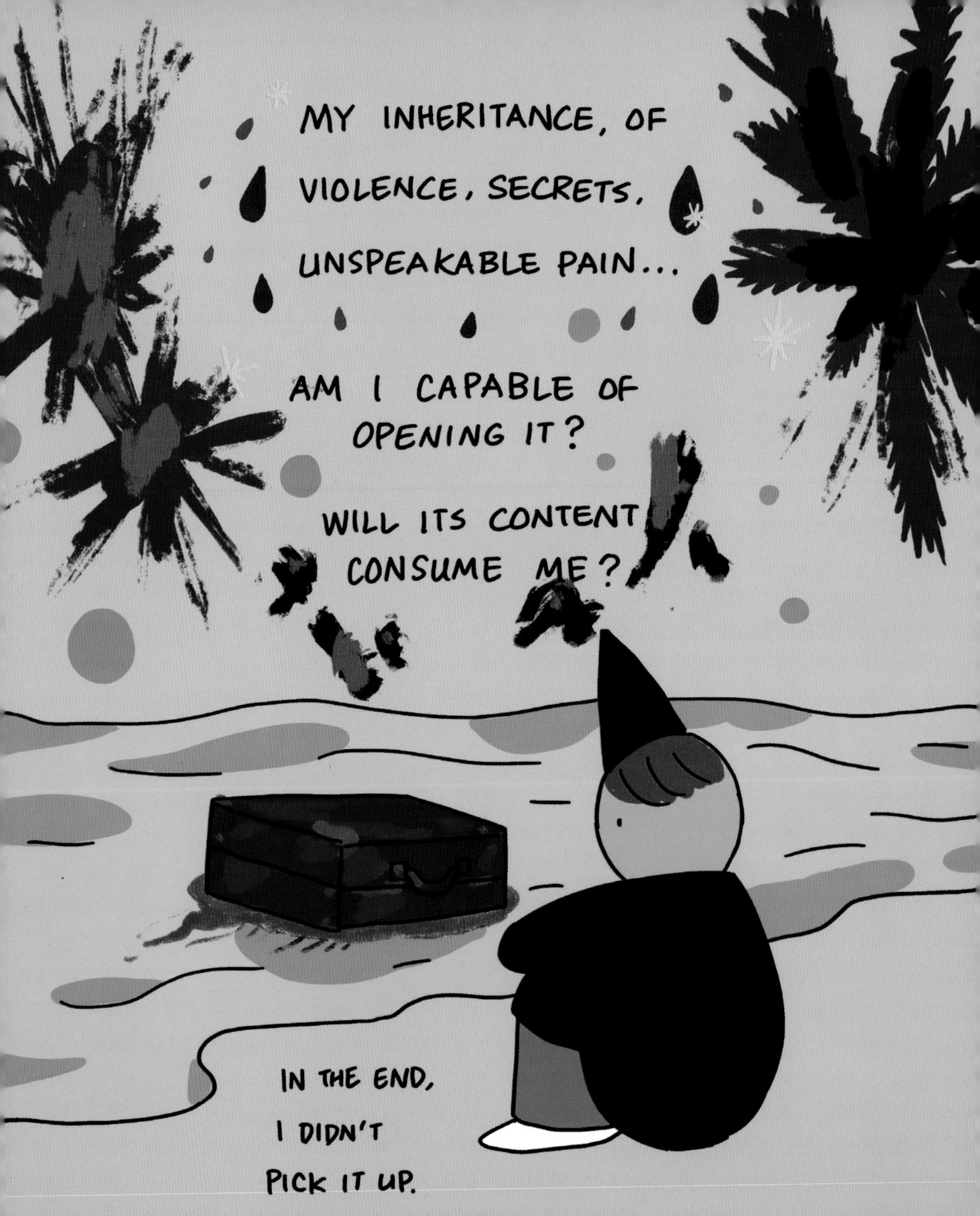
MY INHERITANCE, OF VIOLENCE, SECRETS, UNSPEAKABLE PAIN...
AM I CAPABLE OF OPENING IT?
WILL ITS CONTENT CONSUME ME?
IN THE END, I DIDN'T PICK IT UP.

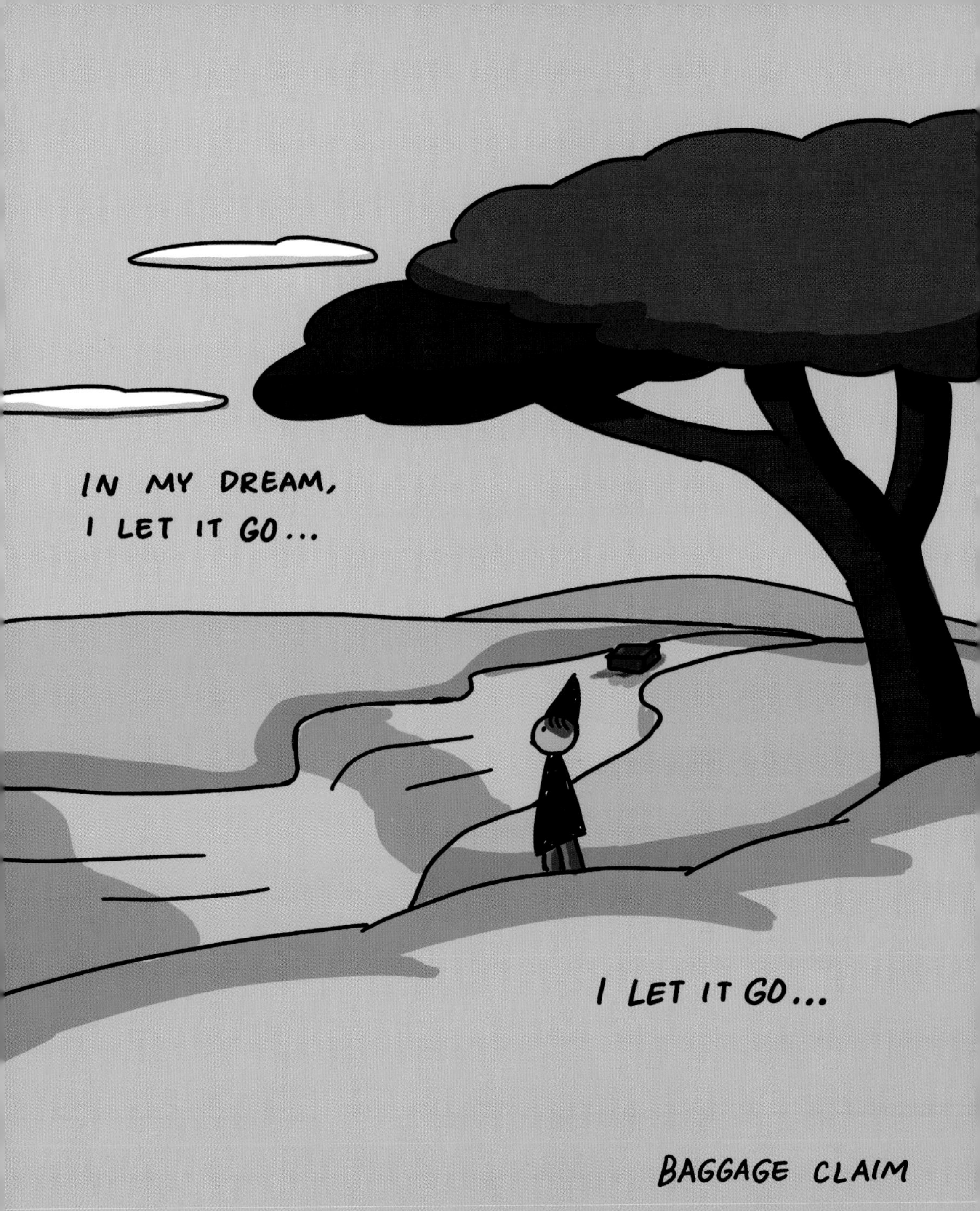
IN MY DREAM,
I LET IT GO...
I LET IT GO...
BAGGAGE CLAIM

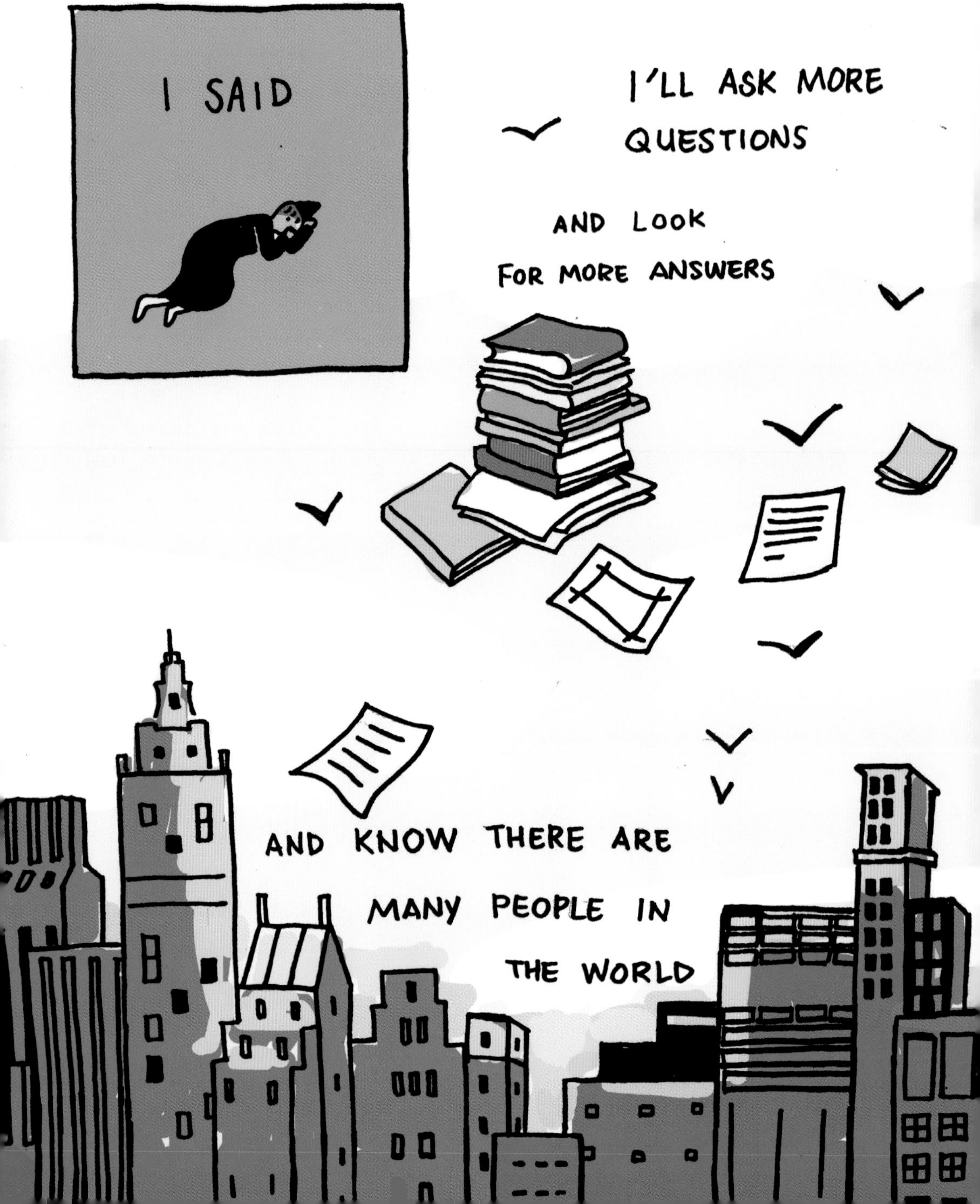
I SAID
I'LL ASK MORE QUESTIONS
AND LOOK FOR MORE ANSWERS
AND KNOW THERE ARE MANY PEOPLE IN THE WORLD

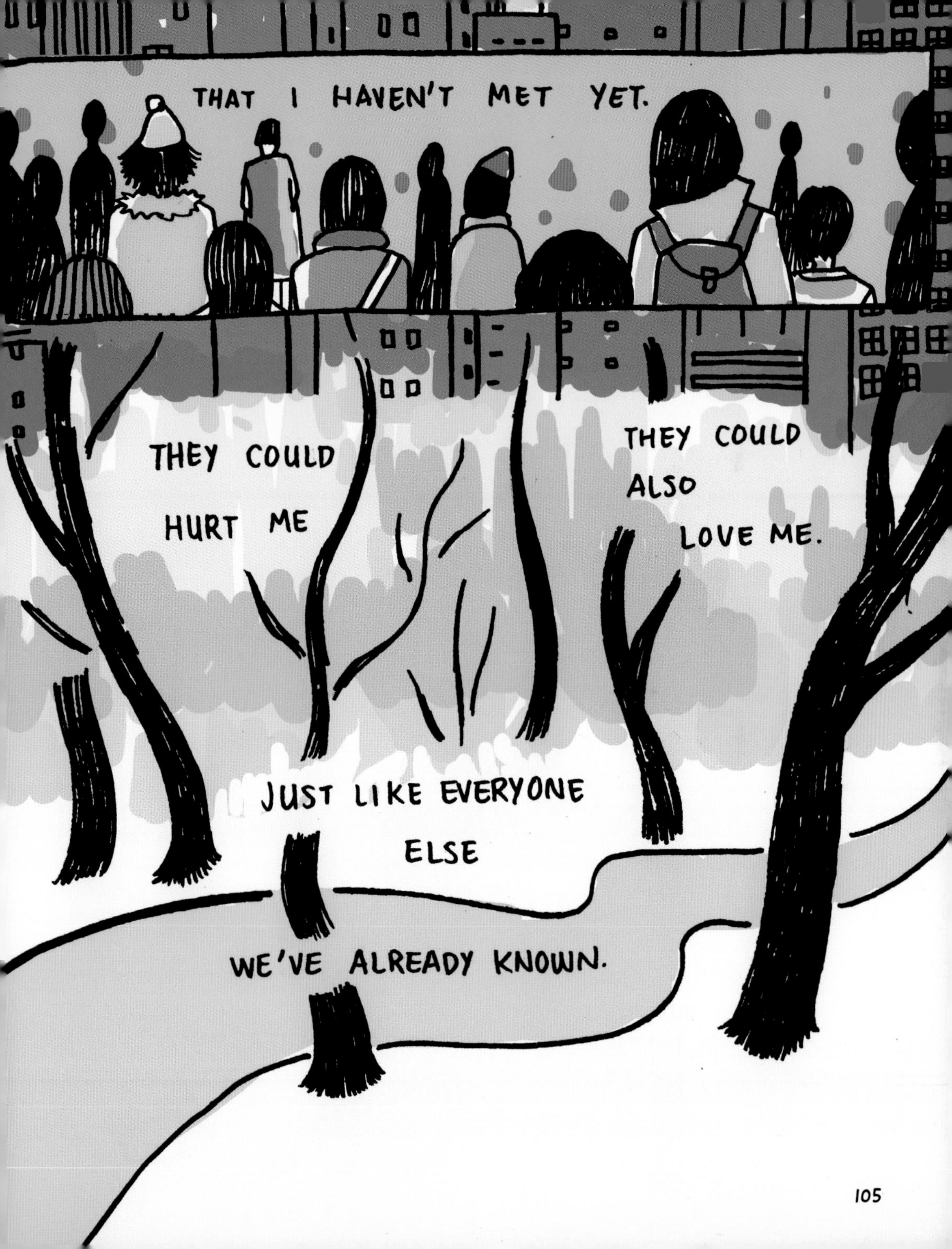
THAT I HAVEN'T MET YET.
THEY COULD HURT ME
THEY COULD ALSO LOVE ME.
JUST LIKE EVERYONE ELSE
WE'VE ALREADY KNOWN.

I FORGAVE SOMEONE
BECAUSE I COULD.

WHEN I COULDN'T

I MADE SURE

TO REMEMBER WHY.

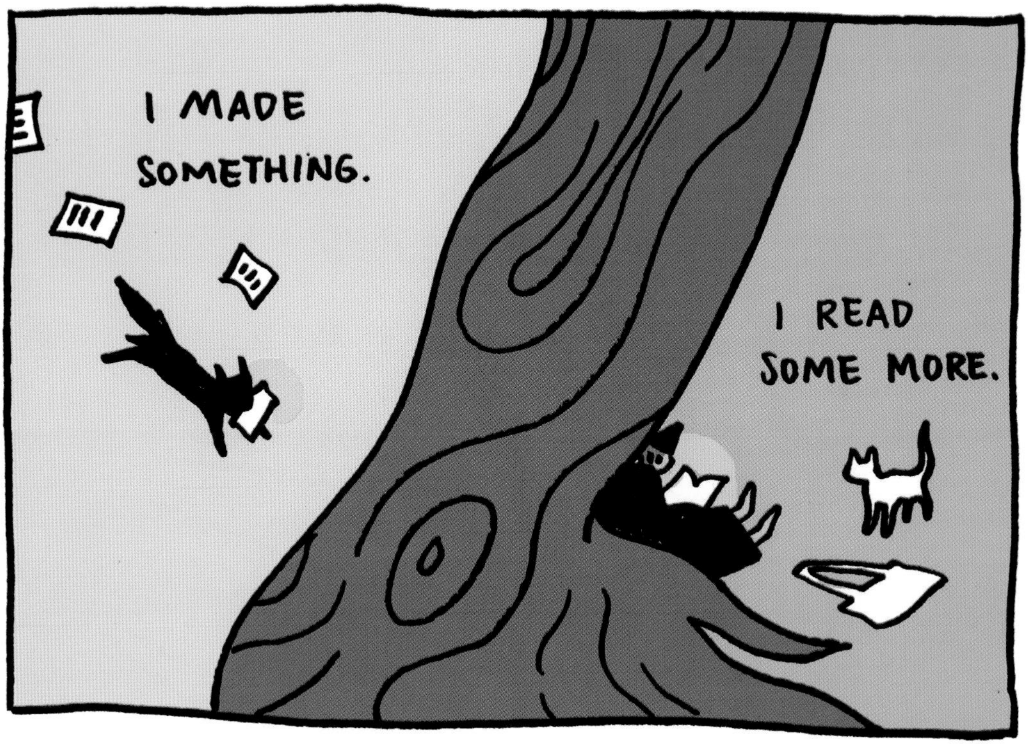
I MADE SOMETHING.
I READ SOME MORE.

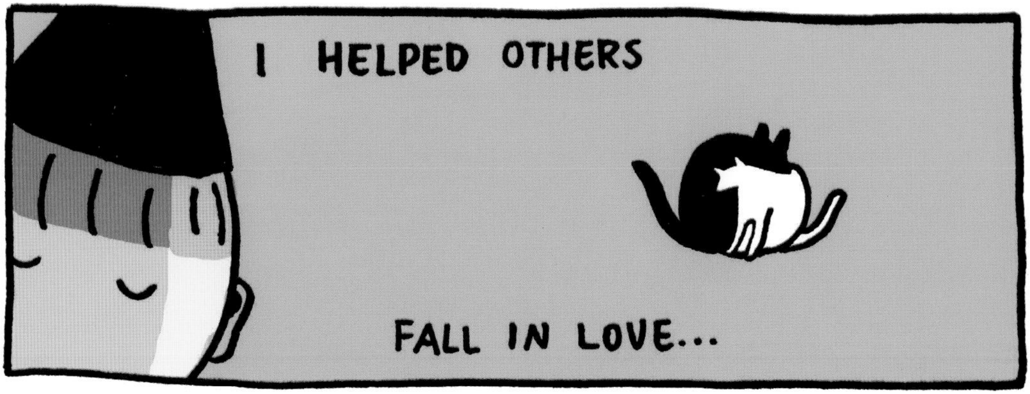
I HELPED OTHERS
FALL IN LOVE...

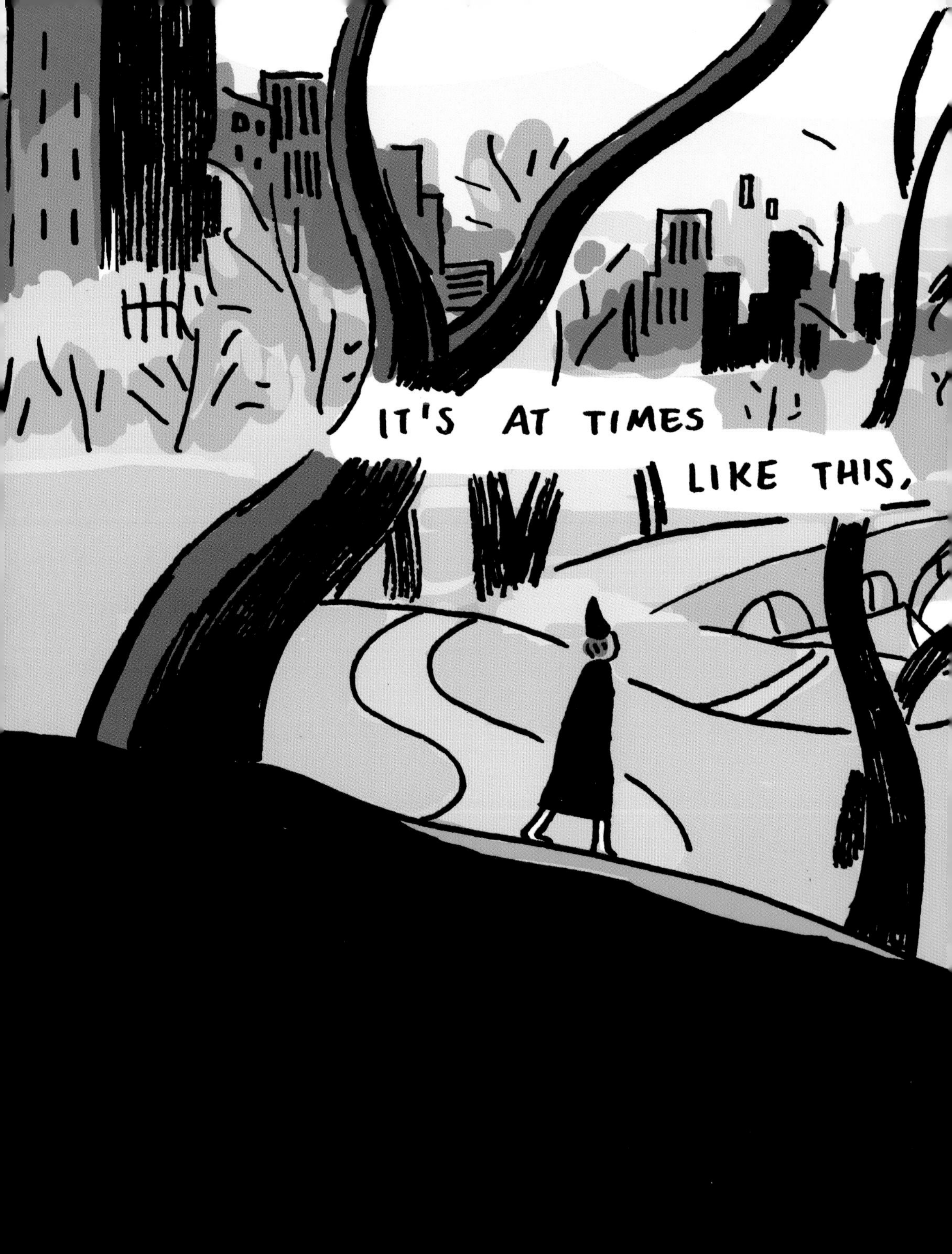
IT'S AT TIMES
LIKE THIS,

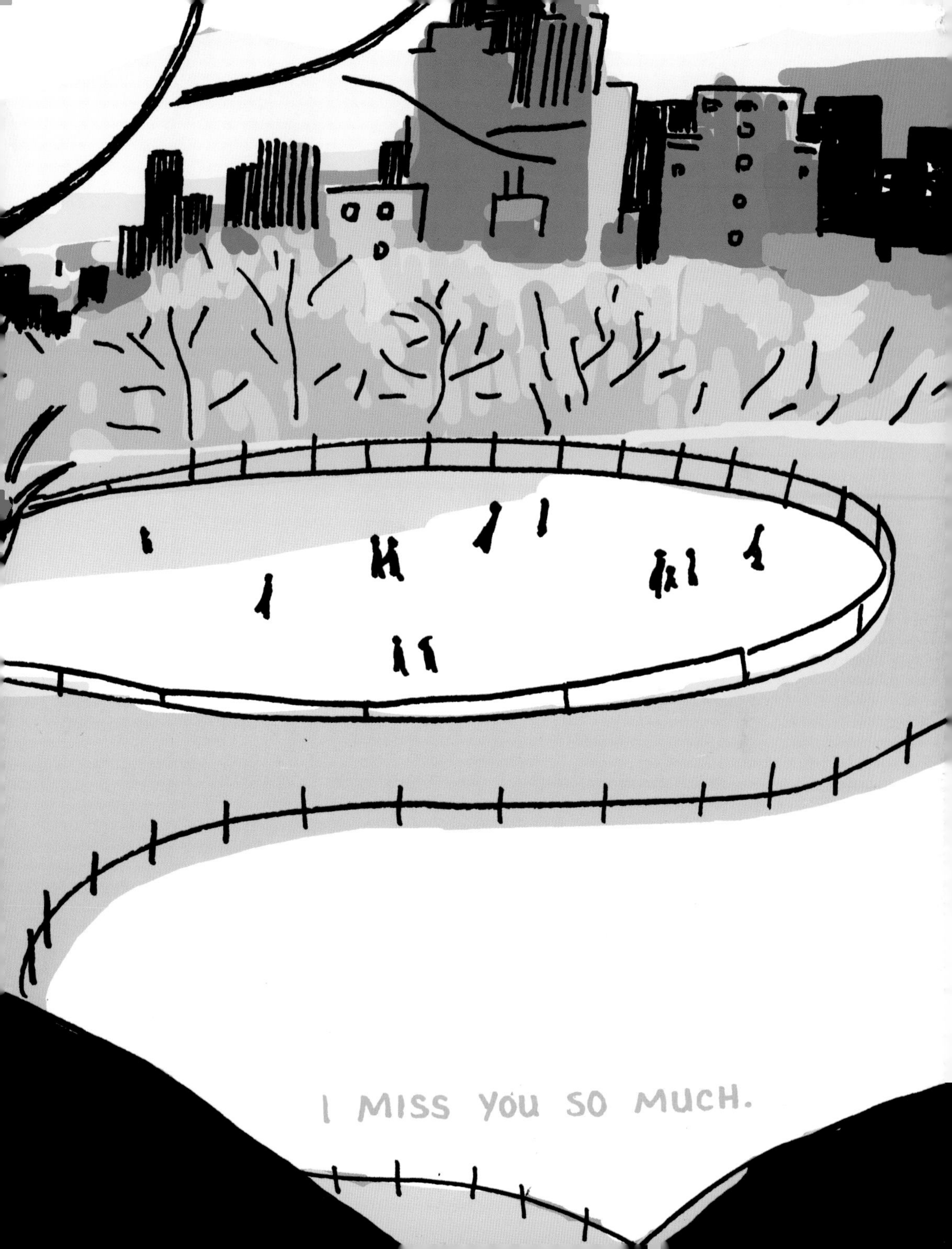
I MISS YOU SO MUCH.

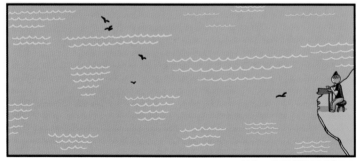

FAMILY REUNION

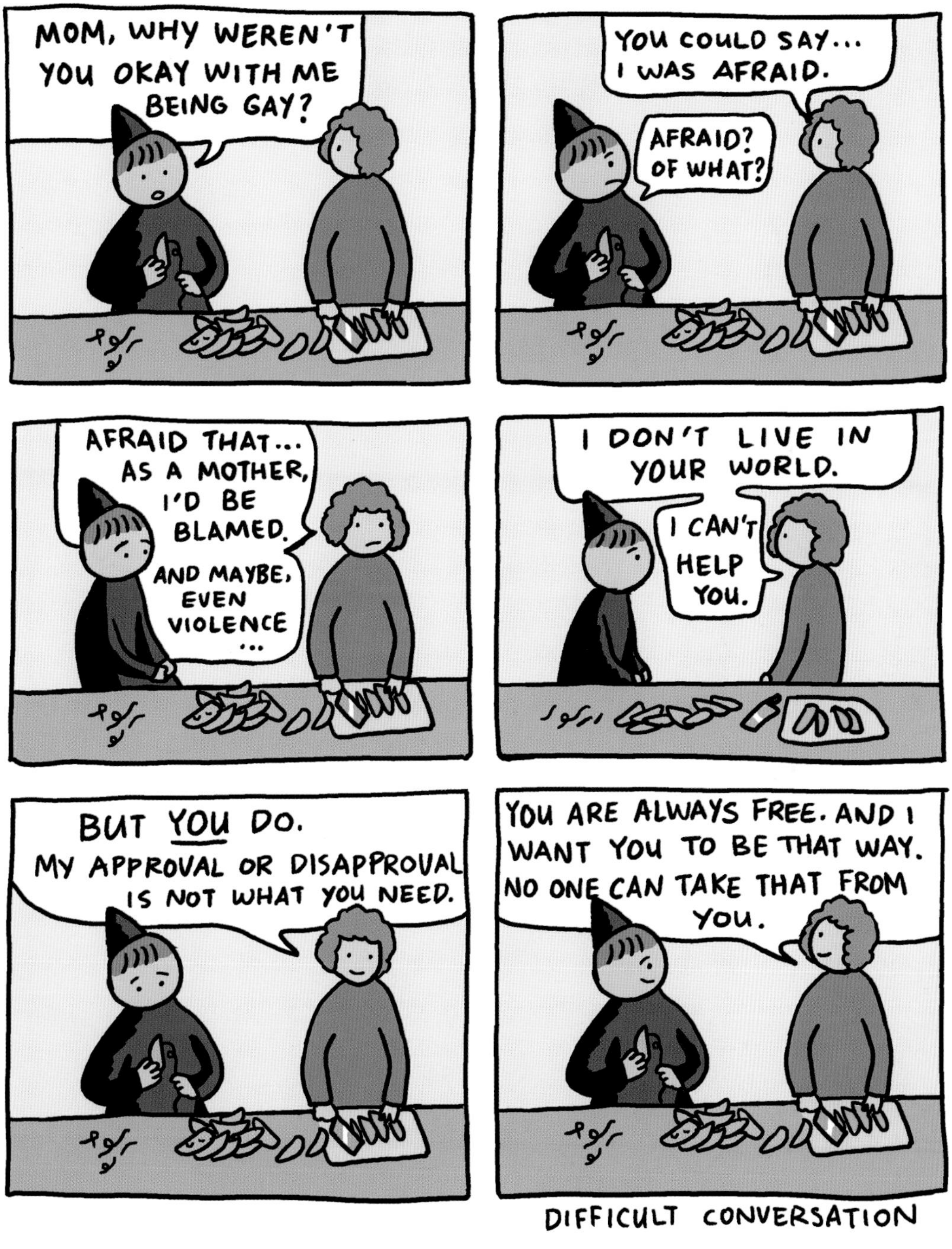
MOM, WHY WEREN'T YOU OKAY WITH ME BEING GAY?
YOU COULD SAY... I WAS AFRAID.
AFRAID? OF WHAT?
AFRAID THAT... AS A MOTHER, I'D BE BLAMED.
AND MAYBE, EVEN VIOLENCE ...
I DON'T LIVE IN YOUR WORLD.
I CAN'T HELP YOU.
BUT YOU DO.
MY APPROVAL OR DISAPPROVAL IS NOT WHAT YOU NEED.
YOU ARE ALWAYS FREE. AND I WANT YOU TO BE THAT WAY.
NO ONE CAN TAKE THAT FROM YOU.

DIFFICULT CONVERSATION

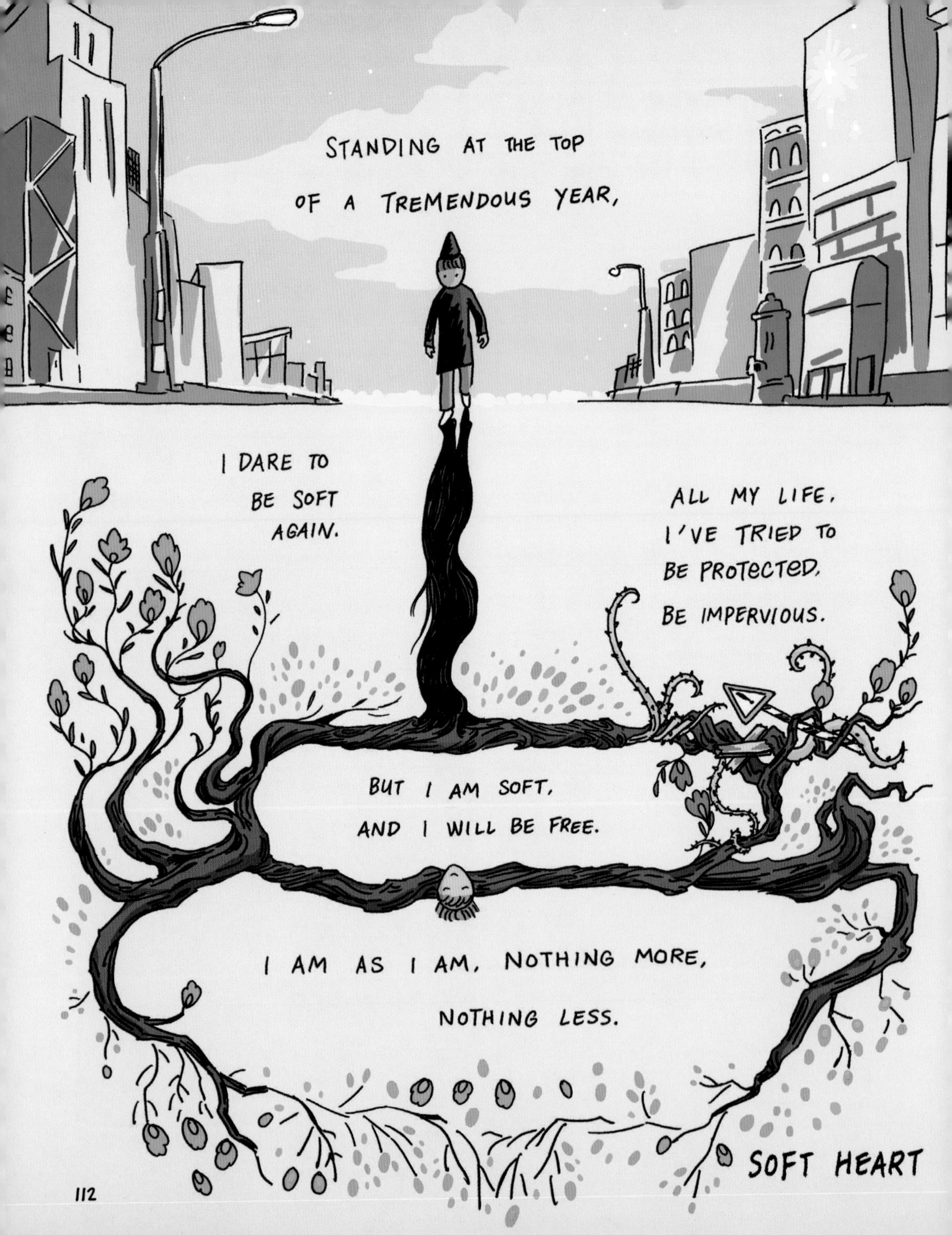
STANDING AT THE TOP
OF A TREMENDOUS YEAR,
I DARE TO
BE SOFT
AGAIN.
ALL MY LIFE,
I'VE TRIED TO
BE PROTECTED,
BE IMPERVIOUS.
BUT I AM SOFT,
AND I WILL BE FREE.
I AM AS I AM, NOTHING MORE,
NOTHING LESS.
SOFT HEART

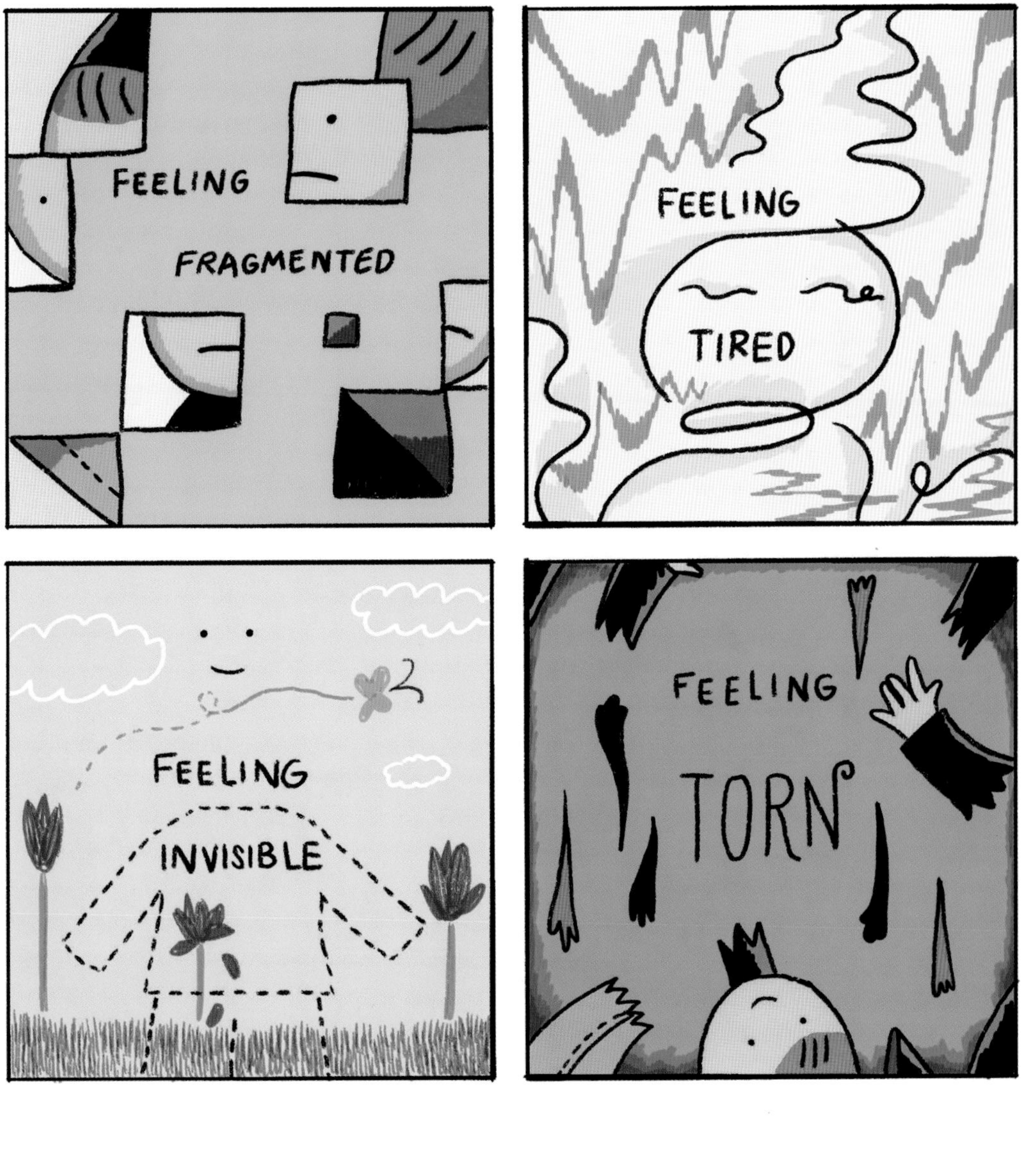
FEELING
FRAGMENTED
FEELING
TIRED
FEELING
INVISIBLE
FEELING
TORN

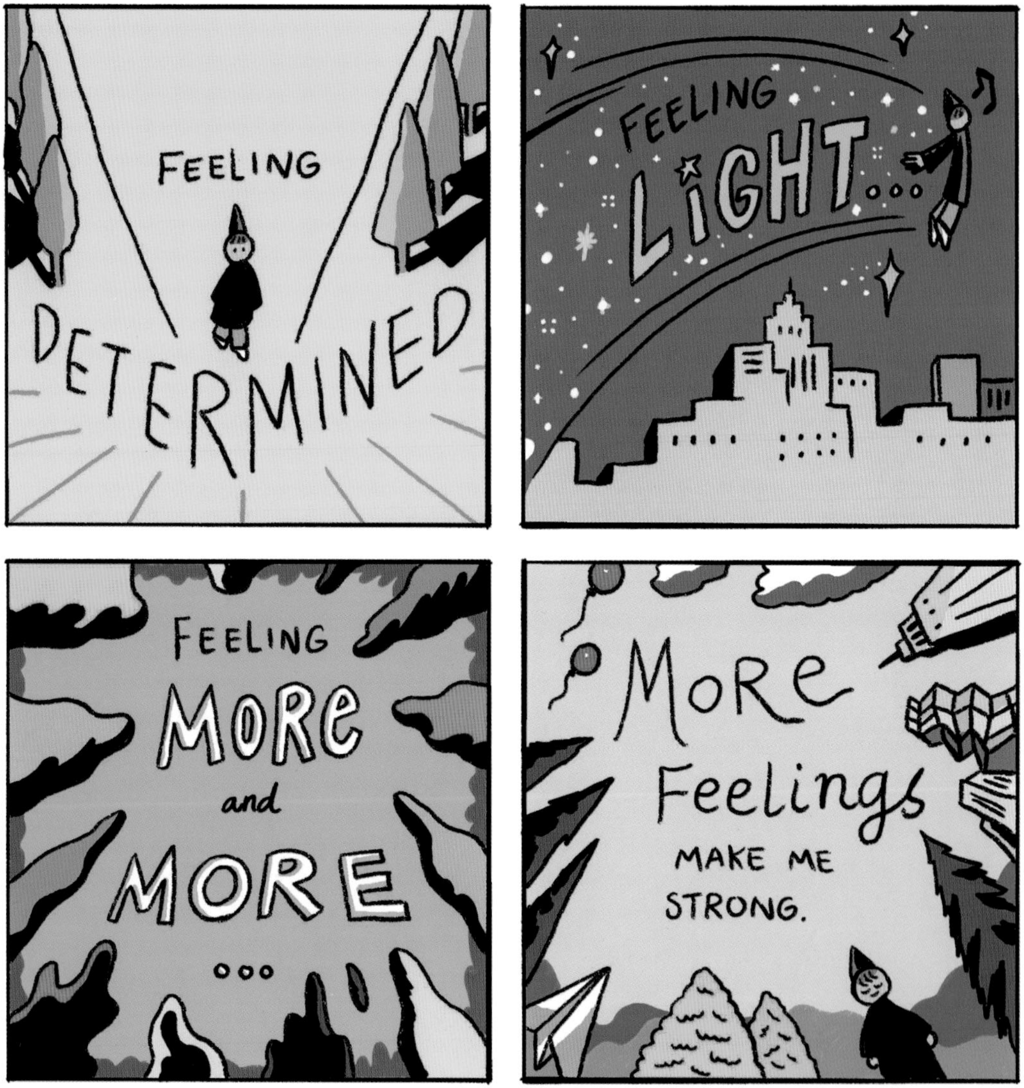
FEELING
DETERMINED
FEELING
LIGHT...
FEELING
MORE
and
MORE
...
MORE
Feelings
MAKE ME
STRONG.

FEELINGS MAKE ME STRONG

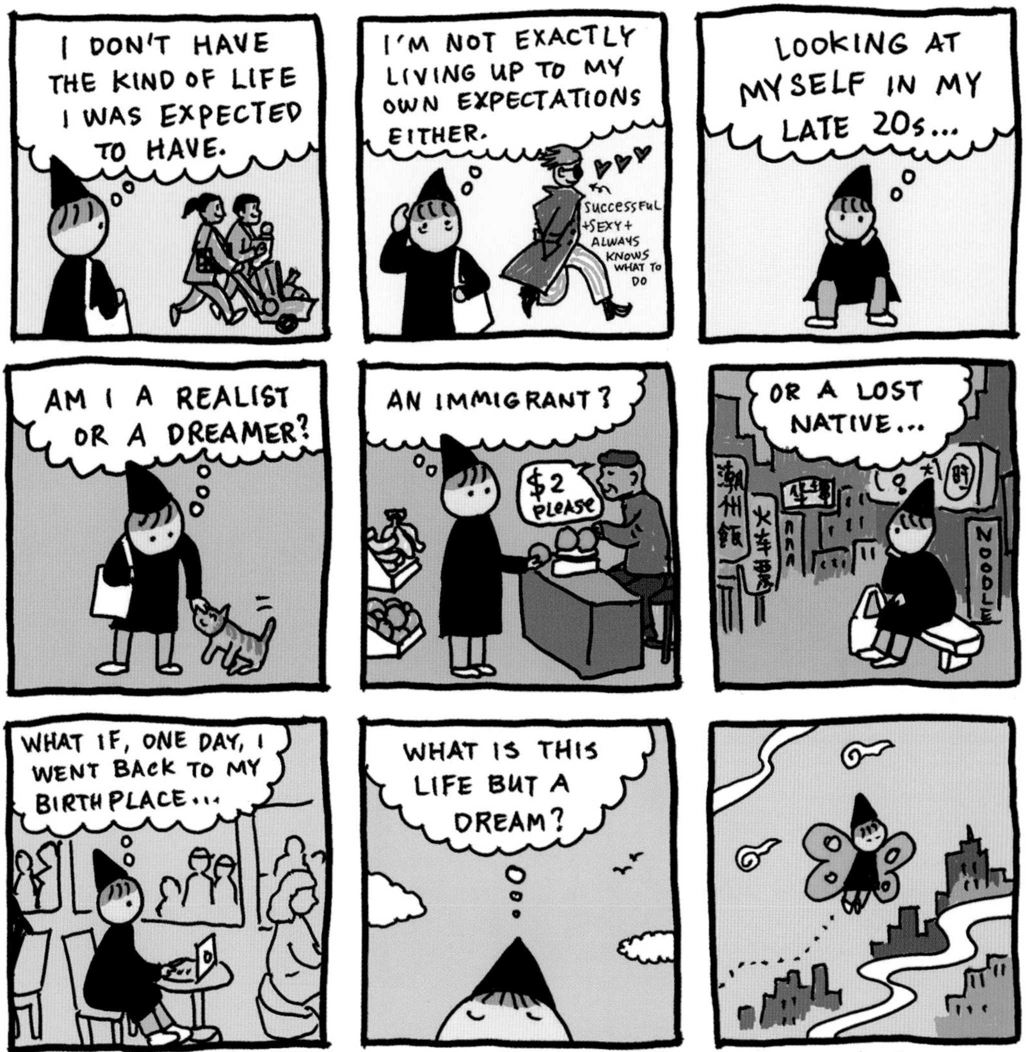
I DON'T HAVE THE KIND OF LIFE I WAS EXPECTED TO HAVE.
I'M NOT EXACTLY LIVING UP TO MY OWN EXPECTATIONS EITHER.
SUCCESSFUL +SEXY+ ALWAYS KNOWS WHAT TO DO
LOOKING AT MYSELF IN MY LATE 20s...
AM I A REALIST OR A DREAMER?
AN IMMIGRANT?
$2 PLEASE
OR A LOST NATIVE...
NOODLE
WHAT IF, ONE DAY, I WENT BACK TO MY BIRTHPLACE...
WHAT IS THIS LIFE BUT A DREAM?

ANYTHING BUT A DREAM

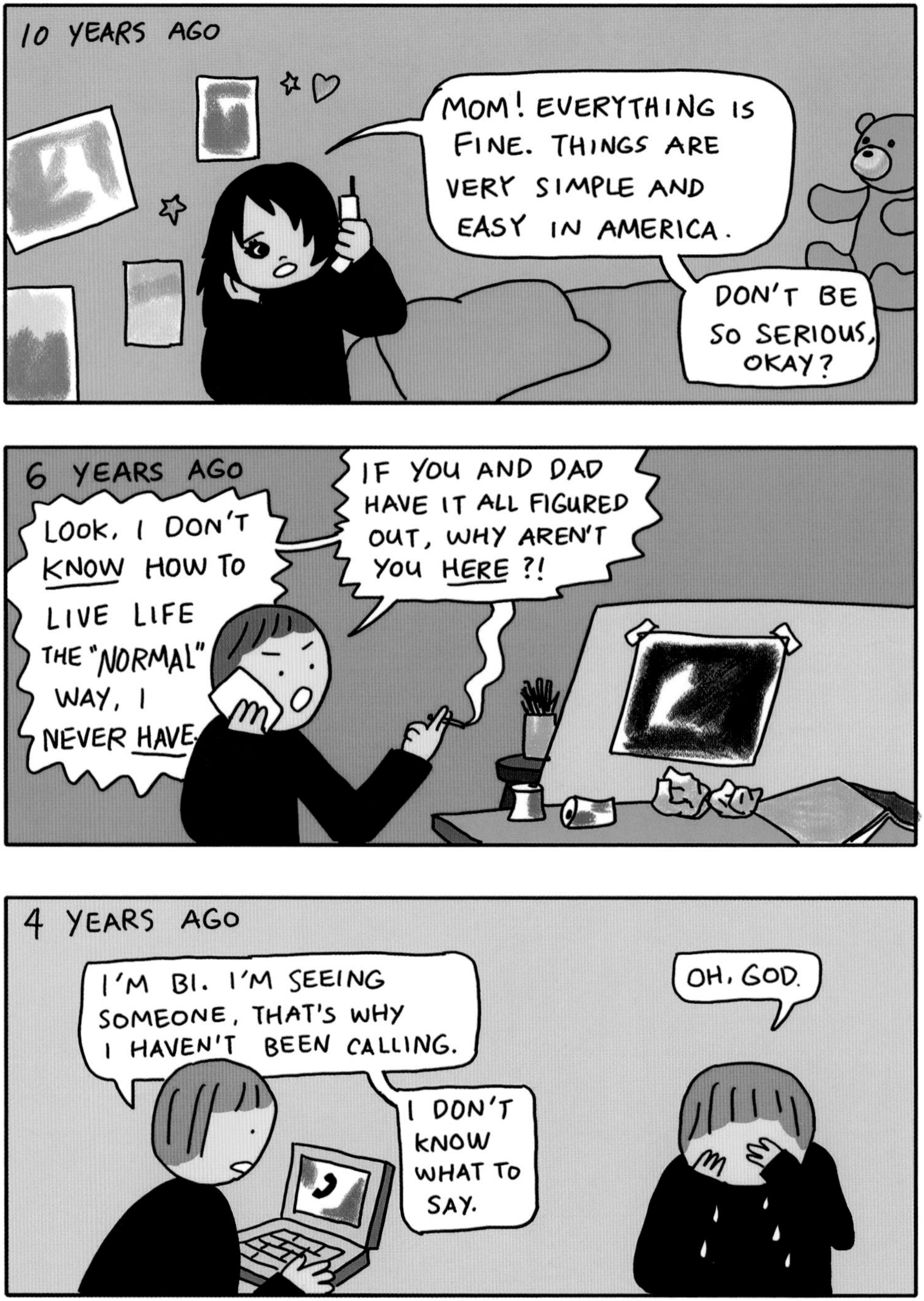
10 YEARS AGO
MOM! EVERYTHING IS FINE. THINGS ARE VERY SIMPLE AND EASY IN AMERICA.
DON'T BE SO SERIOUS, OKAY?
6 YEARS AGO
LOOK, I DON'T KNOW HOW TO LIVE LIFE THE "NORMAL" WAY, I NEVER HAVE.
IF YOU AND DAD HAVE IT ALL FIGURED OUT, WHY AREN'T YOU HERE?!
4 YEARS AGO
I'M BI. I'M SEEING SOMEONE, THAT'S WHY I HAVEN'T BEEN CALLING.
I DON'T KNOW WHAT TO SAY.
OH, GOD.

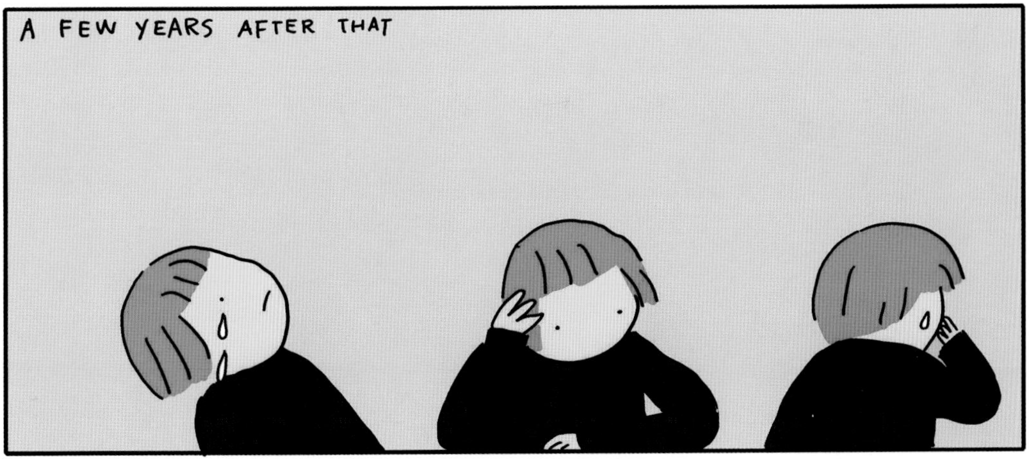
A FEW YEARS AFTER THAT

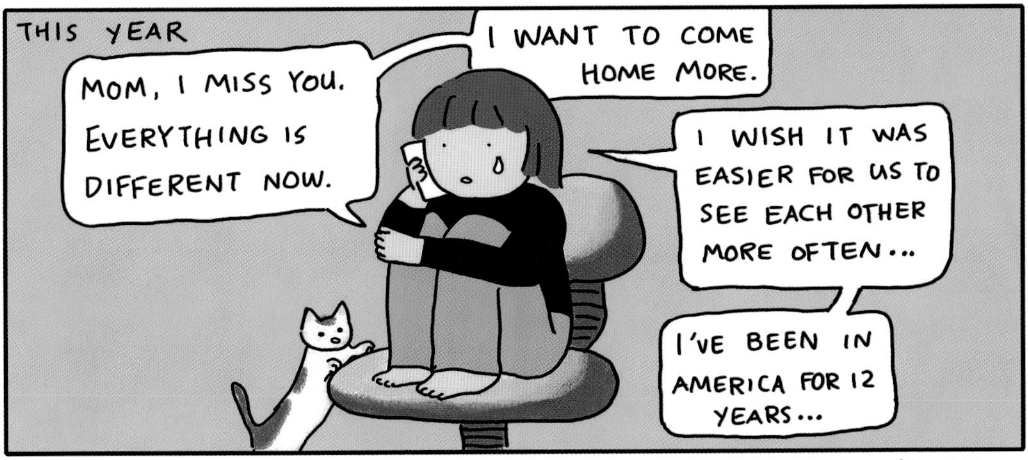
THIS YEAR
MOM, I MISS YOU. EVERYTHING IS DIFFERENT NOW.
I WANT TO COME HOME MORE.
I WISH IT WAS EASIER FOR US TO SEE EACH OTHER MORE OFTEN...
I'VE BEEN IN AMERICA FOR 12 YEARS...

I WANT TO COME HOME

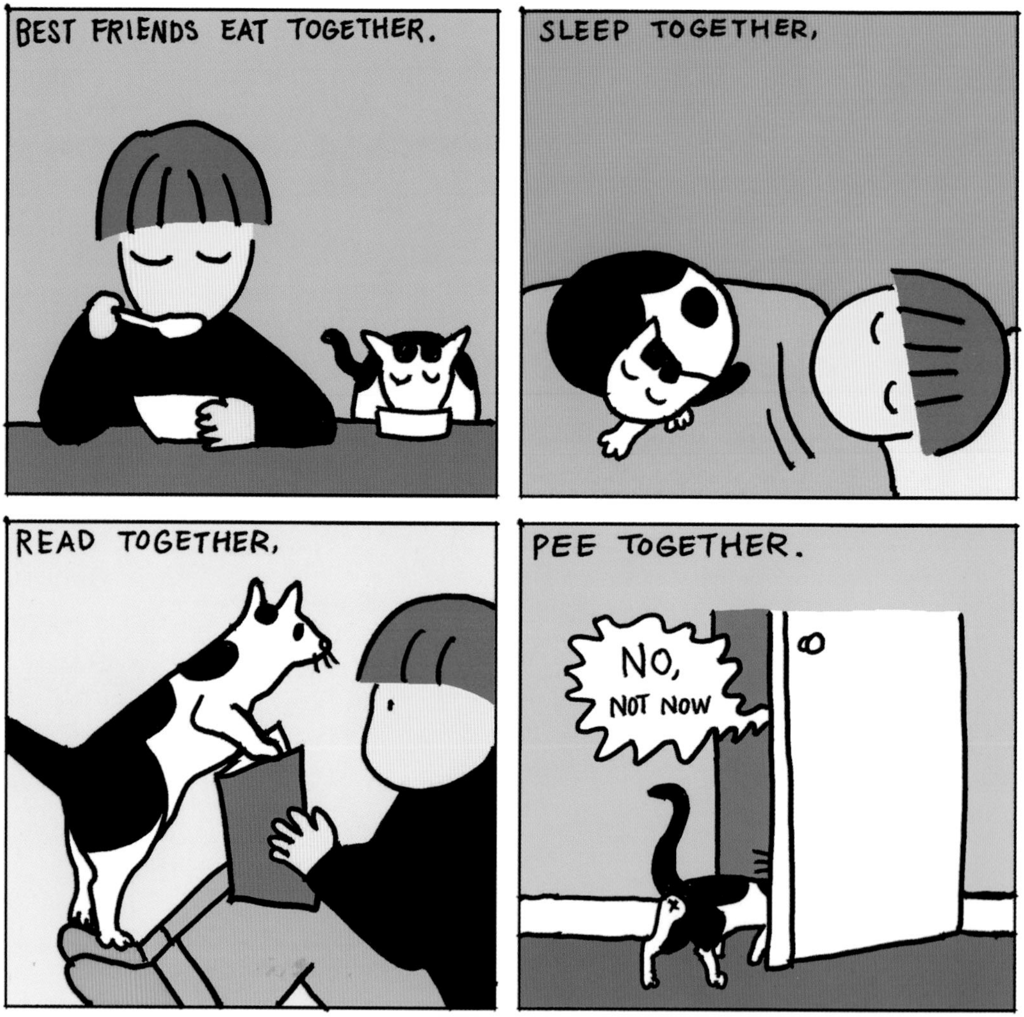
BEST FRIENDS EAT TOGETHER.
SLEEP TOGETHER,
READ TOGETHER,
PEE TOGETHER.
NO, NOT NOW

BEST FRIENDS

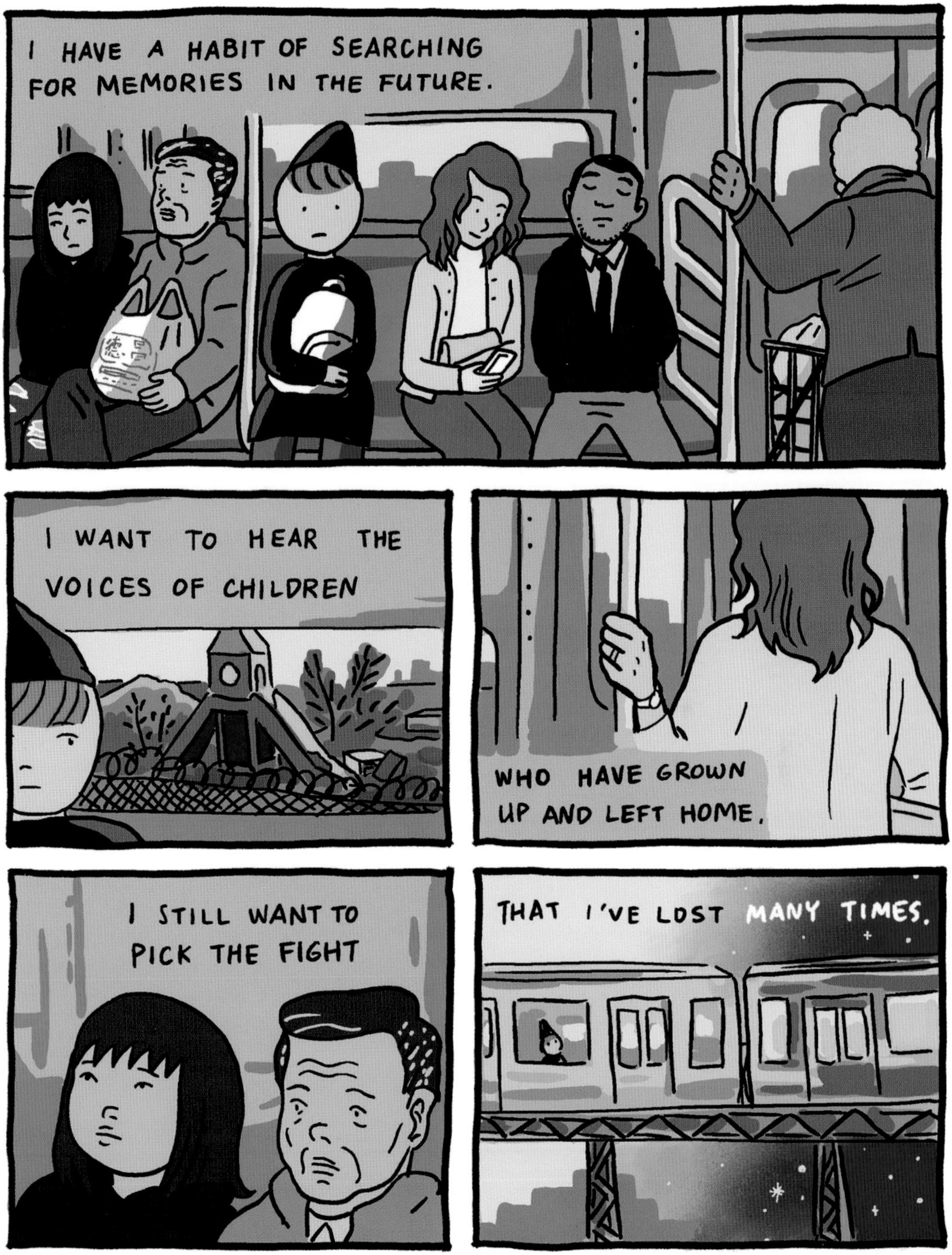
I HAVE A HABIT OF SEARCHING FOR MEMORIES IN THE FUTURE.
I WANT TO HEAR THE VOICES OF CHILDREN
WHO HAVE GROWN UP AND LEFT HOME.
I STILL WANT TO PICK THE FIGHT
THAT I'VE LOST MANY TIMES.

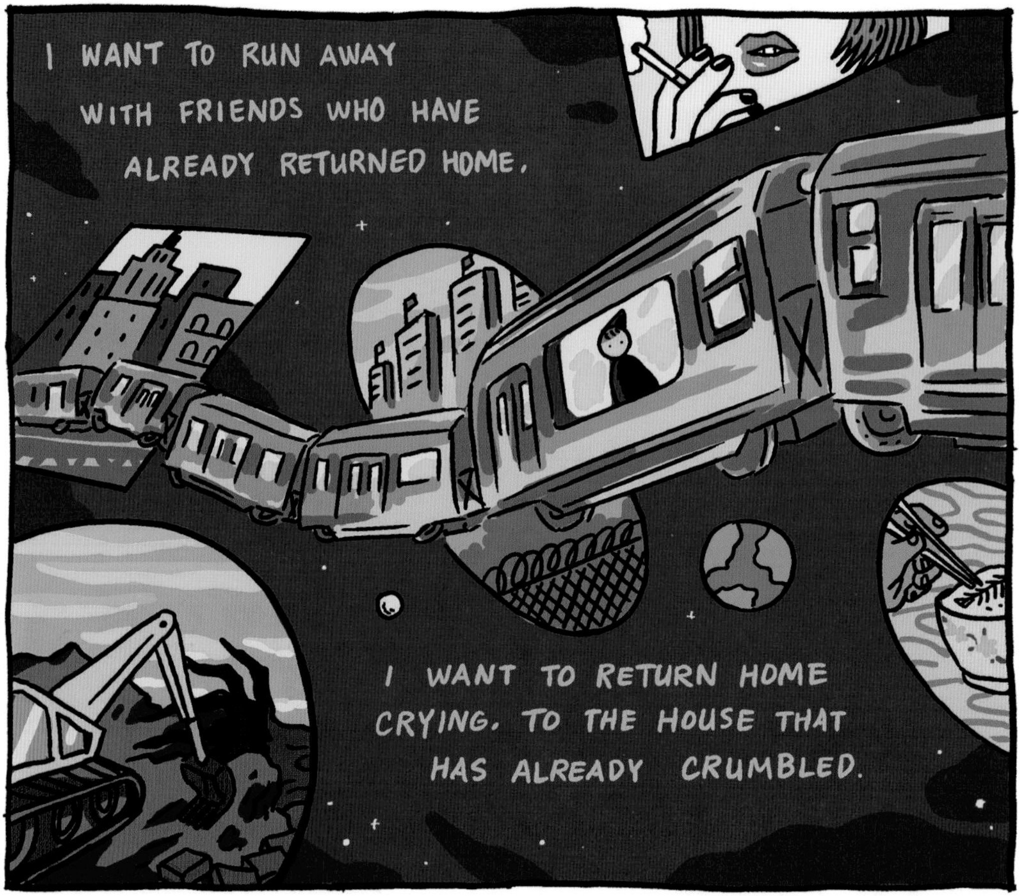
I WANT TO RUN AWAY WITH FRIENDS WHO HAVE ALREADY RETURNED HOME.
I WANT TO RETURN HOME CRYING, TO THE HOUSE THAT HAS ALREADY CRUMBLED.

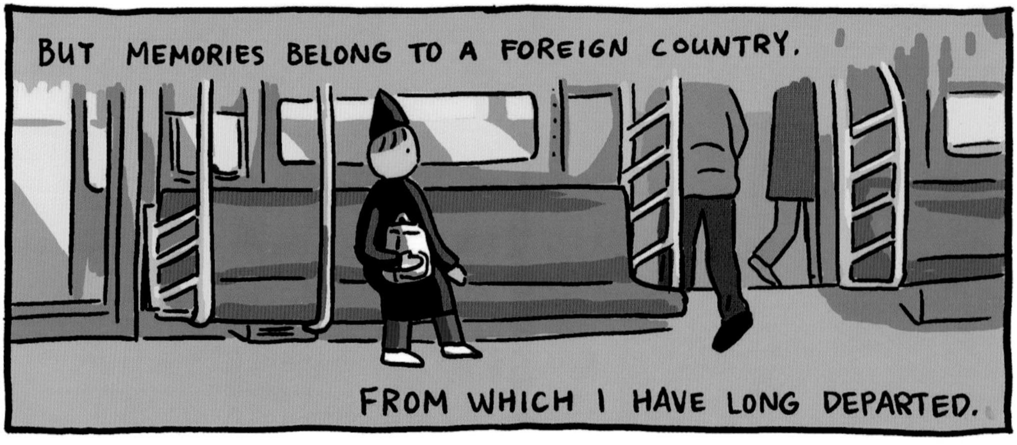
BUT MEMORIES BELONG TO A FOREIGN COUNTRY.
FROM WHICH I HAVE LONG DEPARTED.

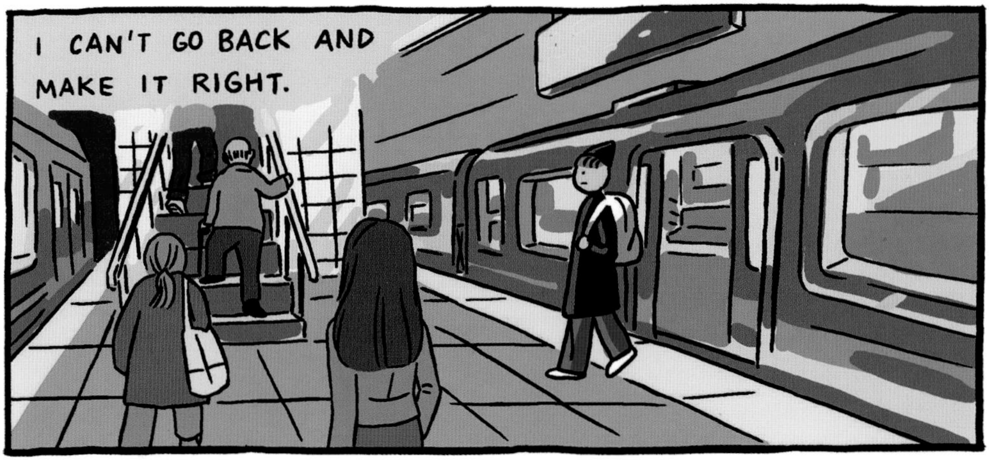
I CAN'T GO BACK AND MAKE IT RIGHT.

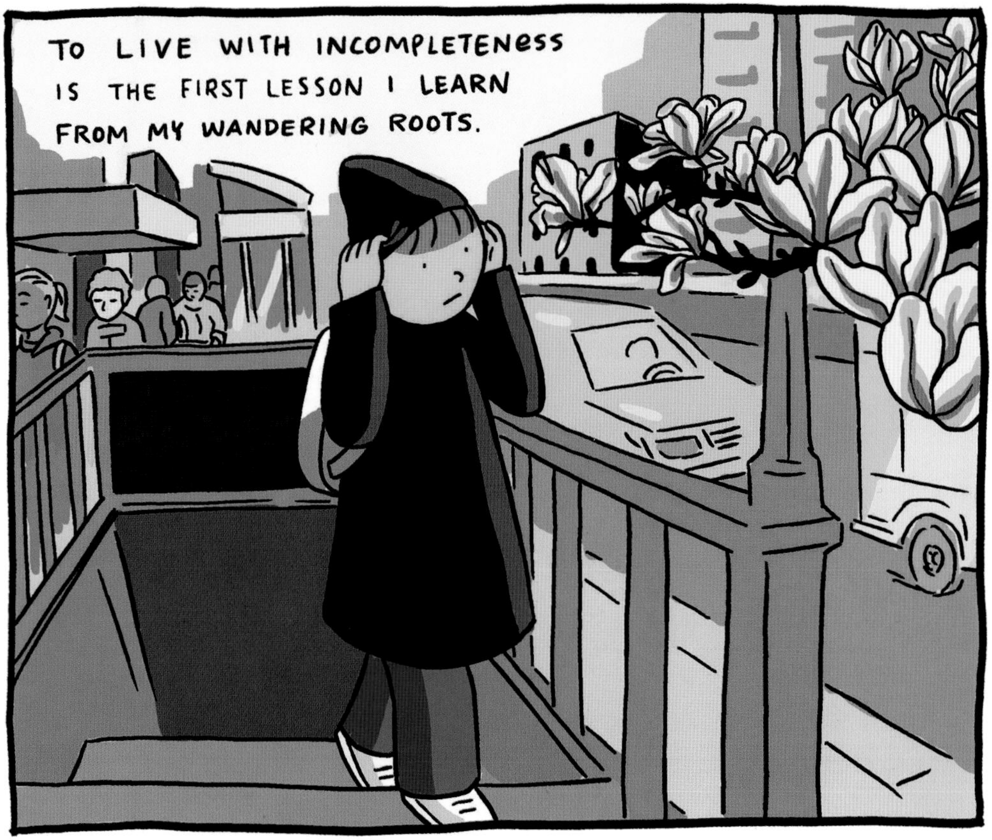
TO LIVE WITH INCOMPLETENESS IS THE FIRST LESSON I LEARN FROM MY WANDERING ROOTS.

MEMORY TRAIN MAKING LOCAL STOPS

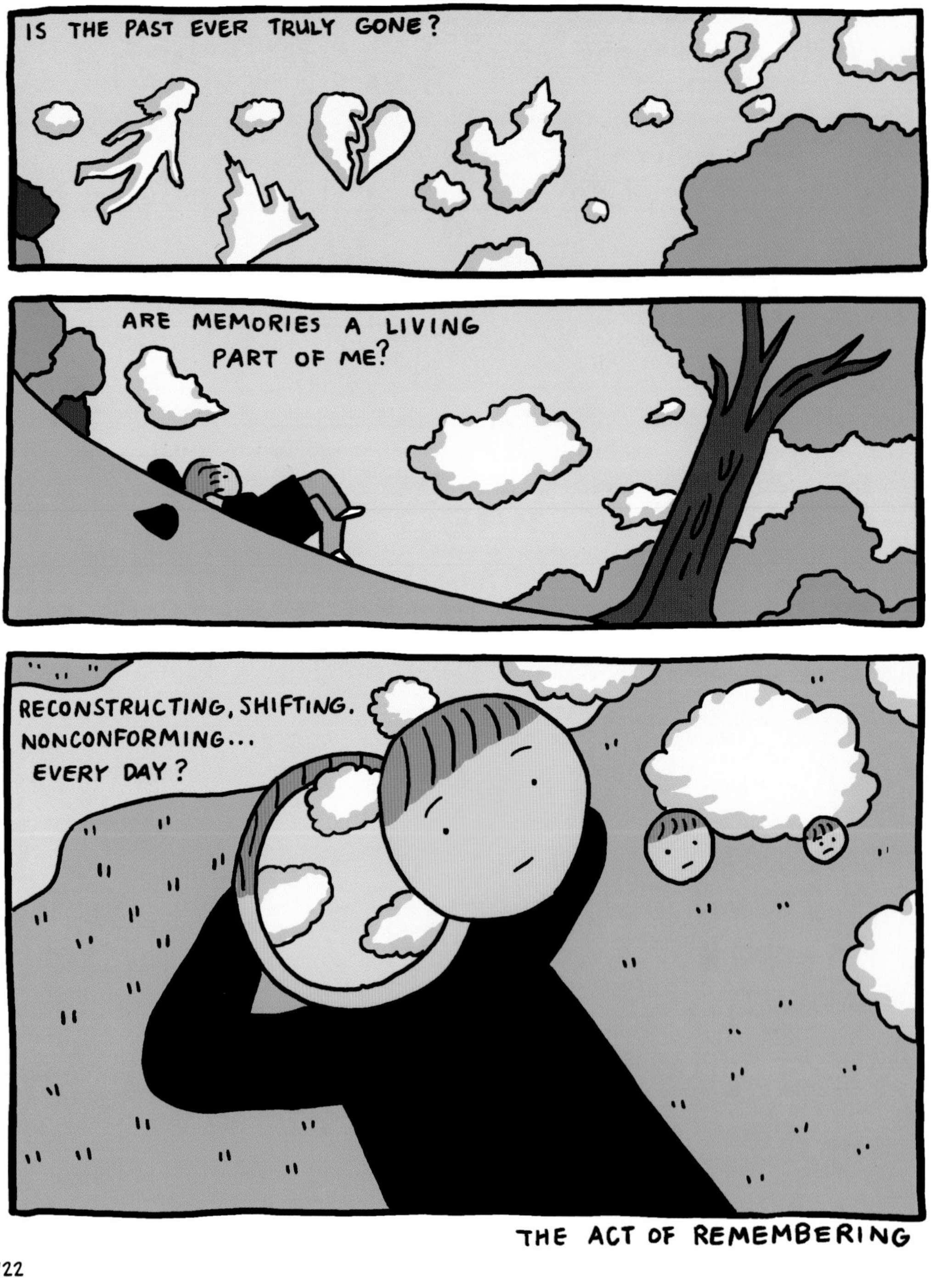
IS THE PAST EVER TRULY GONE?
ARE MEMORIES A LIVING PART OF ME?
RECONSTRUCTING, SHIFTING. NONCONFORMING... EVERY DAY?

THE ACT OF REMEMBERING

I THOUGHT I OWED THE ANSWERS TO A CULTURE, A COUNTRY, A MOVEMENT,

TURNING A VERY PRIVATE PAIN TO A PUBLIC ONE.

THOUGH THIS PUBLIC PAIN URGENTLY DEMANDS AN ANSWER...

I ONLY OWE IT TO MYSELF, FOR NOW.

WHAT AM I MADE OF?

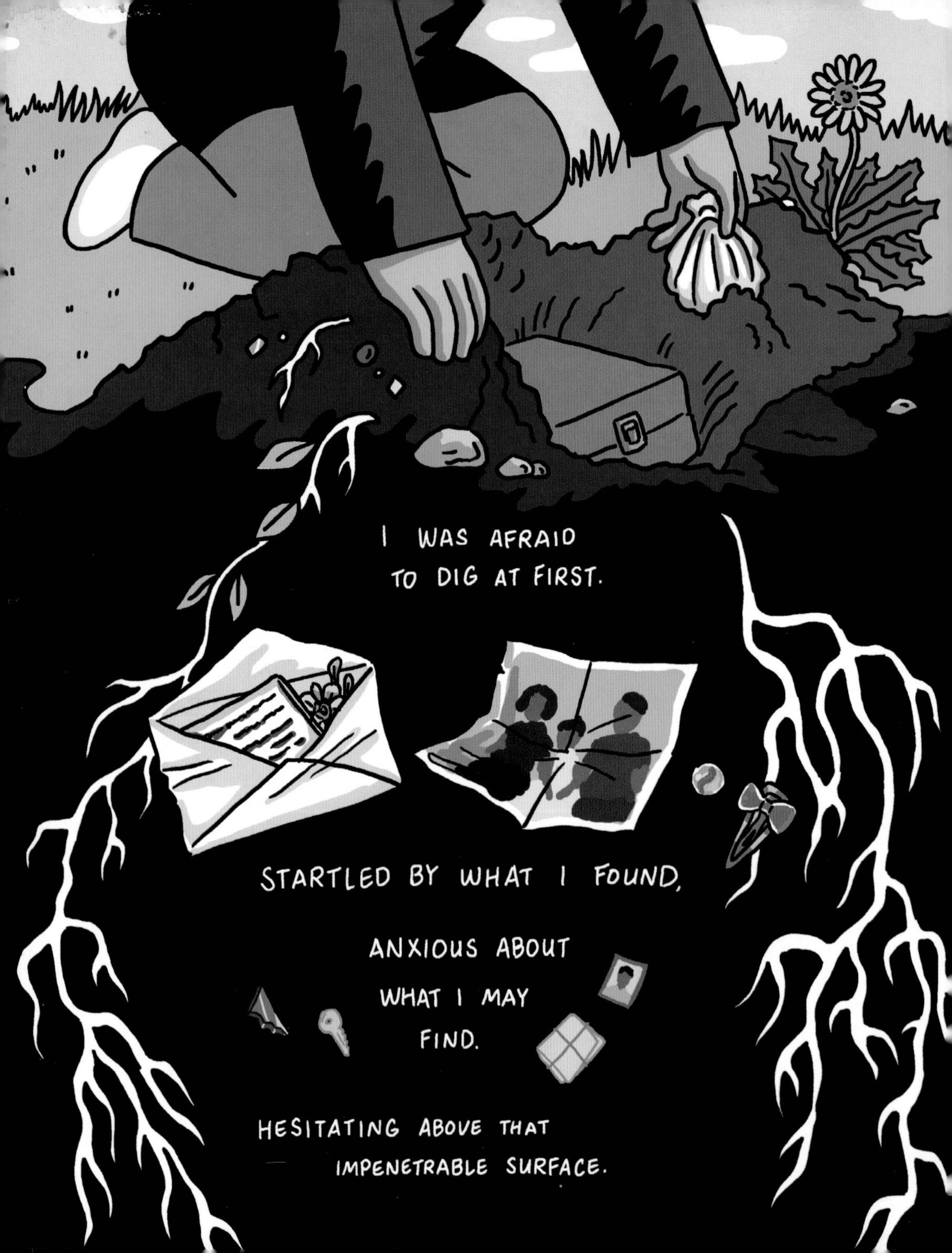
I WAS AFRAID TO DIG AT FIRST.
STARTLED BY WHAT I FOUND,
ANXIOUS ABOUT WHAT I MAY FIND.
HESITATING ABOVE THAT IMPENETRABLE SURFACE.

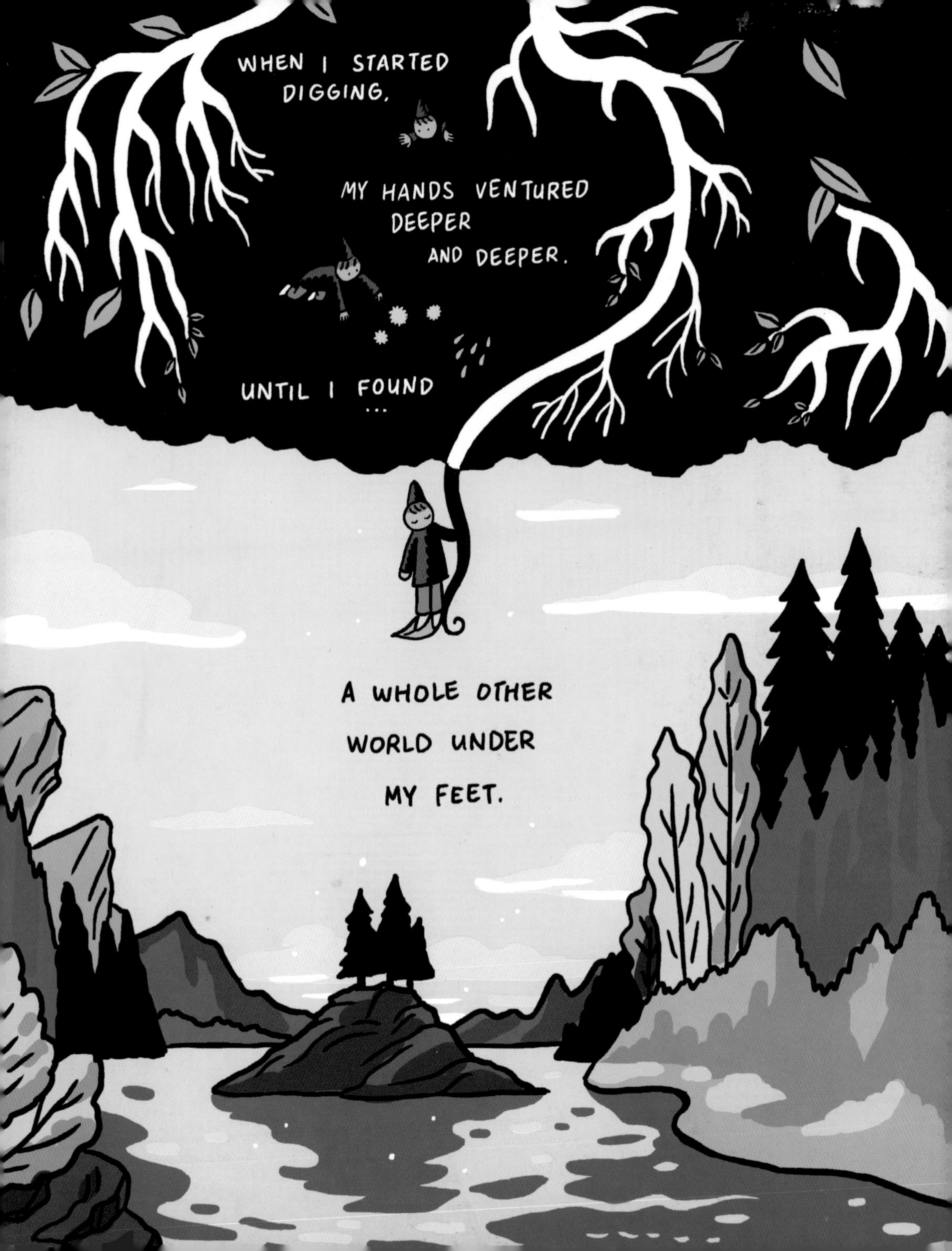
WHEN I STARTED DIGGING,
MY HANDS VENTURED DEEPER AND DEEPER.
UNTIL I FOUND ...
A WHOLE OTHER WORLD UNDER MY FEET.

Andrews McMeel Publishing
a division of Andrews McMeel Universal
1130 Walnut Street, Kansas City, Missouri 64106

www.andrewsmcmeel.com

20 21 22 23 24 TEN 10 9 8 7 6 5 4 3 2 1

ISBN: 978-1-5248-5245-0

Library of Congress Control Number: 2019946582

Editor: Patty Rice
Art Director: Julie Philips
Designer: Sierra S. Stanton
Production Editor: Elizabeth A. Garcia
Production Manager: Tamara Haus